CAKES
to die for!

CAKES
to die for!

BEV SHAFFER

Food Photography and Food Styling by
JOHN R. SHAFFER

PELICAN PUBLISHING COMPANY
GRETNA 2010

*The word "Pelican" and the depiction of a pelican are trademarks
of Pelican Publishing Company, Inc., and are registered in the
U.S. Patent and Trademark Office.*

Library of Congress Cataloging-in-Publication Data

Shaffer, Bev, 1951-
  Cakes to die for! / Bev Shaffer ; food photography and food styling by John
R. Shaffer.
      p. cm.
  Includes bibliographical references and index.
  ISBN 978-1-58980-691-7 (hardcover : alk. paper) 1. Cake. I. Title.
  TX771.S34 2010
  641.8'653—dc22

                          2009050854

Printed in Singapore
Published by Pelican Publishing Company, Inc.
1000 Burmaster Street, Gretna, Louisiana 70053

Join me in rising above the mix!

CONTENTS

ACKNOWLEDGMENTS

Great friends and good people make the completion of a cookbook seem as if it were, well, a piece of cake! I am grateful to a very large group of people for their assistance with this labor of cake love.

Thanks to my husband and dear friend, John, for testing recipes, coordinating the cake testers, styling the food, photographing the food, making dinner, and providing overall support. He even had to schlep in wood from our garage for one of his photo shoots (my general idea, his design), Beyond the Campfire S'Mores Cakes. His food photos always make people want to get out their ingredients and mixing bowls and heat the oven!

Special thanks to my dear friend, Vickie Getz, for her continued support in reading and proofing the manuscript throughout this book-writing process.

Thanks to my cake testers, a willing group who shared my calories and mishaps and oohs and aahs, all of whom had a chance to bake their cakes and eat them, too! They each were assigned a series of recipes, some easy, some difficult, some perfect, some not . . . and agreed, on their own time, to bake and make comments, coordinate pickup and delivery with John, and gain a few pounds along the way. Special thanks go to: Julianna Baillis, Paula Horvath, Lisa Dellafiora, Annette Felton, Barbara Cumming, Lynne Bouton, Tammy Bradfield, Melissa McPherson, Lili Rollins, Darlene Mellon, Pat Beery, Amber Beery, and Vickie Getz.

Warm thanks to everyone at Pelican Publishing Company—from the warehouse staff to the office staff to the production department—for embracing this (and my other cookbooks) and then lavishing it with extraordinary attention. In particular, my appreciation goes to: Milburn and Nancy Calhoun, for their hospitality and support; Kathleen Calhoun Nettleton, assistant to the publisher; Nina Kooij and the editorial staff; Katie Szadziewicz and the promotion department; and Joseph Billingsley and the sales department.

Special thanks to the following for their support of this book: Organic Valley (organic and farmer owned), Florida Crystals (organic and natural sugars made from 100 percent sun-sweetened sugarcane), Bob's Red Mill (whole-grain foods for every meal of the day), Anolon Suregrip bakeware (heavyweight, carbon steel), Emile Henry ceramic baking collection, Rubbermaid (food-storage solutions), and Lodge Cast Iron (America's original cookware).

I know that my cake testers and I have learned a few things while retesting these recipes . . . and we've enjoyed every tasty morsel. Isn't it time you joined us for some cake love?

Apple Sauce Cake

2 cups sifted cake flour
½ teaspoon salt
1 teaspoon baking soda
1 teaspoon baking powder
1 teaspoon cinnamon
½ teaspoon allspice
½ teaspoon nutmeg
¼ teaspoon cloves
½ cup shortening
1 cup sugar
1 egg
1 cup thick strained apple sauce
  (unsweetened)

1 cup Sun-Maid Raisins (Puffed Seeded Muscats)
¾ cup chopped nuts

Sift together first 8 ingredients. Cream shortening. Add sugar and blend well. Add egg and beat until fluffy. Add apple sauce. Gradually add sifted dry ingredients and stir until smooth. Add Raisins and nuts. Bake in a greased 8" square cake pan in a moderate oven (350° F.) for 50 to 60 minutes. While warm sprinkle with confectioners' sugar, or when cool frost as desired.

Smudges and stains and other signs of cake love on this Apple Sauce Cake recipe card from my mom's files hint of a kitchen filled with wonderful memories.

INTRODUCTION: THE ICING ON THE CAKE!

When I was growing up and family would gather for birthday celebrations, one of my uncles would always tell me I was the icing on the cake. I shrugged it off as a ridiculous comment by a quirky man. Thinking back, I should have been proud to be the icing. Birthdays were one of the few times we actually had icing on the cake, not because we were too poor to have icing but because cakes that were made for Sunday dinners and holidays were unfrosted sensations, oftentimes Hungarian or Italian in origin, filled with other flavors and textures. So, yes, icing (I'm now proud to say!) was something special.

My mom, Olga's, Apple Sauce Cake recipe was one such unfrosted sensation. I loved this cake. It was flavorful and full bodied and sweet and spicy and crunchy and fruity . . . and dusted with *lots* of confectioners' sugar that I always managed to get all over me. She made it in a small tube pan and put large chunks of walnuts inside. It was my favorite after-school snack, and as I grew older, I found that a slice with a cup of tea or packed in a work lunch was a delicious treat.

She continued to make this cake even after her stroke kept her from using her right arm and hand, and we were always happy to enjoy a piece or two with her at her home. I miss this cake and my mom. Oh, sure, I could bake it, but it just wouldn't taste the same. The stains on her recipe card are memories: smudges from little fingers, telltale yellowing, and a grease spot or two from whatever shortening Mom happened to be using at the time.

John has similar sweet memories of his mom, Jane, and how she spoiled him with her Butterscotch Sauce (among other things!).

To me, sweet, delicious cakes just like my mom's Apple Sauce Cake are a timeless way to celebrate with family or make any day more memorable. I will share some of that cake love with you . . . and I believe that your most difficult decision will be deciding what chapter will begin this journey for you.

These cakes are a collection of my favorites, from some of my cooking classes and television segments as well as a few clever twists and turns and wonderful crumbs from fellow chefs. Chapters to begin your journey include Layer Cakes, Cupcakes and Baby Cakes, Cheesecakes, Coffeecakes and "Flipped Over" Cakes, Fancy-Schmancy Cakes, One-Pan Wonders, Loaf Cakes and Snack Cakes, Bundt Cakes and Tube Cakes, and My Mixes Cakes Plus Frostings. And just as every good journey begins with a road map, be sure to read "A Slice of Advice" for a tidbit or two that should help you along the way.

So gather up those Organic Valley eggs and unsalted butter, Florida Crystals natural cane sugar, Bob's Red Mill unbleached white flour (my preferences, without apologies), and whatever else you need. Heat the oven. Pull out the stand mixer and plug it in. Let's bake together—it'll be a piece of cake!

This Ricotta Vanilla Bean Pound Cake may look too good to eat—but then you'd be missing some great flavors.

A SLICE OF ADVICE: TIPS TO HELP YOU RISE ABOVE THE MIX!

AN OVERALL SLICE: THINGS I HAVE ASSUMED

You have read the recipe and all your ingredients are measured and prepped ahead (i.e., chopped, toasted, or melted). This is called mise en place.

Your dairy ingredients (milk, eggs, butter, cream cheese) are being used at room temperature unless otherwise called for in my recipe.

Your cake flour, confectioners' sugar, and cocoa powder will be sifted before using.

When my recipe calls for a greased and floured pan, you have tapped out the excess flour so there are no clumps or large amounts of flour remaining in the pan.

Your cake layers will be cooled on a wire rack, allowing for air circulation and no soggy bottoms!

You are using the pan size called for in the recipe.

You've let the oven heat for 15 minutes before baking and your oven temperature is accurate. Test it with an oven thermometer. This detail can be the key to your cake's success.

When I give you a range of times for baking, you will underset your timer and use these times as a guideline. Many things affect baking times, such as correct oven temperature and type of pan used (glass, metal, dark, light).

You won't overbeat your ingredients . . . you are simply mixing everything together until well blended. Unless long beating is required in a specific recipe, overbeating will cause the cake texture to be tough.

FROSTING TIPS

I'll wind up repeating some of these professional frosting tips in other areas of this book, but they're worth highlighting here. They will ensure that your cake looks as delicious as it tastes!

- Cool the cake completely before frosting.
- Dust off any loose crumbs gently with a soft-bristled brush or the flat of your clean hand.
- Freeze layers for several hours or overnight before frosting. Frost them the day you're going to serve the cake. The trick is to frost the layers while they're still frozen, which helps the frosting adhere better to the cake layers.

- Anchor the cake by spreading a dab of frosting in the center of a cake plate or cardboard round.
- Frost in this order: filling, sides, then top.
- Place a thin coat of frosting or filling on the bottom layer. This will help seal in the crumbs.
- Then place a large scoop of frosting or filling on the center of the cake and spread it to the edges with an icing (angled, thin metal) spatula. Level the frosting.
- Slide the top cake layer, bottom side up, on top of the frosted bottom layer, being sure that the layers are aligned. Press the top layer firmly into place.
- Use the best-looking layer on top (check it out . . . one layer always looks better than the other).
- Steady the cake with the palm of your hand while you're frosting the sides.
- Spread a thin coating of frosting on the sides of the cake using short, side-to-side strokes. Refrigerate the cake for 30 minutes to allow the frosting to set.
- Apply a thick coat of frosting to the top and sides of the cake, being sure to coat the cake evenly and smoothly. If necessary, dip the spatula into hot water to create a smooth coat.
- Decorate if you'd like (as simple as chopped nuts or as complex as lattice weave and flowers using a pastry bag).
- There's just a little frosting left? Lick the bowl!

TECHNIQUES

"Cut in the Butter"

Many baking recipes ask you to "cut in" the butter. Basically, this is the method of incorporating solid butter into dry ingredients. For best results, use butter that's well chilled. Do the "cutting in" with a pastry blender or, using a crisscross motion, use two knives to blend the butter into the other ingredients.

Folding Ingredients

Several of my cake recipes call for folding whipped egg whites into a mixture or folding a mixture into whipped egg whites. The basic thing to remember is that you don't want to undo what you've just done. The process needs to be done quickly, gently, and thoroughly so the whites don't deflate.

Here's the process. The lighter mixture is placed on top of the heavier one in a large bowl. Starting at the back of the bowl, use a rubber spatula or whisk to cut down vertically through the two mixtures, across the bottom of the bowl, and up the nearest side. Rotate the bowl a quarter-turn after each series of strokes. This down-across-up-and-over motion gently turns the mixtures over on top of each other, combining them in the process.

Filling Tube Pans and Bundt Pans

To avoid spilling batter down the hole in a tube or Bundt pan, cover the hole with a paper cup while filling the pan.

To prevent air bubbles in a Bundt cake, slowly pour the batter in one area of the pan and allow the batter to flow in and around the Bundt design. Gently tap the filled pan on the counter a few times to release any air bubbles.

To showcase the details of the Bundt-pan design, fill the pan about ¾ full, avoiding overflow. With a spatula, push the batter to the outside of the pan and slightly up the walls. This will give you greater detail on the outside of the baked cake.

Freezing Cakes

Cakes may be frozen either frosted or unfrosted. Buttercream frosting freezes the best, but it's not recommended to freeze egg-white frostings or custard fillings.

To freeze frosted cakes, place in the freezer to harden frosting before wrapping. Place layer cakes in cake containers or bakery boxes to prevent crushing, and overwrap the box. You can freeze a frosted cake for up to 3 months.

You can freeze an unfrosted cake for up to 6 months. Just place the unfrosted cake on a baking sheet, freeze until firm, then seal in a large plastic freezer bag. Or wrap the layers in plastic wrap prior to freezing.

Angel-food cakes are best left in the baking pan or placed in a rigid container to avoid crushing.

Thaw unfrosted cakes at room temperature, covered, for 2 to 3 hours, and then frost as desired. Thaw frosted cakes loosely covered.

Freezing Cake in Slices

After eating only one or two slices from a cake, John and I often prefer to freeze the remainder for another splurge. We slice the cake, and then wrap a sheet of waxed paper around the point and against the sides of each slice. We reassemble the cake, overwrap, and freeze it. Doing this, we can remove as many slices as we like without defrosting the entire cake. I don't recommend this for long-term storage (more than 1 month); the cake will dry out quickly.

Leveling and Splitting a Cake

Level the top of the cake if needed using a long, serrated knife. If the cake top is not too domed, I flip the domed layer over (so I don't waste cake), using the flat bottom as my level cake top.

If you are cutting the cake into layers, measure the height of the cake and cut a small incision into the side to make the desired thickness of your layers. Repeat every 3" around the circumference of the cake. With a long, serrated knife, cut into the cake slowly at the incisions to create 2 even layers, rotating the cake as you cut to keep things uniform and level.

For Almost No-fuss Flouring and Confectioners' Sugar Dusting

Fill empty glass salt or sugar shakers with flour and/or confectioners' sugar and simply shake when you need small amounts of each. Cover the confectioners' sugar shaker with plastic wrap to prevent clumping.

Finishing Touches

Sifted confectioners' sugar and cocoa are simple touches that should be applied at the last minute, using a doily or other items that will leave a fanciful pattern on the cake top once removed.

Using the tines of a fork, make wave designs in the frosting, wiping the fork clean occasionally.

Chopped nuts add flavor, texture, and visual appeal when pressed onto the sides of a cake. Imperfections? Nuts will cover them. To press nuts onto the side of a cake, lift the cake off the stand and hold it by the plate beneath it. Using one hand to hold the cake above a bowl that contains the chopped pistachios, pecans, almonds, or walnuts, use the other hand to press nuts into the frosting, letting the excess fall back into the bowl. You need about 1 cup chopped nuts to cover the sides of a 9" cake.

Toasting Nuts

You should be storing your walnuts, pecans, almonds, etc., in the refrigerator or freezer so they don't become rancid. Just before using, you'll need to toast them to brighten their flavor. I prefer to toast them in a dry skillet over low heat until fragrant, watching carefully so they don't burn. Remove immediately to a large plate or platter and allow to cool completely before chopping or using in the recipe.

Dyeing Frosting

Divide white buttercream frosting or royal icing into separate paper cups with lids (so you can cover to keep from drying out) for each color you will want. Reserve a little plain icing in case you make a mistake. (Hard to believe you could make a mistake, but yes—it happens!)

Dip the end of a toothpick into coloring gel or paste, then dab the color into a paper cup. Use a small spatula to mix the color into the icing until it's thoroughly incorporated and uniform. Want a darker color? Repeat the process, adding just a tiny bit of color at a time. Use a fresh toothpick. Do not put a toothpick that has already stirred icing back into the container of coloring, because this could introduce a tiny amount of icing into the container and cause mold to grow when sealed over time.

Be patient! Adding colors gradually is time consuming, but getting the color right takes time. It's always easier to add more color than to lighten by adding white icing to a dark color.

Think of colors in terms of temperature. If you want a warmer color, add a tiny bit of yellow. If you want a cooler color, add a tiny bit of blue.

Filling a Pastry Bag

To fill a pastry bag with frosting, place an empty pastry bag fitted with a coupler and pastry tip in the center of a tall glass. Open and fold the pastry bag back around the rim of the glass.

When the bag is ⅔ filled, lift it straight out of the glass and gather the end of the bag. Push the frosting down toward the tip to push out any air bubbles, then twist the bag closed.

GOOD THINGS TO KNOW

Watch the Wording of Instructions!

Yes, *there is a difference* if you measure before or after sifting or chopping. If a recipe calls for 1 cup confectioners' sugar, sifted—you measure, then sift. If a recipe calls for 1 cup coarsely chopped dried cranberries—you coarsely chop, then measure.

Do I Have to Sift Flour?

All flour is sifted many times during the milling process, so there's no need to resift flours before using. The exception to this is cake flour, which should always be sifted after measuring.

What's the Best Way to Measure Flour?

To obtain the most accurate measurement of flour, spoon it into a standard dry-ingredient measuring cup and level with a knife or spatula. If the measuring cup is dipped directly into the container—a common mistake—the flour will be packed into the cup and result in extra flour being added to the recipe, which yields tough and dense baked goods.

What Is Cake Flour?

Cake flour is milled from select soft wheat and is especially suited for baking tender, fine-textured cakes as well as biscuits and pastries. (That's not to say you can't get tender results without cake flour!) When substituting cake flour for another flour, increase the amount by 2 tbsp. per cup.

Storing Butter

For the tastiest baked treats, consider these 3 Cs of butter storage: clean, cool, and covered. Refrigerate your butter in either a covered container or its original carton.

To freeze butter, keep it in its original carton and place in a resealable, freezer-safe food bag. This way it will keep in the freezer for up to 9 months.

Butter Measurements
- 2 cups = 4 sticks = 1 lb.
- 1 cup = 2 sticks = ½ lb.
- ½ cup = 1 stick = 8 tbsp. = ¼ lb.
- ⅓ cup = 5⅓ tbsp.
- ¼ cup = ½ stick = 4 tbsp.

No Buttermilk in Your Refrigerator?

Although there's nothing to compare to the taste of real buttermilk, in a pinch you can make a suitable substitute. Use 1 tsp. fresh lemon juice or white vinegar plus milk to make 1 cup. Let stand 10 minutes before using.

What Is Mascarpone?

Mascarpone is a fresh, soft, Italian cheese with a high butterfat content, made from cow's milk enriched with cream. Yum!

What Is Greek Yogurt?

Greek yogurt is a thicker, creamier version of the regular variety, because it has been strained of its whey.

What Is Arrowroot?

This starch thickener has its advantages over cornstarch: it has a more neutral flavor, reheats without apologies, works at a lower temperature, and tolerates acidic ingredients and prolonged cooking better.

What Is Brown Rice Syrup?

Derived from whole or partially polished brown rice, instead of the starch from corn, brown rice syrup is a natural food product that is a delicious substitute for corn syrup. Brown rice syrup is golden, mildly sweet, and caramel flavored. I often completely replace corn syrup with it in my sauces and other desserts, as I find it doesn't yield the sickeningly sweet results that corn syrup does. It is available in natural-food stores and probably the "organic" section of your favorite market.

What Is Barbados Molasses?

Light molasses, often referred to as mild or Barbados molasses, is a subtle, sweet syrup produced from the first boiling of the sugar syrup.

What Is Vanilla Bean Paste?

Vanilla bean paste is a convenient, easy-to-use substitute for whole vanilla beans. I also completely replace vanilla extract with it in some recipes when I want a more intense vanilla flavor.

How Can I Make Vanilla Sugar?

Slice 1 whole vanilla bean down the side and, with the back of the knife, scrape the vanilla seeds into 2 cups granulated sugar. Bury the bean in the sugar and seal the mixture tightly with a lid. Let "steep" for 2 weeks in a cool, dry place out of direct sunlight. Use as you would granulated sugar.

What Is a Bain-Marie?

It's a water bath. It consists of a container (such as a soufflé dish or several ramekins) of food or batter placed in a large shallow pan of warm water, surrounding the food with gentle heat.

Shiny Pans or Dark Pans?

Shiny pans reflect rather than absorb heat. For a pound cake with a tender, delicate crust, bake it in a shiny pan. It's always advisable to lower the oven temperature by 25 degrees when using a dark pan, and watch the baking time carefully so your cake doesn't burn.

Frosting and Icing: What's the Difference?

Just a bunch of letters, my fellow baker—both words have the same meaning. Although frosting/icing can range from thick to thin, it must be thick enough to adhere to the cake yet soft enough to spread easily.

When I Macerate, What Am I Doing?

You're infusing food, usually fruit, with flavor by soaking it in a liquid or allowing it to release its juices and flavor.

Can I Freeze a Cheesecake?

Cheesecakes freeze beautifully. To freeze a cheesecake, place a completely cooled cheesecake, uncovered, in the freezer for 1 hour or until firm. Transfer to a large freezer bag or container. Seal, label, and freeze for up to 1 month. When ready to serve, transfer the cheesecake to a platter and loosely cover. Thaw for 24 hours in the refrigerator.

A CAKE BAKER'S PANTRY

Keep these 13 ingredients on hand. They're found in most recipes in this book.

- Flour, unbleached, all purpose
- Baking powder
- Baking soda
- Sugar, granulated
- Brown sugar
- Confectioners' sugar
- Salt, sea salt preferred
- Arrowroot
- Butter, unsalted please!
- Milk, preferably whole milk
- Eggs, large please!
- Chocolate: bittersweet, semisweet, milk, white, and unsweetened cocoa powder—only the very best will do!
- Vanilla extract, pure please!

CHEF'S HATS

I've taken some time to mark the recipes in this book with chef's hats to indicate their level of difficulty. You should feel free to follow these based on either your skill level or the amount of effort you're in the mood to put into one of my delicious offerings.

🎩 = Easy. You should be able to whip these up in no time!

🎩🎩 = Intermediate. A little more effort and skill are required to complete these cakes.

🎩🎩🎩 = Advanced. These are perfect for more experienced bakers or those willing to take the time to learn.

WEIGHTS AND MEASURES

There's no getting around it—accurate measurement is critical in baking. To achieve consistent results each time you follow a recipe, you must measure correctly.

Measure liquids in standard glass or clear plastic measuring cups designed for liquids. Measure dry or solid ingredients in metal or plastic cups that hold the exact amount specified in a recipe.

Don't shake or pack down dry ingredients. Spoon them in, piling the cup high and light, then level off. Brown sugar is the exception to this rule—press it firmly into the cup with your clean fingers or a spoon, then level off.

Liquid Measure Equivalents

3 tsp.	=			1 tbsp.
2 tbsp.	=			1 fluid oz.
4 tbsp.	=			¼ cup
5 tbsp. + 1 tsp.	=			⅓ cup
8 tbsp.	=	½ cup	=	4 fluid oz.
10 tbsp. + 2 tsp.	=			⅔ cup
12 tbsp.	=			¾ cup
16 tbsp.	=	1 cup	=	8 fluid oz.
¼ cup + 2 tbsp.	=			⅜ cup
½ cup + 2 tbsp.	=			⅝ cup
¾ cup + 2 tbsp.	=			⅞ cup
2 cups	=	16 fluid oz.	=	1 pt.
4 cups	=	2 pt.	=	1 qt.
1 qt.	=			.946 liters (946.3 milliliters)
1 liter	=			1.06 qt.
4 qt.	=			1 gal.

Equivalent Yields

1 medium lemon	=	3 tbsp. fresh lemon juice
1 medium orange	=	¼ cup fresh orange juice
8 egg whites	=	1 cup
¼ lb. (1 stick) butter	=	½ cup = 8 tbsp.
1 lb. (4 sticks) butter	=	2 cups
1 cup (½ pt.) cream	=	2 cups whipped cream
1 lb. granulated sugar	=	2⅓ cups
1 lb. brown sugar	=	2⅓ firmly packed cups
1 lb. confectioners' sugar	=	4 cups, unsifted
4 oz. almond or walnuts	=	1 cup chopped nuts
16 squares graham crackers	=	1 cup crumbs
24 2" vanilla wafers	=	1 cup crumbs
18 2" chocolate wafers	=	1 cup crumbs

Light a candle, sing a song, then serve.

This decorated cupcake is the only acceptable mouse in the house.

CAKES
to die for!

LAYER CAKES

This irresistible Moist, Dark Chocolate Mocha Cake with Raspberry Filling works perfectly when someone answers "Chocolate!" to the question "What kind of cake would you like?"

It *is* possible to create layer cakes with lots of pizzazz, without using a lot of special equipment. Take a few minutes to read through "A Slice of Advice," where you'll find simple decorating ideas for home-style layer cakes you'll be proud to serve.

Keep in mind that baking (just like life itself) isn't always perfect . . . so forgive yourself if your finished product isn't picture perfect. If you've followed my lead and used quality ingredients, you'll know that, taste-wise, your cake will still be unbeatable!

Once you've mastered the art of the cake, mix and match fillings and flavors . . . and don't wait for a landmark celebration to enjoy them.

Moist, Dark Chocolate Mocha Cake with Raspberry Filling

This is my "go to" cake when I need something moist and seductive and loaded with rich chocolate flavor. Try it for your next special (or everyday) occasion and I know you'll agree.

1 cup unsalted butter, room temperature, cut into pieces
3 cups firmly packed light brown sugar
4 large eggs, room temperature
1 tbsp. vanilla extract
3 cups unbleached, all-purpose flour
¾ cup unsweetened cocoa, sifted
1 tbsp. baking soda
½ tsp. salt
1 cup strong-brewed coffee, cooled
1 tsp. espresso powder dissolved in ½ cup milk
1⅓ cups sour cream

FUDGE CREAM CHEESE FROSTING

16 oz. cream cheese, room temperature, cut into pieces
½ cup unsalted butter, room temperature, cut into pieces
8 oz. bittersweet chocolate, melted
½ cup milk, whole or 2 percent
1 tbsp. vanilla extract
6 cups confectioners' sugar, sifted

RASPBERRY FILLING

1½ 10-oz. pkg. frozen raspberries in syrup, thawed
3 tbsp. granulated sugar
3 tbsp. cornstarch or arrowroot

Chocolate-covered espresso beans

Heat oven to 350 degrees. Grease 3 9" round cake pans and cover pan bottoms with a round of parchment paper. Grease and flour the paper and sides of the pans, tapping out excess flour.

In a large bowl of an electric mixer, cream the butter and brown sugar until light and fluffy.

Add the eggs, one at a time, beating well after each addition. Stir in the vanilla. Scrape bowl.

In a medium bowl, whisk together the flour, cocoa, baking soda, and salt. Add the flour mixture to the egg mixture alternately with the coffee, milk mixture, and sour cream. Spread batter into prepared pans. Bake for 30 to 35 minutes or until a toothpick inserted near the center comes out clean.

Cool in pans for 10 minutes. Then run a knife around edge of pans to loosen cakes. Cover a pan with a large, lint-free towel-covered plate and invert pan. Remove pan from cake. Peel off parchment and re-invert cake from plate onto cooling rack. Repeat with remaining cakes. Allow to cool completely on wire racks.

For the Frosting: In a large bowl of an electric mixer, beat the cream cheese and butter until well combined. Scrape bowl. Beat until mixture is fluffy.

Beat in the chocolate, milk, and vanilla until blended. Gradually beat in the confectioners' sugar.

For the Filling: Combine raspberries, sugar, and cornstarch in a medium saucepan. Cook over medium heat, stirring constantly, until mixture comes to a boil. Boil 1 minute; remove from heat. Allow to cool for 15 minutes, then refrigerate until cool.

Spread some frosting and filling between the cake layers and then stack. Frost the sides and top of the cake. Fill a star-tipped pastry bag with remaining frosting and pipe decorations on top of the cake. Refrigerate.

Remove from the refrigerator 30 minutes before serving. Decorate top of cake with the espresso beans. Serves 12-14.

Buttermilk Fudge Cake with a Chocolate "Gloss"

A deep-down, rich chocolate cake with a chocolate "gloss" that thickens like fudge. Yum!

1¾ cups unbleached, all-purpose flour
¾ cup plus 3 tbsp. unsweetened cocoa, sifted
1¼ tsp. baking soda
⅛ tsp. salt
¾ cup unsalted butter, room temperature, cut into pieces
⅔ cup granulated sugar
⅔ cup firmly packed dark brown sugar
2 large eggs
2 tsp. vanilla extract
1½ cups buttermilk

CHOCOLATE "GLOSS"

½ cup unsalted butter, room temperature, cut into pieces
1 cup confectioners' sugar, sifted
2 tsp. vanilla extract
3 oz. unsweetened chocolate, melted and cooled

A SLICE OF ADVICE FROM BEV

"Gloss" thickens quickly, so make it just before you're ready to frost the cake.

Heat oven to 350 degrees. Grease 2 9" round cake pans and cover pan bottoms with a round of parchment paper. Grease the parchment.

In a medium bowl, whisk together the flour, cocoa, baking soda, and salt.

In a large bowl of an electric mixer, cream the butter with the white and brown sugars on medium speed until mixture is light and fluffy. Scrape bowl.

Add the eggs, one at a time, beating well after each addition. Stir in the vanilla.

With the mixer on low, add the dry ingredients alternately with the buttermilk, beginning and ending with the dry ingredients. Mix *just* until blended.

Spread batter into prepared pans; quickly and gently smooth the tops.

Bake until a toothpick inserted in the centers comes out clean, about 20 to 25 minutes.

Cool in pans for 10 minutes. Then run a knife around edge of pans to loosen cakes. Cover a pan with a large, lint-free towel-covered plate and invert pan. Remove pan from cake. Peel off parchment and re-invert cake from plate onto cooling rack. Repeat with remaining cake. Allow to cool completely on wire racks.

For the Chocolate "Gloss": In a large bowl of an electric mixer, cream the butter with the confectioners' sugar until very light. Add the vanilla and melted chocolate, beating until glossy and smooth.

Place one cake layer on a cake stand or serving plate. Spread with a small amount of the gloss. Top with the other layer and frost the sides and then the top, swirling the gloss.

Let the cake stand for at least 30 minutes before slicing, to allow the layers to set. Serves 8.

CAKES TO DIE FOR!

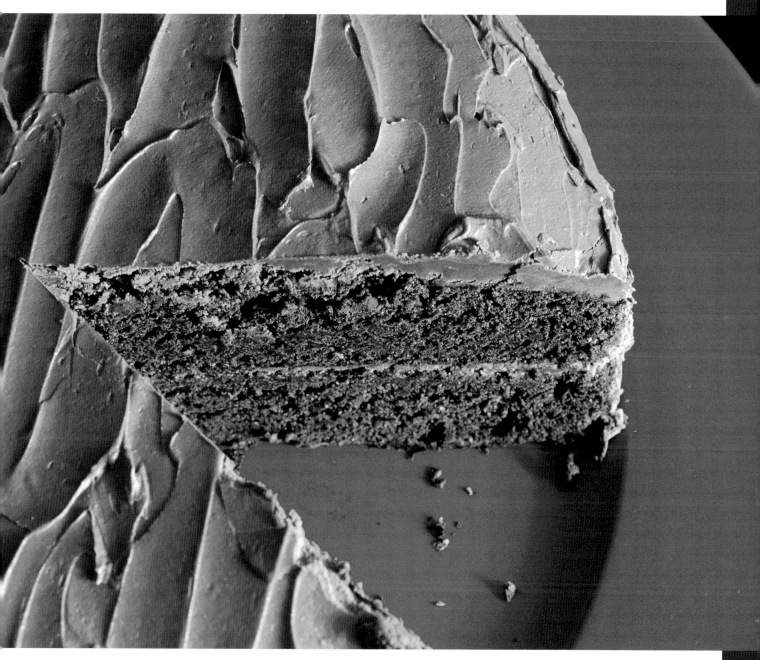

The chocolate "gloss" firms up quickly, adding a fudge-textured frosting to this Buttermilk Fudge Cake.

Marvelous Marble Cake with Chocolate Frosting

The perfect cake for someone who can't decide whether they want a yellow cake or a chocolate cake . . . why not both, combined?!

3 cups unbleached, all-purpose flour
1 tbsp. baking powder
¾ tsp. salt
1 cup milk, whole
2 tsp. vanilla extract
¾ cup unsalted butter, room temperature, cut into pieces
2 cups granulated sugar
4 large eggs
4 oz. bittersweet chocolate, melted

FROSTING

½ cup plus 2 tbsp. heavy cream, divided
4 oz. bittersweet chocolate, coarsely chopped
1 cup unsalted butter, room temperature, cut into pieces
4 cups confectioners' sugar, sifted
1 tsp. vanilla extract
Pinch of salt

Heat oven to 350 degrees. Grease 2 9" round cake pans and cover pan bottoms with a round of parchment paper. Grease and flour paper and pan sides, tapping out excess flour.

In a medium bowl, whisk together the flour, baking powder, and salt. In a small bowl, whisk together the milk and vanilla extract.

In a large bowl of an electric mixer, beat the butter until light and creamy. Add the sugar and beat until mixture is fluffy. Scrape bowl. Beat in the eggs, one at a time, beating well after each addition.

Alternately add the flour mixture and the milk mixture to the butter mixture, just until combined.

In a medium bowl, mix 2 cups batter with the melted chocolate.

Spread yellow batter into prepared pans. Dollop chocolate batter over the batter in both pans and swirl gently with a knife. Bake until a toothpick inserted in the center comes out clean, about 28 to 35 minutes.

Cool in pans for 10 minutes. Then run a knife around edge of pans to loosen cakes. Cover a pan with a large, lint-free towel-covered plate and invert pan. Remove pan from cake. Peel off parchment and re-invert cake from plate onto cooling rack. Repeat with remaining cake. Allow to cool completely on wire racks.

For the Frosting: In a small saucepan, bring ¼ cup heavy cream just to a simmer. Remove from heat and stir in chocolate. Allow to steep for 5 minutes. Whisk until chocolate is melted and smooth. Set aside to cool.

In a large bowl of an electric mixer, beat the butter until creamy. Mix in the sugar and beat until light and fluffy. With mixer on low, beat in the remaining ¼ cup plus 2 tbsp. cream, vanilla, and salt just until combined. Stir in the chocolate-cream mixture until fluffy, being careful not to overbeat.

Spread some frosting between the cake layers, and then stack. Frost the sides and top of the cake. Let cake stand for 1 hour to allow layers to set. Serves 8-10.

CAKES TO DIE FOR!

Butter Cake with Browned Butter Frosting and Bev's Three-Chocolate Bark

Taking a cake from perfect to out of this world is exactly what this three-chocolate candy confection will do. Enjoy your time away.

⅔ cup unsalted butter, room
   temperature, cut into pieces
⅔ cup granulated sugar
2 large eggs
2 tsp. vanilla extract
2 cups unbleached, all-purpose flour
1 tbsp. baking powder
¼ tsp. salt
1 cup milk, whole

BEV'S THREE-CHOCOLATE BARK

½ lb. bittersweet chocolate, coarsely
   chopped
½ lb. milk chocolate, coarsely chopped
½ lb. white chocolate, coarsely chopped
3 tbsp. unsalted butter, divided

BROWNED BUTTER FROSTING

¼ cup unsalted butter, cut into pieces
3 cups confectioners' sugar, sifted
2 tsp. vanilla extract
3 to 4 tbsp. milk, whole

A SLICE OF ADVICE FROM BEV

To be sure you capture the flavor of true white chocolate, be sure cocoa butter is listed on the ingredients label. Otherwise, you're buying sickeningly sweet confectioners' coating.

Heat oven to 350 degrees. Grease and flour 2 8" round cake pans, tapping out excess flour.

In a large bowl of an electric mixer, beat together the butter and sugar until creamy. Scrape bowl. Add eggs and vanilla, continuing to beat until well mixed.

In a medium bowl, whisk together the flour, baking powder, and salt. With mixer on low, alternately add the flour mixture and the milk to the butter mixture, scraping bowl often, until well mixed.

Spread batter into prepared pans. Bake for 25 to 30 minutes or until a toothpick inserted in the center comes out clean.

Cool in pans for 10 minutes. Then run a knife around edge of pans to loosen cakes. Cover a pan with a large, lint-free towel-covered plate and invert pan. Remove pan from cake. Re-invert cake from plate onto cooling rack. Repeat with remaining cake. Allow to cool completely on wire racks.

For Bev's Three-Chocolate Bark: Line a small baking pan with parchment paper. Melt bittersweet chocolate atop a double boiler over simmering water. Once chocolate is melted, quickly stir in 1 tbsp. butter, whisking until smooth.

Spread chocolate smoothly and evenly over the parchment-paper-lined pan (mixture will not reach edges of pan). Refrigerate pan for 10 minutes.

Meanwhile, melt the milk chocolate in a clean pan atop double boiler. Once chocolate is melted, quickly stir in 1 tbsp. butter, whisking until smooth. Spread atop bittersweet chocolate and refrigerate for 10 minutes.

Finally, melt the white chocolate in a clean pan atop double boiler. Once chocolate is melted, quickly stir in remaining 1 tbsp. butter, whisking until smooth. Spread atop milk chocolate and refrigerate until ready to use.

For the Browned Butter Frosting: Melt the butter in a 1½-qt.

saucepan over medium-low heat until light golden brown (3 to 5 minutes). Whisk together the browned butter, confectioners' sugar, and vanilla in a small bowl. Beat at medium speed with an electric mixer, scraping bowl often and gradually adding enough of the milk for desired spreading consistency.

Spread some frosting between the cake layers, and then stack. Frost the sides and top of the cake.

When ready to serve, remove tray of bark from the refrigerator. Flip over atop a large cutting board and carefully peel off parchment paper. Chip apart into irregular-size candy pieces. Place jagged pieces atop cake, and cut cake into slices to serve. Garnish individual plates with additional bark, if desired. Serves 12-14.

Peanut Butter Lover's Cake with Creamy Chocolate Peanut Butter Frosting

Top this cake with mini peanut butter cups for an over-the-top peanut butter and chocolate combination!

¼ cup unsalted butter, room
    temperature, cut into pieces
¼ cup creamy peanut butter
1½ cups firmly packed light brown sugar
2 large eggs
½ cup warm water
1 cup buttermilk
2 cups unbleached, all-purpose flour
1 tsp. salt
1 tsp. baking soda

FROSTING

1 oz. unsweetened chocolate, melted
    and cooled
2 tbsp. unsalted butter, room
    temperature
2 tbsp. creamy peanut butter
2 cups confectioners' sugar, sifted
½ tsp. vanilla extract
3 or 4 tbsp. milk, whole

Heat oven to 350 degrees. Grease and flour 2 9" round cake pans, tapping out excess flour.

In a large bowl of an electric mixer, combine the butter, peanut butter, and brown sugar and beat until blended. Add the eggs, water, buttermilk, flour, salt, and baking soda, beating to combine. Scrape bowl.

Beat mixture on medium-high speed until well combined. Spread batter into prepared pans.

Bake for 25 to 30 minutes or until a toothpick inserted in the center comes out clean.

Cool in pans for 10 minutes. Then run a knife around edge of pans to loosen cakes. Cover a pan with a large, lint-free towel-covered plate and invert pan. Remove pan from cake. Re-invert cake from plate onto cooling rack. Repeat with remaining cake. Allow to cool completely on wire racks.

For the Frosting: In a large bowl of an electric mixer, combine the chocolate, butter, peanut butter, confectioners' sugar, and vanilla and beat on medium speed until blended. Scrape down sides of bowl. Continue beating, adding 3 or 4 tbsp. milk until desired spreading consistency is reached.

Spread some frosting between the cake layers, then stack. Frost the sides and top of the cake. Serves 12.

Combining peanut butter and chocolate brings out the kid in all of us.
Have a giggle fest and laugh about childish things while you share a
slice of this Fluffy Peanut Butter-Frosted Chocolate Cake.

Fluffy Peanut Butter-Frosted Chocolate Cake

A favorite combo, peanut butter and chocolate, makes for a rich and satisfying slice of dessert. This chocolate cake makes a great base for other frostings as well.

1⅔ cups granulated sugar
¾ cup unsalted butter, room temperature, cut into pieces
3 large eggs
1 tsp. vanilla extract
2 cups unbleached, all-purpose flour
⅔ cup unsweetened cocoa, sifted
1¼ tsp. baking soda
½ tsp. baking powder
½ tsp. salt
1⅓ cups milk, whole

FROSTING

1 cup creamy peanut butter
½ cup unsalted butter, room temperature, cut into pieces
2½ cups confectioners' sugar, sifted
2 tsp. vanilla extract
3 to 6 tbsp. milk

Heat oven to 350 degrees. Grease and flour 2 9" square cake pans, tapping out excess flour.

In a large bowl of an electric mixer, combine the sugar and butter and beat at medium speed, scraping bowl often, until mixture is creamy.

Add the eggs and vanilla and continue beating until well mixed.

In a medium bowl, whisk together the flour, cocoa, baking soda, baking powder, and salt. Alternately add the flour mixture and milk to the butter mixture, beating just until blended.

Pour batter into prepared pans. Bake for 30 to 40 minutes or until a toothpick inserted in the center comes out clean.

Cool in pans for 10 minutes. Then run a knife around edge of pans to loosen cakes. Cover a pan with a large, lint-free towel-covered plate and invert pan. Remove pan from cake. Re-invert cake from plate onto cooling rack. Repeat with remaining cake. Allow to cool completely on wire racks.

For the Frosting: In a large bowl of an electric mixer, beat the peanut butter and butter until well combined, scraping bowl often. Beat until creamy. Add the confectioners' sugar, vanilla, and 3 tbsp. milk. Beat until well combined, stopping to scrape bowl. Add milk as needed to reach desired frosting consistency.

Spread some frosting between the cake layers, and then stack. Frost the sides and top of the cake. Refrigerate cake until ready to serve. Serves 8-12.

Celebration! Peppermint Chocolate Cake

This festive cake—deep, dark chocolate stacked high with a sprinkling of peppermint candies—is perfect for any holiday or winter celebration.

1¾ cups boiling water
1½ cups unsweetened cocoa powder, sifted
4 oz. bittersweet chocolate, coarsely chopped
1 cup buttermilk
1 tbsp. vanilla extract
½ tsp. peppermint extract
3 cups cake flour, sifted
2½ tsp. baking soda
1 tsp. salt
2 cups unsalted butter, room temperature, cut into pieces
1½ cups granulated sugar
1½ cups firmly packed dark brown sugar
4 large eggs

PEPPERMINT CREAM-CHEESE FILLING

14 whole, round, hard peppermint candies
1 cup confectioners' sugar, sifted
12 oz. whipped cream cheese, room temperature
4 tbsp. unsalted butter, room temperature
1 tsp. vanilla extract
½ tsp. peppermint extract

CHOCOLATE GLAZE

1¼ cups heavy cream
12 oz. bittersweet chocolate, coarsely chopped
2 tbsp. unsalted butter, room temperature

½ cup coarsely chopped hard peppermint candies

Heat oven to 350 degrees. Grease 3 9" round cake pans and cover pan bottoms with a round of parchment paper. Grease and flour the paper and sides of the pans, tapping out excess flour.

In a heatproof bowl, whisk together the boiling water and cocoa until mixture is smooth. Add the chocolate and let mixture stand for 1 minute. Whisk until smooth, then let stand 5 minutes.

Add buttermilk, vanilla extract, and peppermint extract, whisking to combine.

In a medium bowl, whisk together the flour, baking soda, and salt.

In a large bowl of an electric mixer, beat the butter and sugars until light and fluffy. Scrape bowl. Add eggs, one at a time, beating well after each addition.

With mixer on low, alternately add the flour and chocolate mixtures to the butter mixture, beating just until combined. Spread batter into prepared pans. Quickly and gently smooth tops.

Bake for 38 to 43 minutes or until a toothpick inserted in the center comes out with a few moist crumbs attached.

Cool in pans for 10 minutes. Then run a knife around edge of pans to loosen cakes. Cover a pan with a large, lint-free towel-covered plate and invert pan. Remove pan from cake. Peel off parchment and re-invert cake from plate onto cooling rack. Repeat with remaining cakes. Allow to cool completely on wire racks.

For the Peppermint Cream-Cheese Filling: Pulse the peppermint candies and confectioners' sugar in a food processor until finely ground. Transfer to a medium bowl and stir in cream cheese, butter, and vanilla and peppermint extracts. Mix until well combined.

For the Chocolate Glaze: In a small saucepan, bring the heavy cream to a simmer over medium heat. Remove saucepan from heat and add the chocolate and butter. Whisk until smooth, then transfer mixture to a bowl and allow to cool.

Set a wire rack atop a sheet of waxed paper. Place a platter on the rack, and place 1 cake layer on platter. Spread cake with *half* of the filling, and then top with a second cake layer. Spread with remaining filling and top with third cake layer.

Pour some of the glaze over the top, smoothing onto the sides with a thin, small metal spatula. Continue to pour and spread glaze until cake is evenly coated.

Allow cake to set for 30 minutes. Just before serving, garnish top with chopped peppermint candies. Serves 10-12.

 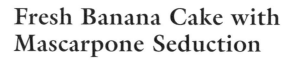

Fresh Banana Cake with Mascarpone Seduction

A banana cake like no other . . . moist, flavorful, and how could you not love that frosting? This is sure to become one of your favorites!

1½ cups unbleached, all-purpose flour
¾ tsp. baking powder
¾ tsp. baking soda
½ tsp. salt
½ cup unsalted butter, room temperature, cut into pieces
¾ cup granulated sugar
2 large egg yolks
1 tsp. vanilla extract
¾ cup mashed, ripe banana
¼ cup plus 2 tbsp. buttermilk
3 large egg whites, room temperature

MASCARPONE FROSTING

1½ cups chilled mascarpone
1¾ cups confectioners' sugar, sifted
1 or 2 large bananas

A SLICE OF ADVICE FROM BEV

One of my cake testers, Barbara, used this method for slicing the layer in half horizontally: "I measured halfway up and placed toothpicks around the layer; then I cut along the toothpick 'line' for even slicing."

Heat oven to 325 degrees. Grease a 9" round cake pan and cover pan bottom with a round of parchment paper. Grease and flour the parchment paper and sides of the pan, tapping out excess flour.

In a medium bowl, whisk together the flour, baking powder, baking soda, and salt.

In a large bowl of an electric mixer, beat the butter and sugar until light and fluffy. Scrape bowl. Beat in the egg yolks and vanilla to blend.

Add the mashed banana and beat until mixture is smooth. Add *half* of the dry ingredients and beat at low speed until the batter is moistened. Scrape bowl. Beat in *half* of the buttermilk, and then add the remaining dry ingredients and remaining buttermilk. Beat until combined.

In a clean bowl of an electric mixer, beat the egg whites until stiff peaks form. Beat *one-fourth* of the egg whites into the batter at low speed.

Using a rubber spatula, gently and swiftly fold in the remainder of the egg whites until no streaks remain. Spread the batter into prepared pan. Quickly smooth top.

Bake for 32 to 35 minutes or until the top is golden and springy and a toothpick inserted in the center comes out clean. (Top may be slightly cracked.)

Cool in pan for 10 minutes. Then run a knife around edge of pan to loosen cake. Cover pan with a large, lint-free towel-covered plate and invert pan. Remove pan from cake. Peel off parchment and re-invert cake from plate onto cooling rack. Allow to cool completely on wire rack.

For the Frosting: In a medium bowl, beat the mascarpone with the confectioners' sugar until frosting is light and fluffy.

Using a long serrated knife, carefully cut the cake horizontally into 2 layers. Place the top layer, cut side up, on a cake stand or large

CAKES TO DIE FOR!

round platter and spread with *half* of the frosting. Slice ½ or 1 banana and arrange in a single layer atop the frosting.

Top with the second cake layer (cut side down) and frost the top. Refrigerate the cake for at least 30 minutes before serving.

Just before serving, thinly slice ½ or 1 banana and place decoratively atop cake. Serves 8-10.

The familiar flavors of a Fresh Banana Cake . . . with all the seduction of creamy, dreamy mascarpone. Caution: don't slip on the peel on your way to being seduced by a slice!

Bev's Banana Split Cake with Ice Cream and Caramel Sauce

The combination of this cake, ice cream, and my caramel sauce will elevate your idea of a banana split to a whole new level!

¾ cup unsalted butter, room temperature, cut into pieces
1 cup granulated sugar
3 large eggs
⅓ cup mashed, ripe banana
⅓ cup sour cream
⅓ cup milk, whole
1 tsp. vanilla extract
2¼ cups unbleached, all-purpose flour
1¼ tsp. baking powder
½ tsp. salt
¼ tsp. baking soda
1½ cups strawberry jam, divided
2 oz. semisweet chocolate, melted and cooled

IN-A-HURRY CARAMEL SAUCE

½ cup unsalted butter, cut into pieces
1¼ cups firmly packed light brown sugar
2 tbsp. brown rice syrup
½ cup heavy cream

Ice cream (vanilla, chocolate, or strawberry)

A SLICE OF ADVICE FROM BEV

This "In-a-Hurry Caramel Sauce" is a favorite from my cookbook *Brownies to Die For!*

Heat oven to 350 degrees. Grease 2 8" round cake pans and cover pan bottoms with a round of parchment paper. Grease and flour paper and pan sides, tapping out excess flour.

In a large bowl of an electric mixer, beat the butter until creamy. Add the sugar, beating until mixture is light and fluffy.

Add the eggs, one at a time, beating well after each addition.

In a medium bowl, stir together the banana, sour cream, milk, and vanilla. In another bowl, whisk together the flour, baking powder, salt, and baking soda.

With mixer on low, alternately beat the flour mixture and the banana mixture into the butter mixture. Scrape bowl.

In a small bowl, combine ⅔ cup batter with ½ cup strawberry jam. In another small bowl, combine ⅔ cup batter with the melted chocolate.

Spread plain batter into prepared pans. Spoon *half* of each flavored batter onto the plain batter in each pan, gently swirling with a knife. Bake for 28 to 35 minutes or until a toothpick inserted near the center comes out clean.

Cool in pans for 10 minutes. Then run a knife around edge of pans to loosen cakes. Cover a pan with a large, lint-free towel-covered plate and invert pan. Remove pan from cake. Peel off parchment and re-invert cake from plate onto cooling rack. Repeat with remaining cake. Allow to cool completely on wire racks.

For the Caramel Sauce: Melt the butter in a medium saucepan. Whisk in the sugar and syrup and bring the mixture to a boil, cooking and stirring until sugar dissolves.

Stir in the heavy cream and return the mixture to a boil. Remove from heat, allowing mixture to cool slightly before using.

Spread remaining strawberry jam between the cake layers, and then stack. Allow cake to set for 30 minutes before slicing. Serve with ice cream and a generous drizzle of Caramel Sauce. Serves 12-14.

CAKES TO DIE FOR!

Cranberry-Amaretto Layer Cake

A delicious alternative to cakes with raspberry or strawberry filling, this tart sweet cake is sure to become a favorite.

3 cups unbleached, all-purpose flour
1 tbsp. baking powder
¾ tsp. salt
1 cup milk, whole
2 tsp. vanilla extract
¾ cup unsalted butter, room
    temperature, cut into pieces
2 cups granulated sugar
4 large eggs

FROSTING

1 cup unsalted butter, room
    temperature, cut into pieces
6 oz. cream cheese, room temperature,
    cut into pieces
4 cups confectioners' sugar, sifted
2 tbsp. amaretto liqueur
1 to 4 tsp. milk, whole

CRANBERRY FILLING

1 cup whole-berry cranberry sauce
2 tbsp. amaretto liqueur
⅓ cup plus 3 tbsp. dried cranberries,
    divided

Heat oven to 350 degrees. Grease 2 9" round cake pans and cover pan bottoms with a round of parchment paper. Grease and flour paper and pan sides, tapping out excess flour.

In a medium bowl, whisk together the flour, baking powder, and salt. In a small bowl, whisk together the milk and vanilla extract.

In a large bowl of an electric mixer, beat the butter until light and creamy. Add the sugar and beat until mixture is fluffy. Scrape bowl. Beat in the eggs, one at a time, beating well after each addition.

Alternately add the flour mixture and the milk mixture to the butter mixture, just until combined. Spread batter into prepared pans.

Bake until a toothpick inserted in the center comes out clean, about 28 to 35 minutes.

Cool in pans for 10 minutes. Then run a knife around edge of pans to loosen cakes. Cover a pan with a large, lint-free towel-covered plate and invert pan. Remove pan from cake. Peel off parchment and re-invert cake from plate onto cooling rack. Repeat with remaining cake. Allow to cool completely on wire racks.

For the Frosting: In a large bowl of an electric mixer, beat the butter and cream cheese until blended. With mixer on low, beat in the confectioners' sugar just until smooth. Blend in the amaretto and enough milk for desired frosting consistency.

For the Cranberry Filling: In a small bowl, combine the cranberry sauce and amaretto.

Spread some frosting between the cake layers, then top with the Cranberry Filling and sprinkle with 3 tbsp. dried cranberries. Top with second cake layer, frosting sides and top of cake. Refrigerate cake for 30 minutes to allow layers to set.

When ready to serve, decorate top with remaining dried cranberries. Serves 8-10.

Chocolate Almond Torte with Cranberry Honey Compote

Many layers and many flavors, including a show-stopping compote on the side that complements each slice perfectly!

⅔ cup unsalted butter, room
    temperature, cut into pieces
1¾ cups granulated sugar
1¾ cups unbleached, all-purpose flour
1¼ tsp. baking soda
1 tsp. salt
¼ tsp. baking powder
4 oz. unsweetened chocolate, melted
1¼ cups water
1 tsp. almond extract
3 large eggs, lightly beaten to blend

WHITE CHOCOLATE FILLING

8 oz. white chocolate, melted
¾ cup unsalted butter, room
    temperature, cut into pieces
¼ tsp. almond extract
½ cup finely chopped almonds

CREAM FILLING AND TOPPING

2 cups heavy cream, whipped
1 tbsp. granulated sugar
¼ tsp. almond extract

CRANBERRY HONEY COMPOTE

12 oz. cranberries, fresh or frozen
1 cup apple cider or natural apple juice
½ cup honey
4 cinnamon sticks, broken in half and
    placed in a large tea infuser
1 tbsp. freshly grated orange zest
⅛ tsp. ground cloves
1 tbsp. crystallized (candied) ginger,
    finely chopped
½ cup dried cranberries

Heat oven to 350 degrees. Grease and flour 4 9" round cake pans, tapping out excess flour.

In a large bowl of an electric mixer, beat the butter and sugar until light and fluffy. With mixer on low, beat the flour, baking soda, salt, baking powder, chocolate, water, almond extract, and eggs into the butter mixture until moistened.

Scrape bowl. Beat mixture at high speed for 4 minutes. Spread batter into prepared pans. Layers will be very thin.

Bake for 15 to 23 minutes or until a toothpick inserted in the center comes out clean.

Cool in pans for 10 minutes. Then run a knife around edge of pans to loosen cakes. Cover a pan with a large, lint-free towel-covered plate and invert pan. Remove pan from cake. Re-invert cake from plate onto cooling rack. Repeat with remaining cakes. Allow to cool completely on wire racks.

For the White Chocolate Filling: In a medium bowl, combine the white chocolate, butter, and almond extract. Beat until smooth and creamy; stir in the almonds to blend.

For the Cream Filling and Topping: In a medium bowl, blend together the whipped cream, sugar, and almond extract, just until combined.

Place one cake layer on a cake stand or serving plate. Spread with *half* of the White Chocolate Filling. Top with a second cake layer and spread with *half* of the Cream Filling and Topping.

Repeat cake layers. Frost the sides and top with the Cream Filling and Topping. Keep refrigerated until ready to serve.

For the Cranberry Honey Compote: In a large saucepan, combine the fresh or frozen cranberries, cider or juice, honey, cinnamon pieces (in a tea infuser for easy removal), zest, cloves, and ginger. Bring to a boil over medium heat.

CAKES TO DIE FOR!

A SLICE OF ADVICE FROM BEV

If you find yourself with leftover Cranberry Honey Compote, be very happy! This tart-sweet mixture is perfect with many of the other cakes in this book, an assortment of cheeses, or grilled salmon or pork.

Simmer, stirring occasionally, until berries burst and sauce thickens slightly, about 20 minutes. Simmer just until desired thickness is reached. Remove from heat. Remove cinnamon pieces and stir in dried cranberries.

Allow to cool to room temperature or, if made ahead, keep covered and refrigerated until ready to serve. Makes about 2½ cups.

Serve cake with compote on the side. Serves 12.

There's just one slice left? Go for it! No one ever regrets biting into this
Chocolate Almond Torte with Cranberry Honey Compote.

Macadamia nuts' buttery rich flavor is a perfect match for white chocolate. One bite of this Macadamia Madness with White Chocolate Frosting layer cake and you'll be hooked!

Macadamia Madness with White Chocolate Frosting

The richness of macadamia nuts and the decadence of white chocolate frosting join for a beautiful layer cake. If you're in a festive mood, it makes the perfect base for a decorated cake.

2 cups unbleached, all-purpose flour
1 tbsp. baking powder
¼ tsp. salt
¾ cup unsalted butter, room temperature, cut into pieces
1½ cups granulated sugar
1 tsp. vanilla extract
1 cup milk, whole
5 large egg whites, room temperature
¼ cup finely ground roasted and salted macadamia nuts
2 tsp. freshly grated orange zest

WHITE CHOCOLATE FROSTING

½ cup unsalted butter, room temperature, cut into pieces
2 tsp. vanilla extract
6 cups confectioners' sugar, sifted, divided
⅓ cup milk, whole, divided
6 oz. white chocolate, melted

A SLICE OF ADVICE FROM BEV

You don't have 3 cake pans? Divide the batter evenly into thirds. Bake 2 pans of batter and refrigerate the remaining batter. While the 2 baked layers are cooling, prepare a pan as above and bake the third layer.

Heat oven to 350 degrees. Grease 3 8" round cake pans and cover pan bottoms with a round of parchment paper. Grease and lightly flour the paper and sides of pans, tapping out excess flour.

In a medium bowl, whisk together the flour, baking powder, and salt.

In a large bowl of an electric mixer, beat the butter until light. Scrape bowl. Add the sugar and vanilla, beating until well combined.

Alternately add the flour mixture and the milk to the butter mixture, beating on low just until combined. Scrape bowl.

In another bowl, beat the egg whites on high speed until stiff peaks form. Gently stir about 1 cup of the beaten egg whites into the batter to lighten.

Fold the remaining beaten egg whites into the batter. Fold in the macadamia nuts and orange zest. Spread batter into prepared pans.

Bake for 25 minutes or until cakes spring back when lightly touched.

Cool in pans for 10 minutes. Then run a knife around edge of pans to loosen cakes. Cover a pan with a large, lint-free towel-covered plate and invert pan. Remove pan from cake. Peel off parchment and re-invert cake from plate onto cooling rack. Repeat with remaining cakes. Allow to cool completely on wire racks.

For the White Chocolate Frosting: In a large bowl of an electric mixer, beat the butter and vanilla on medium speed until blended. Gradually beat in 3 cups confectioners' sugar with *half* the milk, stirring to combine. Beat in the melted white chocolate. Scrape bowl.

Beat in the remaining confectioners' sugar. If necessary, add 1 or 2 tbsp. milk to reach desired spreading consistency.

Spread some frosting between the cake layers, and then stack. Frost the sides and top of the cake. Serves 12.

Marmalade-Topped Sweet Potato Cake with Cinnamon-Infused Whipped Cream

Don't care for sweet potatoes? Forget about it! You'll only notice that this cake is rich and moist with a delightful marmalade topping.

2½ cups unbleached, all-purpose flour
1 tsp. baking powder
½ tsp. baking soda
½ tsp. salt
1¼ cups granulated sugar
1 cup unsalted butter, room temperature, cut into pieces
4 large eggs
1 cup cooked, mashed sweet potato
1 tbsp. freshly grated orange zest
¼ cup milk, whole

TOPPING

½ to ¾ cup orange marmalade, divided
1 cup heavy cream, whipped with dash of cinnamon

A SLICE OF ADVICE FROM BEV

For best flavor and cake texture, use the dark, orange-fleshed sweet potato for this recipe.

A dollop (a word I just love) is a small quantity of a substance. So a dollop of whipped cream would be a good-sized dessert spoonful.

Heat oven to 350 degrees. Grease 2 9" round cake pans.

In a medium bowl, whisk together the flour, baking powder, baking soda, and salt.

In a large bowl of an electric mixer, combine the sugar and butter, beating until creamy. Scrape bowl.

Add eggs, one at a time, beating well after each addition.

Add sweet potato and orange zest. With mixer on low, alternately add flour mixture and milk until well combined. Scrape bowl.

Spread batter into prepared pans. Bake for 30 to 35 minutes or until a toothpick inserted in the center comes out clean.

Cool in pans for 10 minutes. Then run a knife around edge of pans to loosen cakes. Cover a pan with a large, lint-free towel-covered plate and invert pan. Remove pan from cake. Re-invert cake from plate onto cooling rack. Repeat with remaining cake.

Spread *half* of the marmalade atop each warm cake. Allow to cool completely on wire racks. Keep as 2 cakes or stack. Serve each slice with a dollop of the whipped cream. Serves 16.

Not a sweet potato fancier? No matter . . . try a slice of this Marmalade-Topped Sweet Potato Cake with Cinnamon-Infused Whipped Cream and you'll convince yourself otherwise.

Ginger has heat and bite and tang. Combine those profiles with a
Lemon Cream-Cheese Frosting, as I have in this Tang of Ginger Cake,
and you'll soon crave this peppery, slightly sweet cake.

The Tang of Ginger Cake with Lemon Cream-Cheese Frosting

This is a moist cake with a bold ginger flavor. The lemon in the frosting makes a delicious counterpoint to the zing of the fresh ginger.

2½ cups unbleached, all-purpose flour
1 tsp. ground ginger
½ tsp. ground cinnamon
½ tsp. ground allspice
¼ tsp. freshly ground black pepper
1 cup firmly packed light brown sugar
1 cup unsalted butter, room temperature, cut into pieces
1 cup light corn syrup or brown rice syrup
2 large eggs, room temperature
2 tsp. baking soda
1 cup boiling water
½ cup peeled and finely grated fresh ginger

FROSTING

8 oz. cream cheese, room temperature, cut into pieces
4 tbsp. unsalted butter, room temperature, cut into pieces
2¾ cups confectioners' sugar, sifted
1 tsp. pure lemon extract

Heat oven to 325 degrees. Grease 2 9" square cake pans and cover pan bottoms with a square of parchment paper. Lightly grease again and set pans aside.

In a medium bowl, whisk together the flour, ginger, cinnamon, allspice, and pepper.

In a large bowl of an electric mixer, beat together the brown sugar and butter until fluffy and combined. Add the syrup and eggs, stirring to combine. Scrape bowl.

In a large measuring cup, combine the baking soda with the boiling water, whisking to blend. Add the water mixture and fresh ginger to the large bowl, stirring to blend well. Scrape bowl.

Sprinkle half of the flour mixture evenly over the top of the liquid mixture; mix to blend. Add remaining dry ingredients and mix, stopping to scrape sides and bottom of bowl, until well combined.

Spread batter into prepared pans. Bake for 25 to 35 minutes or until a toothpick inserted in the center comes out clean. (Top of the cakes may still appear somewhat moist.)

Cool in pans for 10 minutes. Then run a knife around edge of pans to loosen cakes. Cover a pan with a large, lint-free towel-covered plate and invert pan. Remove pan from cake. Peel off parchment and re-invert cake from plate onto cooling rack. Repeat with remaining cake. Allow to cool completely on wire racks.

For the Frosting: In a large bowl of an electric mixer, beat the cream cheese until smooth. Scrape bowl. Add the butter, beating until smooth and mixture is incorporated.

Stir in the confectioners' sugar and lemon extract until well combined. Mix until desired spreading consistency is reached.

Spread some frosting between the cake layers, and then stack. Frost the sides and top of the cake. Serves 12.

Festive Gingerbread Cake with Brown Sugar Buttercream Frosting

A simply incredible frosting that complements a mild, delicate, and delicious gingerbread cake very, very well.

2½ cups unbleached, all-purpose flour
2 tsp. baking powder
2 tsp. ground ginger
1 tsp. baking soda
1 tsp. ground cinnamon
½ cup unsalted butter, room temperature, cut into pieces
½ cup firmly packed light brown sugar
1 cup molasses
2 large eggs
1 cup boiling water

BROWN SUGAR BUTTERCREAM FROSTING

1½ cups plus 1 tbsp. firmly packed light brown sugar
½ cup egg whites (from about 4 large eggs), room temperature
1½ cups unsalted butter, room temperature, cut into pieces
2½ tsp. vanilla extract

A SLICE OF ADVICE FROM BEV

When it comes to molasses, I prefer the taste of light molasses, which comes from the first boiling of the sugar syrup and is lighter in both flavor and color. My favorite is sold as Barbados molasses.

Heat oven to 350 degrees. Grease and flour 2 9" round cake pans, tapping out any excess flour.

In a medium bowl, whisk together the flour, baking powder, ginger, baking soda, and cinnamon. Set aside.

In a large bowl of an electric mixer, beat together the butter, brown sugar, and molasses until well mixed. Add eggs, beating until well combined.

Add flour mixture alternately with boiling water, beating on low speed after each addition, until smooth. Spread batter into prepared pans.

Bake for 20 to 22 minutes or until a toothpick inserted in the centers comes out clean. Cool in pans for 10 minutes. Remove from pans and cool completely on a wire rack.

For the Frosting: In a large bowl, thoroughly whisk together the brown sugar and egg whites.

Set the bowl over a pot of boiling water. Whisking constantly, heat the mixture until all the sugar crystals have dissolved and the mixture is hot. (Be sure to get this mixture as hot as you can, being careful not to cook the eggs!)

Remove the bowl from atop the boiling water. With an electric mixer and whisk attachment, beat on high speed until the mixture forms a stiff meringue and the bottom of the bowl comes to room temperature (this will take about 10 minutes).

Stop the mixer and replace the whisk attachment with regular beaters. With mixer on low speed, add the butter, a few pieces at a time. When all the butter is incorporated, mix on medium speed until fluffy.

Turn the mixer to low and add the vanilla, mixing to blend. Scrape bowl, then continue to mix until frosting has a smooth, creamy texture.

Spread some frosting between the cake layers, and then stack. Frost the sides and top of the cake. Refrigerate cake until ready to serve. Serves 12.

*(Jump! Jump!) Apparently not even a missing slice from this
Festive Gingerbread Cake will stop this running gingerbread man from
leaping out of my* Cookies to Die For! *book and into this book!*

Pumpkin Patch Spice Cake with Maple Cream-Cheese Frosting

You can smell autumn in the air with each bite of this spicy layer cake!

3 cups unbleached, all-purpose flour
2 tsp. baking powder
1 tsp. baking soda
1 tbsp. ground cinnamon
2 tsp. ground ginger
1¾ tsp. ground allspice
1 tsp. salt
½ tsp. freshly grated nutmeg
1½ cups granulated sugar
1 cup firmly packed light brown sugar
1 cup light olive oil
4 large eggs
15-oz. can pumpkin puree
1 tbsp. vanilla extract
1 tbsp. freshly grated orange zest

MAPLE CREAM-CHEESE FROSTING

8 oz. cream cheese, room temperature, cut into pieces
10 tbsp. unsalted butter, room temperature, cut into pieces
1 tbsp. maple extract
1 tbsp. pure maple syrup
½ tsp. vanilla extract
4½ cups confectioners' sugar, sifted

TOPPING

Dried cranberries
Candy corn

A SLICE OF ADVICE FROM BEV

If you find yourself with a little of the Cranberry Honey Compote left over from my Chocolate Almond Torte (see index), slather some atop the frosting between the layers of this cake. It's delicious!

Heat oven to 350 degrees. Grease 2 9" round cake pans and cover pan bottoms with a round of parchment paper. Grease and flour paper and pan sides, tapping out excess flour.

In a medium bowl, whisk together the flour, baking powder, baking soda, cinnamon, ginger, allspice, salt, and nutmeg.

In a large bowl of an electric mixer, beat the granulated and brown sugar with the olive oil until combined. Add the eggs, one at a time, beating well after each addition.

Mix in the pumpkin, vanilla, and orange zest, beating until combined. Scrape bowl. Beat in flour mixture just until incorporated. Spread batter into prepared pans.

Bake for 50 to 60 minutes or until a toothpick inserted in the center comes out clean.

Cool in pans for 20 minutes. Then run a knife around edge of pans to loosen cakes. Cover a pan with a large, lint-free towel-covered plate and invert pan. Remove pan from cake. Peel off parchment and re-invert cake from plate onto cooling rack. Repeat with remaining cake. Allow to cool completely on wire racks.

For the Maple Cream-Cheese Frosting: In a large bowl of an electric mixer, beat the cream cheese and butter until smooth. Mix in the maple extract, syrup, and vanilla extract.

With mixer on low, add *half* of the confectioners' sugar, mixing just until blended and smooth. Scrape bowl. Mix in remaining confectioners' sugar, beating just until smooth.

Spread some frosting between the cake layers, and then stack. Frost the top of the cake. Refrigerate cake for 30 minutes to allow to set.

Just before serving, decoratively garnish with dried cranberries and candy corn. Serves 8-10.

CAKES TO DIE FOR!

Patriot's Cake (Red, White, and Blue)

This is the perfect summertime cake for those Memorial Day, Fourth of July, and Labor Day get-togethers.

2¾ cups cake flour, sifted
2 tsp. baking powder
¼ tsp. salt
10 tbsp. unsalted butter, room temperature, cut into pieces
1¾ cups granulated sugar
3 large eggs
1 tsp. freshly grated orange zest
1 tsp. vanilla extract
1¼ cups milk, whole

BLUEBERRY FILLING

3 cups fresh blueberries, divided
⅔ cup granulated sugar
5 tbsp. water, divided
3 tbsp. cornstarch or arrowroot
1 tbsp. fresh lemon juice

TOPPING

1 cup heavy cream
2 tbsp. confectioners' sugar, sifted
1 pt. fresh strawberries, hulled and sliced

A SLICE OF ADVICE FROM BEV

Zest is the perfumy, outermost skin layer of citrus fruit, which is removed with the aid of a zester, Microplane, paring knife, or vegetable peeler. Only the colored portion of the citrus skin (not the white pith, which is bitter) is considered the zest. The aromatic oils in citrus zest are what add so much flavor to cakes and other dishes.

Heat oven to 350 degrees. Grease 3 8" round cake pans and cover pan bottoms with a round of parchment paper. Grease and flour the paper and sides of pans, tapping out excess flour.

In a medium bowl, whisk together the flour, baking powder, and salt.

In a large bowl of an electric mixer, beat the butter and sugar until light and fluffy. Add eggs, one at a time, beating well after each addition.

Mix in zest and vanilla. With mixer on low, alternately beat milk and dry ingredients into the butter mixture until well combined.

Spread batter into prepared pans. Bake for 22 to 28 minutes or until cakes spring back when lightly touched.

Cool in pans for 10 minutes. Then run a knife around edge of pans to loosen cake. Cover a pan with a large, lint-free towel-covered plate and invert pan. Remove pan from cake. Peel off parchment and re-invert cake from plate onto cooling rack. Repeat with remaining cakes. Allow to cool completely on wire racks.

For the Blueberry Filling: In a large saucepan, gently stir together 2 cups blueberries, the sugar, and 2 tbsp. water. Bring mixture to a full boil, gently stirring occasionally.

While mixture cooks, in a small bowl whisk together the cornstarch or arrowroot and remaining 3 tbsp. water. Add to blueberry mixture, stirring constantly, and return to a boil.

Reduce heat to low and cook 2 minutes, stirring. Remove from heat; stir in lemon juice and remaining 1 cup blueberries. Transfer to a shallow container and refrigerate, uncovered, for 1 hour to allow mixture to set.

Place one cake layer on a cake stand or serving platter. Spread *half* of the filling on top. Arrange second cake layer on top, then spread with remaining filling. Top with third cake layer. Cover and let stand for 3 hours at room temperature (or up to 24 hours refrigerated) to set.

For the Topping: In a large bowl of an electric mixer, beat the heavy cream with the confectioners' sugar until stiff peaks form. Spread on top of cake. Decoratively top cake with sliced strawberries. Serves 8-12.

Sweet-Tart Lemon-Orange Cake with Matching Frosting

Bright flavors of lemon and orange highlight this "breath of spring" cake, perfect for an Easter celebration or bridal shower.

2⅔ cups unbleached, all-purpose flour
2 tsp. baking powder
¼ tsp. baking soda
¾ cup unsalted butter, room temperature, cut into pieces
6 large egg yolks or 3 large eggs
1⅔ cups granulated sugar
1 cup milk, whole
2 tsp. freshly grated lemon zest
2 tsp. freshly grated orange zest
2 tbsp. fresh lemon juice
2 tbsp. fresh orange juice

CITRUS WHIPPED CREAM FROSTING

2 cups heavy cream
1 cup confectioners' sugar, sifted
½ tsp. lemon extract
1 tbsp. freshly grated lemon zest
1 tbsp. freshly grated orange zest

A SLICE OF ADVICE FROM BEV

Using just the egg yolks produces a more golden-colored, richly flavored cake.

If Meyer lemons are in season, use their lemony zest and juice for a refreshing, sweet-tart flavor.

Heat oven to 350 degrees. Grease and flour 2 9" round cake pans, tapping out excess flour.

In a medium bowl, whisk together the flour, baking powder, and baking soda.

In a large bowl of an electric mixer, beat butter with egg yolks until creamy and combined. Scrape bowl.

Mix in the sugar, beating until mixture is light and fluffy. Alternately add the flour mixture with the milk to the butter mixture, mixing just until combined. Stir in lemon zest, orange zest, lemon juice, and orange juice to blend.

Spread batter into prepared pans. Bake for 20 to 25 minutes or until a toothpick inserted near the center comes out clean.

Cool in pans for 10 minutes. Then run a knife around edge of pans to loosen cakes. Cover a pan with a large, lint-free towel-covered plate and invert pan. Remove pan from cake. Re-invert cake from plate onto cooling rack. Repeat with remaining cake. Allow to cool completely on wire racks.

For the Citrus Whipped Cream Frosting: In a large bowl of an electric mixer, whip the heavy cream, confectioners' sugar, lemon extract, lemon zest, and orange zest until stiff peaks form.

Spread some frosting between the cake layers, and then stack. Frost the sides and top of the cake. Refrigerate cake until ready to serve. Serves 12.

Hints of Apple Cinnamon Cake with Cider Browned Butter Frosting

Perfect for any fall occasion, this cake will simply impress!

3¾ cups unbleached, all-purpose flour
1 tbsp. plus 1 tsp. baking powder
1 tbsp. plus 1 tsp. ground cinnamon
1 tsp. baking soda
1 tsp. salt
½ tsp. ground cloves
1 cup unsalted butter, room
 temperature, cut into pieces
3 cups firmly packed light brown sugar
4 large eggs
1 cup unsweetened applesauce
2 of your favorite tart, firm apples,
 peeled and cut into ½" chunks

CIDER BROWNED BUTTER FROSTING

½ cup unsalted butter, cut into pieces
4½ cups confectioners' sugar, sifted
6 to 8 tbsp. apple cider or natural apple
 juice

Dried apple rings or apple chips
 (optional)

Heat oven to 350 degrees. Grease 3 9" round cake pans and cover pan bottoms with a round of parchment paper. Grease parchment paper.

In a medium bowl, whisk together the flour, baking powder, cinnamon, baking soda, salt, and cloves.

In a large bowl of an electric mixer, beat together the butter and brown sugar until light and fluffy.

With mixer on low speed, add the eggs, one at a time, mixing well after each addition. Scrape bowl.

Alternately add the flour mixture and the applesauce to the butter mixture, beating after each addition until thoroughly combined.

Stir in the apples just until incorporated. Spread batter into prepared pans.

Bake for 32 to 42 minutes or until a toothpick inserted in the center comes out clean.

Cool in pans for 10 minutes. Then run a knife around edge of pans to loosen cakes. Cover a pan with a large, lint-free towel-covered plate and invert pan. Remove pan from cake. Peel off parchment and re-invert cake from plate onto cooling rack. Repeat with remaining cakes. Allow to cool completely on wire racks.

For the Cider Browned Butter Frosting: Melt the butter in a 1½-qt. saucepan over medium-low heat until light golden brown (3 to 5 minutes). Whisk together the browned butter, confectioners' sugar, and 6 tbsp. apple cider or juice in a medium bowl. Beat at medium speed with an electric mixer, scraping bowl often and gradually adding enough apple cider or juice to reach desired spreading consistency.

Spread some frosting between the cake layers, and then stack. Frost the sides and top of the cake. Refrigerate for 30 minutes to allow cake to firm before serving. Just before serving, decorate top of cake with apple rings or chips, if desired. Serves 10-12.

Tender Sponge Cake with Sinfully Good Lemon Curd Filling

What makes this cake so good? Layers of rich, "eggy" sponge cake surround an unbelievably sinful made-from-scratch lemon curd, better than any lemon meringue filling you've tasted!

½ cup cake flour, sifted
¼ cup unbleached, all-purpose flour
1 tsp. baking powder
¼ tsp. salt
3 tbsp. milk, whole
2 tbsp. unsalted butter
½ tsp. vanilla extract
5 large eggs, room temperature, divided
¾ cup granulated sugar, divided

LEMON CURD FILLING

¾ cup granulated sugar
¼ cup cornstarch or arrowroot
⅛ tsp. salt
1 cup cold water
4 large egg yolks
2 tsp. freshly grated lemon zest
⅓ cup fresh lemon juice
2 tbsp. unsalted butter

TOPPING

Confectioners' sugar, sifted
Fresh seasonal fruit: strawberries,
    blackberries, mangoes, peaches

A SLICE OF ADVICE FROM BEV

Lemon Curd Filling can be made ahead and refrigerated overnight.

Heat oven to 350 degrees. Grease 2 9" round cake pans and cover pan bottoms with a round of parchment paper. Grease parchment paper.

In a medium bowl, whisk together the flours, baking powder, and salt.

In a small saucepan over low heat, combine the milk and butter and stir just until the butter melts. Remove from heat and add vanilla; cover and keep warm.

Separate 3 eggs, placing whites in a bowl of a large electric mixer fitted with the whisk attachment. Reserve the remaining 3 egg yolks and 2 whole eggs in another bowl.

Beat the whites on high speed until foamy. Gradually add 6 tbsp. sugar and continue to beat the whites to soft peaks, being careful not to overbeat.

In another bowl, beat the yolks and whole egg mixture with the remaining 6 tbsp. sugar. Beat on medium-high speed until eggs are very thick and a pale yellow color. (This will take about 5 minutes with a stand mixer and longer with a hand mixer.)

Add the beaten eggs to the whites. Sprinkle flour mixture over the beaten eggs and whites, and *fold very gently 12 times* with a large rubber spatula.

Make a well in one side of the batter and pour milk mixture into the bowl. Continue folding until batter shows no trace of flour, and whites and whole eggs are evenly mixed, about 10 additional strokes.

Immediately pour batter into prepared pans. Bake until cake tops are a light brown, feel firm, and spring back when touched, 15 to 17 minutes.

Immediately run a knife around edge of pans to loosen cakes. Cover a pan with a large, lint-free towel-covered plate and invert pan. Remove pan from cake. Peel off parchment and re-invert cake from plate onto cooling rack. Repeat with remaining cake. Allow to cool completely.

For the Filling: In a large saucepan, bring the sugar, cornstarch, salt, and water to a simmer over medium heat, whisking. When mixture begins to simmer and turn translucent, whisk in the egg yolks, one at a time. Whisk in the zest, lemon juice, and finally the butter.

Bring mixture to a simmer, whisking constantly. Remove from heat and transfer to a bowl. Place a piece of plastic wrap directly on the surface to prevent a skin from forming. Allow to cool to room temperature and let stand.

Place one cake layer on a cake stand or large plate. Carefully spoon filling over layer and spread evenly almost up to the cake's edge. Place the second layer on top, making sure layers line up.

Dust top with confectioners' sugar and decorate base with fresh seasonal berries or sliced fruit. Serves 12.

Tender Sponge Cake layers cradle an incredibly tart,
Sinfully Good Lemon Curd Filling. Got berries?

CUPCAKES AND BABY CAKES

*There are enough Sunshine Key Lime Cupcakes in this dish to
share with a few of your friends.*

"Baby cakes, you've got the cutest little baby cakes."

"What . . . it's 'face'? Really. I always thought it was baby cakes!"

Baby cakes and cupcakes are perfect for buffets, small parties, kids' birthdays, gifts from your kitchen, and those annoying people who always say, "No, really—just one bite!"

This selection of cupcakes and baby cakes will bring a smile to your lips, before and after tasting. Who could resist enjoying the likes of Blackberry Cupcakes with Candied Violets, Momma's Midnight Macaroon Madness, or Gooey Pecan Cupcakes, to name just a few?

"Baby cakes, you've got the cutest little . . . "

Blackberry cupcakes with edible Candied Violets, fading into the distance, make a very, very special dessert!

CAKES TO DIE FOR!

Blackberry Cupcakes with Candied Violets

A mouthful of goodness with a violet crunch . . . these are perfect for your favorite guests (or when you're treating yourself to something very special).

1⅓ cups unbleached, all-purpose flour
2 tsp. baking powder
¼ tsp. salt
¼ cup unsalted butter, room temperature, cut into small pieces
⅔ cup granulated sugar
1 large egg
⅔ cup milk, whole
1 tsp. vanilla extract
⅔ cup blackberry jam or preserves

ICING

2½ cups confectioners' sugar, sifted
½ tsp. vanilla extract
2 to 3 tbsp. milk

30 candied violets

Heat oven to 325 degrees. Line 30 1¾" muffin cups with miniature paper liners.

In a medium bowl, whisk together the flour, baking powder, and salt.

In a large bowl of an electric mixer, beat the butter and sugar until light and fluffy. Scrape bowl.

Alternately beat in egg, milk, and vanilla with the flour mixture until combined. Scrape bowl.

Spoon 1 scant teaspoon batter into each muffin cup. Add ½ tsp. blackberry jam or preserves and top with ½ tsp. additional batter.

Bake 10 to 12 minutes or until a toothpick inserted in the center of the cakes comes out clean.

Cool on a wire rack 10 minutes, then remove from muffin cups and cool completely, in paper liners, on a wire rack.

For the Icing: In a small bowl, whisk together the confectioners' sugar, vanilla, and 2 tbsp. milk. Whisk in additional milk as needed until icing reaches drizzling consistency.

Ice each cupcake. Allow icing to set for 10 minutes, then top each cupcake with a candied violet before serving. Serves 30.

Apple "Flipped Over" Cupcakes

A comfort dessert with all the right flavors—perfect for a Sunday brunch.

1 tbsp. unsalted butter
2 large crisp-tart apples, peeled, cored, and thinly sliced
2 tbsp. firmly packed light brown sugar
½ tsp. ground cinnamon

CUPCAKES

1½ cups unbleached, all-purpose flour
¾ cup granulated sugar
¾ tsp. baking powder
¼ tsp. baking soda
¼ tsp. salt
⅛ tsp. ground ginger
3 tbsp. unsalted butter, melted
¼ tsp. vanilla extract
3 large eggs, lightly beaten
¾ cup plain, low-fat yogurt

Heat oven to 350 degrees.

Heat the butter in a small skillet over medium-high heat. Once melted, add the apples, brown sugar, and cinnamon and cook just until apples are tender.

Divide the apple mixture evenly among 12 nonstick muffin cups.

For the Cupcakes: In a large mixing bowl, whisk together the flour, sugar, baking powder, baking soda, salt, and ginger.

Stir in the melted butter, vanilla, eggs, and yogurt, until mixture is well combined. Scrape bowl.

Spoon the batter evenly over the apples.

Bake for 21 to 29 minutes or until a toothpick inserted in the center of the cakes comes out clean.

Cool in pan 10 minutes, then quickly run a knife around the inside edge of each muffin cup. Place a large baking sheet atop pan and, using potholders and both hands, hold sheet and pan firmly together and invert. Shake gently, which should allow cupcakes to settle on sheet.

Gently remove cupcakes from pan, reapplying to the cakes any fruit that remains in the pan. Cool 30 minutes.

Serve warm, topped with ice cream or freshly whipped, cinnamon-scented cream, if desired. Serves 12.

*Did that missing piece of apple make its way onto the bottom of one of these
Apple "Flipped Over" Cupcakes?*

Pineapple "Flipped Over" Cupcakes with Whipped Cream Topping

Best eaten the same day they're made, these cupcakes have shades of caramel flavor throughout.

⅓ cup plus 3 tbsp. unsalted butter, divided
¼ cup firmly packed light brown sugar
2 tsp. molasses, preferably Barbados
6 ½"-thick slices fresh or canned pineapple
¾ cup unbleached, all-purpose flour
½ cup finely ground toasted macadamia nuts
1½ tsp. baking powder
¼ tsp. ground ginger
3 tbsp. granulated sugar
2 large eggs
½ cup milk, whole

WHIPPED CREAM TOPPING

½ cup heavy cream
2 tsp. granulated sugar
1 tbsp. finely chopped crystallized ginger

A SLICE OF ADVICE FROM BEV

Toast the macadamia nuts in a dry skillet just until fragrant. Remove from skillet to a large plate and allow to cool completely. Then—and only then—grind. Toasting the nuts brings out their maximum nutty flavor.

Heat oven to 350 degrees.

In a small saucepan, combine ⅓ cup butter, brown sugar, and molasses and cook, stirring, over low heat until butter is melted.

Divide molasses mixture among 6 jumbo muffin cups. If necessary, cut pineapple slices to fit into bottoms of muffin cups. Place pineapple on top of molasses mixture in cups. Set aside.

In a medium bowl, whisk together the flour, macadamia nuts, baking powder, and ginger.

In a large bowl of an electric mixer, beat the remaining 3 tbsp. butter and the sugar until light and fluffy. Scrape bowl.

With mixer on low, beat in 1 whole egg and 1 egg yolk. Alternately add the flour mixture and milk to the butter mixture, beating just until combined.

In a small bowl with an electric mixer, beat 1 egg white until stiff peaks form. Fold beaten white into batter, then spoon batter over pineapple in muffin cups, filling about ¾ full.

Bake for 19 to 26 minutes or until tops spring back when lightly touched.

Let stand 5 minutes on a wire rack, then run a knife around the inside edge of cups. Place a large tray atop pan and, using potholders and both hands, hold tray and pan firmly together and invert. Shake gently, which should allow cakes to settle on tray.

Gently remove pan, reapplying to cupcakes any fruit that remains in the pan. Cool 30 minutes.

For the Whipped Cream Topping: In a large bowl of an electric mixer, whip the heavy cream with the sugar until soft peaks form. Quickly and gently fold in the crystallized ginger.

When ready to serve, top the warm cupcakes with a dollop of the cream. Serves 6.

CAKES TO DIE FOR!

Banana Cupcakes with Maple Frosting

A moist, flavorful, and utterly divine cupcake . . . with a rich Maple Frosting!

2 tsp. baking soda
3¼ cups plus 1½ tbsp. unbleached, all-purpose flour
1 cup unsalted butter, room temperature, cut into pieces
2½ cups granulated sugar
4 large eggs
1 cup sour cream
1 tbsp. vanilla extract
6 very ripe, medium bananas

MAPLE FROSTING

3¾ cups confectioners' sugar, sifted
6 tbsp. unsalted butter, room temperature, cut into pieces
1 tsp. maple flavoring
5 to 6 tbsp. sour cream

Coarsely chopped walnuts, toasted (optional)

A SLICE OF ADVICE FROM BEV

You'll probably have some of this frosting leftover, which will only give you an excuse to make more Banana Cupcakes!

Heat oven to 350 degrees. Line 24 muffin cups with paper liners.

In a medium bowl, whisk together the baking soda and flour.

In a large bowl of an electric mixer, beat the butter and sugar until light and fluffy. Scrape bowl.

Add the eggs, one at a time, beating well after each addition. With mixer on low, add the sour cream and vanilla and beat until well combined. Add the flour mixture just until blended.

Peel and mash the bananas. Quickly and gently stir in the banana mash. Do not overmix.

Spoon the batter into prepared muffin cups. Bake for 18 to 26 minutes or until cupcakes spring back when lightly touched in the center and a toothpick comes out clean.

Cool on a wire rack 10 minutes, then remove from muffin cups and cool completely, in paper liners, on a wire rack.

For the Maple Frosting: In a large bowl of an electric mixer, beat together the confectioners' sugar, butter, and maple flavoring until mixed. With mixer on medium, blend in the sour cream until frosting is smooth and reaches desired spreading consistency.

Slather desired amount of Maple Frosting atop each cupcake and allow to set. Garnish with chopped walnuts, if desired. Serves 24 (okay, who are we kidding? . . . serves more like 12!).

Sunshine Key Lime Cupcakes

These key lime favorites are a small bite of warm, ocean breezes and days of sunshine, perfect for a spring baby or wedding shower.

1¾ cups unbleached, all-purpose flour
1 tsp. baking powder
⅛ tsp. salt
½ cup unsalted butter, room temperature, cut into pieces
1¼ cups granulated sugar
2 large eggs
2½ tbsp. fresh lime juice or key lime juice
1 tbsp. freshly grated lime zest
¾ cup buttermilk

FROSTING

8 oz. cream cheese, room temperature, cut into pieces
1½ cups confectioners' sugar, sifted
½ cup unsalted butter, room temperature, cut into pieces
1 tbsp. freshly grated lime zest
1 tsp. fresh lime juice

A SLICE OF ADVICE FROM BEV

After you add the buttermilk, the batter may look curdled. Don't be alarmed; calmly continue with recipe.

Heat oven to 350 degrees. Line 12 muffin cups with paper liners.

In a medium bowl, whisk together the flour, baking powder, and salt.

In a large bowl of an electric mixer, beat the butter and sugar until light and fluffy. Scrape bowl.

Add eggs, one at a time, beating well after each addition. Add the lime juice, lime zest and buttermilk, beating until blended. Scrape bowl.

With mixer on medium, beat in the flour mixture until blended. Scrape bowl. Spoon batter into each muffin cup, filling ¾ full.

Bake 21 to 24 minutes or until cake tester inserted into center comes out clean.

Cool on a wire rack 10 minutes, then remove from muffin cups and cool completely, in paper liners, on a wire rack.

For the Frosting: In a large bowl of an electric mixer, beat together the cream cheese, confectioners' sugar, butter, lime zest and vanilla until well combined and mixture is smooth. Scrape bowl.

Frost Baby Cakes and allow to set 30 minutes. Serves 12.

Strawberry-Topped Cupcakes with Bittersweet Ganache

These little wonders combine my two favorite flavors—chocolate and strawberry—and eating just one is very, very difficult!

1 cup unbleached, all-purpose flour
½ tsp. baking powder
¼ tsp. baking soda
⅛ tsp. salt
½ cup unsalted butter, cut into pieces
1 cup granulated sugar
⅓ cup unsweetened cocoa powder, sifted
1 large egg
1 tsp. vanilla extract
¾ cup milk, whole

BITTERSWEET GANACHE

1 cup heavy cream
10 oz. bittersweet chocolate, coarsely
    chopped
3 tbsp. unsalted butter, room
    temperature, cut into pieces

TOPPING

½ cup strawberry fruit spread or jam
1 qt. fresh organic strawberries, gently
    washed and dried

Heat oven to 350 degrees. Line 12 muffin cups with paper liners.

In a medium bowl, whisk together the flour, baking powder, baking soda, and salt.

In a large saucepan, melt the butter. Remove from heat.

Whisk in the sugar and cocoa powder until smooth. Add the egg and vanilla, beating just until combined. Alternately add the flour mixture and the milk to the chocolate mixture, beating by hand after each addition.

Spoon batter into prepared muffin cups, filling each ⅔ full. Bake for 14 to 21 minutes or until a toothpick inserted near the center of the cakes comes out clean.

Cool on a wire rack 10 minutes, then remove from muffin cups and cool completely, in paper liners, on a wire rack.

For the Bittersweet Ganache: In a small saucepan, bring the heavy cream to a simmer. Remove and pour atop the bittersweet chocolate in a large bowl. Allow to steep for 5 minutes, then whisk until chocolate is melted and mixture is smooth.

Whisk is butter, a piece at a time, until ganache is smooth and glossy.

When ready to serve, place cakes on rack atop a large piece of waxed paper. Peel cupcake liners down, leaving them still attached at the bottom. Spread 1 tsp. strawberry fruit spread or jam atop each cake.

Spoon ganache over cupcakes, coating all sides. Hull each strawberry and thinly slice, cutting to but not through the top. Gently fan strawberries. Place a fresh strawberry on top of each cake. Drizzle gently with a little additional ganache. Serves 12.

Pace yourself! One of these Mini Chocolate Chip Sour Cream Cupcakes with Chocolate Buttercream Frosting should satisfy your sweet tooth.

Mini Chocolate Chip Sour Cream Cupcakes with Chocolate Buttercream Frosting

These bite-size morsels are moist and chocolaty . . . the perfect solution for a chocolate craving.

3 oz. unsweetened chocolate, coarsely chopped
2 cups unbleached, all-purpose flour
¼ tsp. baking powder
¼ tsp. baking soda
¼ tsp. salt
½ cup unsalted butter, room temperature, cut into pieces
1 cup granulated sugar
2 large eggs
1 tsp. vanilla extract
½ cup sour cream
¼ cup mini chocolate chips

CHOCOLATE BUTTERCREAM FROSTING

4 cups confectioners' sugar, sifted
½ cup unsalted butter, room temperature, cut into pieces
¼ cup plus 1 tbsp. milk, whole, plus additional as needed
2 oz. unsweetened chocolate, melted
1 oz. milk chocolate, melted
½ tsp. vanilla extract

Heat oven to 325 degrees. Line 36 mini muffin cups with miniature paper liners.

Melt the chocolate in a double boiler. Remove double boiler top and wipe on towel to remove any excess water. Allow to cool.

In a medium bowl, whisk together the flour, baking powder, baking soda, and salt.

In a large bowl of an electric mixer, beat the butter and sugar until light and fluffy. Scrape bowl.

Add the cooled chocolate and the eggs, one at a time, beating well after each addition. With mixer on low, add the vanilla and sour cream. Stir in the flour mixture and the chocolate chips.

Spoon the batter into the muffin cups, filling ⅔ full. Bake for 9 to 14 minutes or until done. Cool on a wire rack 10 minutes, then remove from muffin cups and cool completely, in paper liners, on a wire rack.

For the Chocolate Buttercream Frosting: In a large bowl of an electric mixer, beat the confectioners' sugar, butter, milk, melted chocolates, and vanilla until combined. Scrape bowl.

Beat in 1 or 2 tbsp. additional milk as needed to reach desired frosting consistency. Using a pastry bag fitted with a star tip, pipe onto the cupcake tops. Serves 36.

Hazelnut Cream Cupcakes with Hazelnut Cream-Cheese Frosting

Another use for that fabulous shot of syrup you get in your favorite coffee drink . . . cupcakes!

3 cups unbleached, all-purpose flour
1 tsp. baking powder
½ tsp. baking soda
½ tsp. salt
2 cups granulated sugar
1½ cups unsalted butter, room temperature, cut into pieces
6 large eggs, separated
2 tbsp. hazelnut syrup
1½ tsp. vanilla extract
1 cup buttermilk
2 cups sweetened shredded coconut, toasted
1 cup hazelnuts, toasted and skinned, coarsely chopped, plus additional for garnish

HAZELNUT CREAM-CHEESE FROSTING

16 oz. cream cheese, room temperature, cut into pieces
1½ cups unsalted butter, room temperature, cut into pieces
3 tbsp. hazelnut syrup
2 tbsp. heavy cream
4 cups confectioners' sugar, sifted

Heat oven to 325 degrees. Line 24 muffin cups with paper liners.

In a large bowl, whisk together the flour, baking powder, baking soda, and salt.

In a large bowl of an electric mixer, cream the sugar and butter together until light and fluffy. Scrape bowl.

Add the egg yolks, one at a time, beating well after each addition. With mixer on low, stir in hazelnut syrup and vanilla until combined.

Alternately add the flour mixture and the buttermilk to the batter, blending well.

In a clean large bowl of an electric mixer, beat the egg whites until stiff peaks form. Fold a third of the whites into batter just until blended.

Quickly and gently fold remaining whites, with the coconut and hazelnuts, into batter just until blended. Spoon batter into prepared muffin cups, filling ⅔ full.

Bake for 18 to 24 minutes or until a toothpick inserted in the center of the cakes comes out clean.

Cool on a wire rack 10 minutes, then remove from muffin cups and cool completely, in paper liners, on a wire rack.

For the Hazelnut Cream-Cheese Frosting: In a large bowl of an electric mixer, beat the cream cheese and butter until light and fluffy. Scrape bowl. Beat in the hazelnut syrup, heavy cream, and confectioners' sugar until frosting is smooth and well blended.

Frost the cupcakes and sprinkle with chopped hazelnuts. Serves 24.

Momma's Midnight Macaroon Madness

This is the perfect dessert treat when you have leftover egg whites—a simple-to-make taste tidbit, even at midnight.

¾ cup unbleached, all-purpose flour
1⅓ cups granulated sugar, divided
½ tsp. baking powder
¼ tsp. salt
6 large egg whites, room temperature
½ tsp. cream of tartar
1 tsp. almond or vanilla extract
1 cup unsweetened or sweetened flaked coconut

A SLICE OF ADVICE FROM BEV

Did you know you can freeze egg whites (to gather enough to make this recipe)? When you have leftover whites, lightly beat them, place them in a freezer container, and freeze. When you're ready to use the frozen whites, thaw them in the refrigerator and use just as you would fresh egg whites.

Heat oven to 350 degrees. Line 18 muffin cups with paper liners.

In a medium bowl, whisk together the flour, 1 cup sugar, baking powder, and salt.

In a large bowl of an electric mixer, beat the egg whites, cream of tartar, and extract until foamy. With mixer on high, gradually add the remaining sugar until stiff peaks form.

Quickly and gently fold the flour mixture and the coconut into the egg white mixture, just until blended.

Spoon into prepared muffin cups, filling each ⅔ full. Bake for 22 to 36 minutes or until light golden with a dry top crust.

Cool on a wire rack 10 minutes, then remove from muffin cups and cool completely, in paper liners, on a wire rack. Serves 18.

Pecan Cupcakes with Jane's Butterscotch Sauce

These are fanciful little plates of goodness—drizzled, restaurant style, with my mother-in-law, Jane's, decadent butterscotch sauce.

1 cup unsalted butter, room temperature, cut into pieces
1½ cups granulated sugar
2½ tsp. baking powder
1 tsp. vanilla extract
½ tsp. salt
3 large eggs
2¼ cups unbleached, all-purpose flour
½ cup pecan pieces, toasted then finely chopped
1¼ cups milk, whole

JANE'S BUTTERSCOTCH SAUCE

6½ tbsp. unsalted butter, cut into pieces
⅔ cup light corn syrup
1¼ cup firmly packed light brown sugar
¾ cup evaporated milk

Confectioners' sugar, sifted

A SLICE OF ADVICE FROM JOHN

I've taken over from Bev to tell you that this is my absolute favorite butterscotch sauce recipe, made for me by my mom many years ago and eaten with Mary Cole's vanilla ice cream as a special treat after Sunday dinner. It never lasted for long in the "icebox" . . . and that fact is still true to this day!

Heat oven to 350 degrees. Grease and flour 24 muffin cups, tapping out excess flour.

In a large bowl of an electric mixer, beat the butter and sugar until light and fluffy. Scrape bowl.

Beat in baking powder, vanilla, and salt. Add eggs, one at a time, beating well after each addition.

In a medium bowl, whisk together the flour and pecans. With mixer on low, alternately add the flour mixture and milk to butter mixture until combined. Scrape bowl.

Spoon batter into prepared muffin cups. Bake for 16 to 19 minutes or until a toothpick inserted in the centers comes out clean.

Cool in pan 10 minutes, then quickly run a knife around inside of muffin cups. Remove from pan and cool completely on a wire rack.

For Jane's Butterscotch Sauce: In a medium saucepan, cook the butter, corn syrup, and brown sugar over medium-high heat to the soft-ball stage (238 degrees on a candy thermometer). Remove from heat and cool slightly. Whisk in evaporated milk until smooth.

When ready to serve, drizzle some of Jane's Butterscotch Sauce on a small dessert plate in a decorative pattern. Place a Pecan Cupcake atop plate and dust with some sifted confectioners' sugar. Repeat with remaining cupcakes. Pass additional sauce, especially if John is around! Serves 24, with enough sauce left over for another batch or an ice-cream sundae.

Jane's Butterscotch Sauce will need to be licked off the plate . . . once your Pecan Cupcake is eaten and no one is looking! (Yes, it sounds like something John would do.)

Warm from the oven, these Gooey Pecan Cupcakes are intoxicating, with hints of butterscotch and caramel and with toasted nuts set atop moist spongelike cakes.

Gooey Pecan Cupcakes

If you love sticky buns, you'll love these cupcakes. No yeast or rising is involved, and they reheat beautifully right from the freezer (in the event of a few surprise guests).

⅔ cup firmly packed light brown sugar
½ cup unsalted butter, cut into pieces
⅓ cup honey
1½ cups coarsely chopped pecans, toasted
1 tsp. freshly grated orange zest
2½ cups unbleached, all-purpose flour
1 tsp. baking powder
½ tsp. baking soda
½ tsp. salt
3 large eggs
2 cups granulated sugar
1 cup light olive oil
8 oz. sour cream
2 tsp. vanilla extract

Heat oven to 350 degrees. Grease 12 jumbo muffin cups or large custard cups. Place on a large, foil-lined baking sheet.

In a medium saucepan, heat the brown sugar, butter, and honey, stirring over medium heat, until mixture is smooth and butter is melted. Remove from heat and stir in pecans and orange zest.

In a medium bowl, whisk together the flour, baking powder, baking soda, and salt.

In a large bowl of an electric mixer, combine eggs and granulated sugar. With mixer on medium, beat until mixture is thick and lemon colored. Add oil, sour cream, and vanilla, beating until combined.

With mixer on low, add flour mixture just until smooth. Scrape bowl.

Place 2 tbsp. pecan mixture on the bottom of each muffin or custard cup. Spoon a generous ⅓ cup batter into each cup.

Bake for 24 to 31 minutes (watching carefully the last 5 minutes) or until a toothpick inserted in the centers comes out clean.

Let stand 5 minutes on a wire rack, then run a knife around the inside edge of cups. Place a large tray atop rack of cups and, using potholders and both hands, hold tray and rack firmly together and invert. Shake gently, which should allow cakes to settle on tray.

Gently remove cups, reapplying to the cakes any pecan mixture that remains in the cups. Serve warm. Serves 12.

Seductive Soufflé (Chocolate and Strawberry) Baby Cakes with Raspberry Coulis

What a bright and flavorful combination of fruits, perfect with warm chocolate baby soufflé cakes.

7½ oz. bittersweet chocolate, finely chopped
15 tbsp. unsalted butter, cut into pieces
½ cup strawberry jam or preserves
6 large eggs, separated
¾ cup granulated sugar
2 tsp. vanilla extract

COULIS

¼ cup granulated sugar
½ cup water
2½ cups frozen, unsweetened red raspberries, thawed

Confectioners' sugar, sifted

Heat oven to 300 degrees. Butter and sugar 12 5-oz. ramekins, tapping out excess sugar.

In a medium saucepan, melt the chocolate and butter, whisking until smooth. Remove from heat and stir in the strawberry jam. Set aside until cooled.

Place egg yolks in a large bowl. With a handheld electric mixer, beat the sugar and vanilla into the yolks until very thick and pale.

Whisk in the cooled chocolate mixture.

In a large bowl of an electric mixer, beat the egg whites to soft peaks. Gently fold them into the egg yolk/chocolate mixture.

Spoon batter into prepared ramekins. Bake for 23 to 26 minutes or until puffed and just set.

Cool on a wire rack 10 minutes. Quickly run a knife around inside of ramekins, then invert onto dessert plates.

For the Coulis: In a blender, puree the sugar, water, and berries until smooth. Strain through a fine sieve into a medium bowl.

When ready to serve, dust cakes with confectioners' sugar. Drizzle some of the coulis around the edges of the plated cakes. Serve immediately. Serves 12.

Seductive Soufflés right out of the oven.

CAKES TO DIE FOR!

Pour that Raspberry Coulis on! I'm ready to be seduced by these Seductive Soufflé (Chocolate and Strawberry) Baby Cakes.

Pudding Quiche Cakes with Berries

Little individual dessert cakes, loaded with assorted fresh seasonal berries.

2 large eggs
¼ cup granulated sugar
1 tsp. vanilla extract
⅛ tsp. salt
1 cup milk, whole
½ cup unbleached, all-purpose flour
½ tsp. baking powder
3 cups fresh seasonal red raspberries,
    black raspberries, and/or blueberries,
    gently washed and dried

Confectioners' sugar, sifted

Heat oven to 400 degrees. Grease 6 6-oz. individual quiche dishes. Set dishes atop a large baking sheet.

In a medium bowl, whisk together the eggs, sugar, vanilla, and salt until mixture is light and frothy.

Whisk in the milk until blended, then whisk in the flour and baking powder until smooth.

Divide berries among the prepared dishes, then spoon batter atop berries. Bake for 15 to 20 minutes or until puffed and golden brown.

Serve warm, dusted generously with confectioners' sugar. Serves 6.

Baby Cheesecakes with Easy Apricot Compote

Delicious reduced-fat minis are topped with a compote that's simple to make from canned apricots.

1 cup plain, low-fat yogurt
4 oz. Neufchatel cheese, room
    temperature, cut into pieces
½ cup granulated sugar
1 large egg
1 large egg white
1 tbsp. flour
1 tsp. freshly grated lemon zest
1 tsp. fresh lemon juice

EASY APRICOT COMPOTE

15¼-oz. can apricot halves in light syrup
½ cup dried cranberries
¼ cup finely chopped dried apricots

Heat oven to 350 degrees. Grease 6 2-oz. custard cups.

Drain yogurt in a fine-mesh strainer lined with cheesecloth, set atop a bowl, for 1 hour.

In a large bowl of an electric mixer, beat the Neufchatel and sugar until light and fluffy. Scrape bowl.

With mixer on medium, blend in the egg, egg white, flour, lemon zest, and lemon juice until combined. Quickly and gently stir in the strained yogurt (discarding the liquid).

Spoon evenly into prepared cups. Place the cups in a roasting pan and add enough hot water to the pan to come 1" up the sides of the cups.

Bake for 29 to 37 minutes or just until set. Turn oven off and allow cheesecakes to remain in the oven for 45 minutes, keeping oven door closed.

Remove cheesecakes from water bath and allow to cool 30 minutes on a wire rack. Refrigerate for 1 hour.

For the Easy Apricot Compote: Strain liquid from the apricots into a small saucepan, reserving apricot halves. Add the cranberries and the dried apricot pieces and bring mixture to a boil. Reduce heat to medium low and cook just until cranberries soften.

Remove from heat and allow to cool completely. Dice the apricot halves and gently stir into the liquid.

When ready to serve, top each cheesecake with a generous spoonful of the Easy Apricot Compote. Serves 6.

*My own Gingerbread Baby Cheesecake? You shouldn't have
(but I'm secretly so glad you did!).*

Gingerbread Baby Cheesecakes

These are perfect as individual desserts or to share with someone special. The silky texture of cheesecake, the spicy flavors of gingerbread, and the snap and crunch of the cookie and nut crust make for a perfect fall dessert.

¼ cup unsalted butter
1 cup crushed gingersnap cookies
¼ cup finely chopped toasted pecans
3 tbsp. granulated sugar

GINGERBREAD FILLING

24 oz. cream cheese, room temperature, cut into pieces
¾ cup granulated sugar
1 tbsp. unbleached, all-purpose flour
3 large eggs
¼ cup molasses, preferably Barbados
1 tsp. ground ginger
¼ tsp. ground cinnamon

TOPPING

Fresh whipped cream
Freshly grated nutmeg
Candied ginger, coarsely chopped

A SLICE OF ADVICE FROM BEV

If you don't have 4" springform pans, use an 8" springform to make a large version. Bake for at least 1 hour, or until cheesecake appears set around the edges. Cool completely on a wire rack, then cover and refrigerate overnight to allow cheesecake to set up before serving.

Heat oven to 300 degrees.

In a small saucepan, melt the butter. Remove from heat and allow to cool slightly. In a small bowl, combine the cookie crumbs, pecans, and sugar. Stir in the melted butter until well combined. Press mixture onto bottoms and ½" to 1" up sides of 4 4" springform pans. Bake for 5 minutes. Cool in pans on a wire rack.

For the Gingerbread Filling: In a large bowl of an electric mixer, beat the cream cheese, sugar, and flour just until creamy. Scrape bowl.

Add eggs, one at a time, beating well after each addition. Beat in the molasses, ginger, and cinnamon.

Spread filling onto prepared crusts. Bake for 39 to 42 minutes or until centers appear nearly set. Cool in pans on a wire rack.

Cover loosely with waxed paper and refrigerate cheesecakes overnight. When ready to serve, run a knife around the inside edge of pans and carefully remove the springform sides.

Garnish cheesecakes with whipped cream, freshly grated nutmeg, and candied ginger. Serves 4 to 8.

Orange-Ricotta Baby Cheesecakes

Orange marmalade, fresh orange juice, and the zest of orange give these little babies their bright flavor.

⅔ cup granulated sugar
½ cup fresh orange juice
4 tsp. freshly grated orange zest
16 oz. cream cheese, room temperature, cut into pieces
1 cup ricotta cheese
2 large eggs
1 large egg white

Orange marmalade

A SLICE OF ADVICE FROM BEV

When making cheesecakes, remember that all dairy ingredients (eggs, cream cheese, etc.) should be at room temperature before using. And *don't* overbeat the batter—too much air whipped into the mixture is the number-one cause of cracking cheesecake tops.

Heat oven to 425 degrees. Grease 6 6-oz. custard cups or ramekins. Place cups or ramekins atop a baking sheet.

In a large bowl of an electric mixer, beat the sugar, orange juice, and zest until sugar dissolves.

With mixer on low, add the cream cheese and ricotta cheese, beating until smooth.

Add the eggs and egg white, beating until well blended. Scrape bowl.

Spoon batter into prepared cups. Bake 16 to 19 minutes or until puffed and light golden.

Cool on a wire rack for 30 minutes, then refrigerate, uncovered, until cold. When ready to serve, spread some orange marmalade atop each little cheesecake. Serves 6.

Mini White Chocolate Swirl Cheesecakes

These mini cheesecakes are just enough of a sweet thing . . . especially when they're swirled with the very best white chocolate!

Melted butter
16 oz. cream cheese, room temperature, cut into pieces
⅔ cup granulated sugar
1½ tsp. vanilla extract
⅛ tsp. salt
2 large eggs
½ cup coarsely chopped white chocolate, melted
2¼ tsp. unbleached, all-purpose flour
½ tsp. ground cinnamon
½ tsp. espresso powder

A SLICE OF ADVICE FROM BEV

When buying white chocolate, be sure cocoa butter is included in the ingredients. Otherwise, it's not even chocolate.

Heat oven to 300 degrees. Line 12 muffin cups with *foil* muffin liners. Brush each foil liner lightly with melted butter.

In a large bowl of an electric mixer, beat the cream cheese until smooth and fluffy. Scrape bowl.

Beat in the sugar, vanilla, and salt until well blended. Scrape bowl. Add the eggs, one at a time, beating just until blended. Do not overbeat.

Transfer ⅔ cup of the batter to a small bowl. Add the white chocolate, flour, cinnamon, and espresso powder. Stir by hand until well blended.

Divide the plain batter among the muffin cups. Divide the white chocolate batter evenly on top of the plain batter.

Quickly and gently drag the tip of a toothpick or paring knife through the 2 batters in a random swirl pattern to create a marbled effect.

Bake for 14 to 19 minutes or until centers of cheesecakes barely jiggle when nudged.

Cool on a wire rack 10 minutes. Carefully remove from muffin cups and cool completely, in foil liners, on a wire rack. Cover and refrigerate at least 8 hours or overnight, until very cold. Serves 12.

Lick-Your-Fingers Coconut Snowballs with Marshmallow Frosting

First, it will be difficult to get past the simply delicious chocolate baby cakes that come out of your oven. Second, be prepared to lick your fingers . . . Marshmallow Frosting is sticky! And third, these are so much fun to eat.

1 cup unsalted butter, room temperature, cut into pieces
10½ oz. bittersweet or semisweet chocolate, finely chopped
2¼ cups boiling water
2¾ cups plus 1 tbsp. unbleached, all-purpose flour
1½ tsp. baking soda
2 cups plus 2 tbsp. granulated sugar
3 large eggs

MARSHMALLOW FROSTING

6 tbsp. water
1¼ cups light corn syrup
¾ cup plus 1 tbsp. granulated sugar
4 large egg whites
Pinch of cream of tartar
Pinch of salt
2 tsp. vanilla extract

Sweetened coconut flakes

A SLICE OF ADVICE FROM BEV

Marshmallow Frosting is very sticky to spread, so if you have a disposable pastry bag, piping it and then coating immediately with coconut flakes works very well.

Coat the Marshmallow Frosting generously with the coconut flakes. This helps the frosting adhere to the snowballs.

Heat oven to 300 degrees. Grease 24 4-oz. round-bottom custard cups. Set cups atop a baking sheet.

Place the butter and chocolate in a large bowl and pour in the boiling water. Allow mixture to steep for 5 minutes, then whisk until butter and chocolate are melted.

In a medium bowl, whisk together the flour, baking soda, and sugar. Add slowly to the chocolate mixture, mixing until smooth.

Whisk the eggs in a small bowl and add to the chocolate mixture. Spoon batter into prepared cups.

Bake for 15 to 22 minutes or until cakes spring back when lightly touched.

Cool on a wire rack 10 minutes. Quickly run a knife around inside of cups, then remove cakes from cups and cool completely on a wire rack.

For the Marshmallow Frosting: In a medium saucepan, combine the water, corn syrup, and sugar and cook over medium heat, stirring constantly, to hard-ball stage (252- to 268-degree range on a candy thermometer).

In a large bowl of an electric mixer, beat the egg whites, cream of tartar, and salt until soft peaks form. Slowly pour the hot sugar mixture down the side of the bowl. With mixer on high, continue to whip until mixture begins to cool. Add vanilla.

Carefully spread (using a small tapered pastry knife) or pipe a very thin layer of Marshmallow Frosting around the entire surface of each cake. Roll cakes in coconut flakes, patting them lightly to form as perfect a snowball as possible (remembering that snowballs are not perfect!). Serves 24.

Your idea of the childhood treat will never be the same after you eat one of these Coconut Snowballs with Marshmallow Frosting. Licking your fingers is mandatory!

Personal Coconut Pound Cakes

The perfect complement to these personal pound cakes is a generous dollop of your favorite fruit spread, preserves, or jam.

1½ cups granulated sugar
¾ cup unsalted butter, room temperature, cut into pieces
3 oz. cream cheese, room temperature, cut into pieces
¼ cup sweetened cream of coconut
3 large eggs
1 tsp. vanilla extract
1½ cups unbleached, all-purpose flour
1 cup unsweetened, flaked coconut

Fruit spread, preserves, or jam

Heat oven to 350 degrees. Line 16 muffin cups with paper liners.

In a large bowl of an electric mixer, beat together the sugar, butter, and cream cheese until mixture is light and fluffy. Scrape bowl.

With mixer on low, add the cream of coconut, eggs, and vanilla, beating until smooth. Scrape bowl.

With mixer on low, stir in the flour and coconut just until blended.

Spoon batter into prepared muffin cups, filling each ¾ full. Bake for 25 to 39 minutes or until a light golden brown and a toothpick inserted in the centers comes out clean.

Cool on a wire rack 10 minutes, then remove from muffin cups and cool completely, in paper liners, on a wire rack. Serve warm, topped with the fruit spread, preserves, or jam of your choice. Serves 16.

Little Quarter-Pound Cakes

The perfect little pound cake—delectable with tea, coffee, or a tall glass of organic milk!

1 cup unsalted butter, room temperature, cut into pieces
1 cup granulated sugar plus additional for sprinkling pans
1½ tsp. freshly grated lemon zest
2 tsp. vanilla extract
5 large eggs, separated
2 cups unbleached, all-purpose flour
¼ tsp. salt

A SLICE OF ADVICE FROM BEV

The batter will be stiff and a little difficult to work with, but don't despair!

Heat oven to 350 degrees. Grease and sprinkle with sugar 8 small loaf pans, tapping out excess sugar. Place loaf pans atop a baking sheet.

In a large bowl of an electric mixer, beat the butter and sugar until light and fluffy. Scrape bowl.

Beat in the lemon zest and vanilla until mixed. Add the egg yolks, one at a time, beating well after each addition. Scrape bowl.

With mixer on low, add the flour and beat just until blended. Don't overmix.

In another clean large bowl, beat the egg whites with the salt just until stiff peaks begin to form. Fold the whites, a third at a time, into the flour mixture.

Once whites have been blended into the flour mixture, spoon into the prepared pans, filling each ⅔ full.

Bake 34 to 46 minutes or until lightly golden and a toothpick inserted in the centers comes out clean.

Cool in pans for 10 minutes. Then run a knife around inside edge of pans to loosen cakes. Remove from pans and allow to cool completely on wire racks. Serves 8.

Blueberry-Cornmeal Yogurt Shortcakes

Yogurt replaces the fat in these biscuits, and they bake up crisp on the outside, moist on the inside.

1 cup unbleached, all-purpose flour
1 cup plain, low-fat yogurt
2 tbsp. granulated sugar

BLUEBERRY FILLING

3 cups blueberries, gently washed and dried
2 tbsp. granulated sugar
½ tsp. freshly grated lemon zest

YOGURT SHORTCAKES

¾ cup unbleached, all-purpose flour
½ cup cornmeal
2 tsp. baking powder
½ tsp. baking soda
½ tsp. ground cinnamon
½ tsp. salt

TOPPING

Half-and-half
3 tbsp. thinly sliced almonds, toasted
Vanilla ice cream or peach sorbet
Turbinado sugar

In a medium bowl, stir together the flour and the yogurt until smooth. Sprinkle with the sugar. Cover bowl and let stand in a warm place overnight.

For the Blueberry Filling: One hour before serving, toss the berries with the sugar and zest, mashing them lightly. Cover.

Heat oven to 425 degrees. Line a baking sheet with parchment paper.

In a medium bowl, whisk together the flour, cornmeal, baking powder, baking soda, cinnamon, and salt.

Stir this flour mixture into the yogurt mixture just until blended.

Turn the dough out onto a lightly floured surface and pat into an 8" by 4" rectangle. Cut the dough into 2" squares and place on baking sheet, being sure to leave at least 1½" between squares.

Brush the shortcakes lightly with the half-and-half, and then sprinkle with the sliced almonds.

Bake for 10 to 14 minutes or until shortcakes are light golden. Cool 15 minutes on a wire rack.

When ready to serve, split the shortcakes and place the bottoms on dessert plates. Spoon some of the berries and their juices over each bottom, adding a spoonful of the ice cream or sorbet. Top with the shortcake lids and sprinkle with turbinado sugar. Serves 8.

CAKES TO DIE FOR!

Kiwi Shortcakes with Lemon Cream

Small cakes with the crisp crunch of turbinado sugar, filled with tart sweet kiwi pieces and a silky lemon cream. Sorry, strawberries!

1½ cups unbleached, all-purpose flour
¾ cup cake flour, sifted
3 tbsp. granulated sugar
2 tsp. baking powder
½ tsp. salt
6 tbsp. unsalted butter, cold, cut into pieces
1 cup heavy cream
1½ tbsp. unsalted butter, melted
2 tbsp. turbinado sugar

LEMON CREAM

1½ tsp. freshly grated lemon zest, divided
¼ cup fresh lemon juice
2½ tbsp. granulated sugar
1 large egg
1 large egg yolk
3 tbsp. unsalted butter, divided
1 cup heavy cream

KIWI FILLING

10 ripe kiwi, peeled and diced
2 tbsp. turbinado sugar

A SLICE OF ADVICE FROM BEV

Meyer lemons have a sweet, tart flavor with a tangerine-like scent and would be perfect for the Lemon Cream if they're in season (October through May).

Heat oven to 375 degrees. Line a baking sheet with parchment paper.

In a medium bowl, whisk together the flours, sugar, baking powder, and salt. With a pastry blender, add the butter until mixture is crumbly.

Stir in the heavy cream *just* until dough gathers together. Quickly and gently knead the dough on a lightly floured surface just until it comes together.

Roll dough into a 6½" round, about ¾" thick. Using a 2½" biscuit cutter, cut 6 shortcakes from dough (gathering any scraps and lightly rerolling once if needed).

Place the shortcakes on prepared baking sheet. Brush with melted butter, then sprinkle with turbinado sugar. Bake for 22 to 34 minutes or until golden. Cool on a wire rack.

For the Lemon Cream: In a small saucepan, combine *half* of the lemon zest, the lemon juice, sugar, egg, egg yolk, and 1 tbsp. butter. Whisk over medium heat until mixture is thickened.

Strain lemon mixture into a medium bowl. Whisk in the remaining zest and 2 tbsp. butter. Press a piece of plastic wrap directly onto the hot surface. Refrigerate for 25 minutes or until cool.

In a large bowl of an electric mixer, whip the heavy cream until soft peaks form. Fold the lemon mixture into the whipped cream. Refrigerate, covered, for 30 minutes.

For the Kiwi Filling: In a large bowl, toss together the kiwi pieces and sugar. Let stand 20 minutes.

When ready to serve, split the shortcakes in half and arrange their bottoms on dessert plates. Place a generous spoonful of the Lemon Cream on each biscuit, then top with the kiwis and their juices and replace shortcake tops. Serves 6.

CHEESECAKES

I'll take that piece of Chocolate Peanut Butter Cheesecake with a Touch of Ganache!
(On second thought, you take that piece and I'll take the rest.)

Cheesecakes have always been surrounded by a sense of intrigue . . . the thought that they're filled with such sensuous pleasure yet are so difficult to make.

Truth be told, they're extremely easy to make. They even freeze beautifully, for that spur-of-the-moment party dessert . . . topped with fresh seasonal fruit or some leftover ganache in your refrigerator or cut into small pieces to serve a crowd.

Enjoy my decadent, creamy selection of America's favorite dessert today!

Chocolate Peanut Butter Cheesecake with a Touch of Ganache

Every bite is a peanut butter cup lover's fantasy: a silky smooth filling with layers of chocolate and peanut butter!

2 cups graham cracker crumbs
⅓ cup firmly packed light brown sugar
⅓ cup unsalted butter, melted

CHOCOLATE LAYER

6 oz. semisweet chocolate, coarsely
    chopped
6 tbsp. unsalted butter, cut into pieces
½ cup granulated sugar
2 large eggs
2 tbsp. unbleached, all-purpose flour

PEANUT BUTTER LAYER

24 oz. cream cheese, room temperature,
    cut into pieces
1½ cups firmly packed light brown sugar
¾ cup creamy peanut butter
3 large eggs
1 large egg yolk
⅓ cup heavy cream

A TOUCH OF GANACHE

3 oz. semisweet chocolate, coarsely
    chopped
3 tbsp. heavy cream

TOPPING

Chocolate-covered peanut butter cups,
    chopped in large pieces
Roasted, salted peanuts, coarsely
    chopped

Heat oven to 300 degrees.

In a small bowl, combine the graham cracker crumbs and brown sugar. Add the melted butter, stirring to combine. Press crust onto the bottom and 1" up the sides of a 9" springform pan.

Bake for 5 to 6 minutes. Cool pan on wire rack. Leave oven on.

For the Chocolate Layer: In a medium saucepan, melt the chocolate and butter over low heat, stirring until melted and smooth. Whisk in the sugar, eggs, and flour until combined. Spread chocolate onto the cooled crust. Bake for 15 minutes. Cool on wire rack. Leave oven on.

For the Peanut Butter Layer: In a large bowl of an electric mixer, beat the cream cheese and brown sugar until creamy. Beat in the peanut butter until combined. Scrape bowl.

With mixer on low, beat in the eggs and egg yolk, one at a time, beating well after each addition. Stir in the heavy cream. Spread batter over cooled chocolate layer and bake for 70 minutes.

Remove from the oven and quickly run a knife around the inside edge of pan (leaving springform sides intact). Let cool completely on a wire rack.

For a Touch of Ganache: In a small saucepan over medium heat, combine the chocolate and the cream, stirring until mixture is melted and smooth. Spread over cooled cheesecake. Cover loosely with waxed paper and refrigerate cheesecake overnight.

When ready to serve, run a knife around the inside edge of pan and carefully remove the springform sides. Garnish top with peanut butter cup pieces and chopped peanuts. Serves 12-14.

Swirl me up some of this Chocolate Raspberry Swirl Cheesecake.

Chocolate Raspberry Swirl Cheesecake

A subtle, tasty swirl of chocolate raises this raspberry cheesecake to a whole new creamy level!

⅓ cup graham cracker crumbs

CHOCOLATE RASPBERRY SWIRL FILLING

32 oz. cream cheese, room temperature, cut into pieces
1⅓ cups granulated sugar
4 large eggs
2 tbsp. raspberry liqueur
2 tbsp. chopped fresh red raspberries
1½ tsp. freshly grated orange zest
3 oz. semisweet chocolate, melted

Heat oven to 325 degrees. Lightly grease bottom of a 9" springform pan. Wrap the outside of pan with foil, being sure bottom and sides of pan are completely covered (to prevent water from seeping into the pan).

Sprinkle graham cracker crumbs over bottom of pan.

For the Chocolate Raspberry Swirl Filling: In a large bowl of an electric mixer, beat the cream cheese until creamy. Gradually add sugar, beating well to combine. Scrape bowl.

Add eggs, one at a time, beating well after each addition. Add raspberry liqueur, chopped raspberries, and zest; beat until combined. Scrape bowl.

In a small bowl, reserve 1¼ cups batter. Spread remaining batter onto crumb-lined pan.

Gently stir melted chocolate into reserved batter. Drop spoonfuls of chocolate batter onto batter in pan. Using a knife, gently swirl the chocolate batter through the cheesecake batter to marble.

Place the springform into a larger pan. Carefully pour boiling water in the second pan until it comes halfway up the sides of the springform. Bake for 1 hour or until set. Cool in pan on wire rack, then refrigerate overnight.

When ready to serve, run a knife around the inside edge of pan and carefully remove the springform sides. Serves 12-14.

Thin Chocolate-Chipped Raspberry Cheesecake Triangles with Butter Crust

The line forms here for these delicate pieces of chocolate- and raspberry-studded cheesecake on a buttery crust.

1 cup unbleached, all-purpose flour
½ cup unsalted butter, room temperature, cut into pieces
¼ cup granulated sugar
1 large egg yolk

CHEESECAKE FILLING

16 oz. cream cheese, room temperature, cut into pieces
½ cup granulated sugar
2 large eggs, lightly beaten
12 oz. frozen red raspberries in syrup, thawed and undrained
½ cup semisweet mini chocolate chips

Heat oven to 350 degrees.

In a small bowl, mix together the flour, butter, sugar, and egg yolk until a soft dough forms. Press evenly onto the bottom of an ungreased 13" by 9" baking pan.

Prick dough lightly all over with a fork. Bake for 12 to 15 minutes or until crust is a light golden brown. Cool on a wire rack.

For the Cheesecake Filling: In a large bowl of an electric mixer, beat the cream cheese until smooth and fluffy. Beat in the sugar and eggs. Scrape bowl.

Stir in raspberries and chocolate chips. Spread batter over crust.

Bake for 20 to 25 minutes or just until center is set. Cool completely on a wire rack, then cover and refrigerate at least 4 to 12 hours until chilled.

When ready to serve, cut into 5 rows by 3 rows, then cut squares into triangles and serve. Serves 15+.

Cranberry Chocolate Cheesecake with Cranberry Sauce and Fudge Sauce

A drizzle of this and a drizzle of that with a slice of rich, cranberry-infused chocolate cheesecake—life is good!

9 oz. chocolate wafers
6 tbsp. unsalted butter, melted
2 tsp. granulated sugar

CRANBERRY CHOCOLATE CHEESECAKE FILLING

24 oz. cream cheese, room temperature, cut into pieces
½ cup granulated sugar
6 oz. semisweet chocolate, melted and cooled
½ cup 100 percent unsweetened cranberry juice
4 large eggs
½ cup heavy cream

CRANBERRY SAUCE

2 12-oz. pkg. frozen cranberries, thawed
½ cup granulated sugar
2 tbsp. 100 percent unsweetened cranberry juice

FUDGE SAUCE

4 oz. bittersweet chocolate, coarsely chopped
⅓ cup unsalted butter, cut into pieces
1⅓ cups confectioners' sugar, sifted
¾ cup half-and-half
1 tsp. vanilla extract

TOPPING

1 cup heavy cream, whipped
½ cup fresh cranberries, wetted, rolled in sugar, and frozen

A SLICE OF ADVICE FROM BEV

The Cranberry Sauce and the Fudge Sauce can be prepared 1 day ahead. Cover and refrigerate, but bring to room temperature before using.

Heat oven to 350 degrees. Grease a 9" springform pan (with 2½" sides).

In a food processor, grind the chocolate wafers to fine crumbs. Pulse in the melted butter and sugar until moist crumbs form. Press onto bottom and 1½" up sides of pan.

For the Cranberry Chocolate Cheesecake Filling: In a large bowl of an electric mixer, beat the cream cheese until creamy. Add the sugar, chocolate, and juice, mixing until well blended.

With mixer on low, add the eggs, one at a time, just until blended. Scrape bowl. Stir in the cream.

Spread batter onto prepared crust. Bake for 55 to 60 minutes or until center appears nearly set. (Center will still jiggle but not be liquidy.) Transfer to a wire rack and cool in pan. Cover loosely with waxed paper and refrigerate cheesecake overnight.

For the Cranberry Sauce: In a medium saucepan, combine the cranberries, sugar, and juice. Cook over medium heat just until cranberries soften and begin to pop. Set aside to cool for 10 minutes, and then strain mixture through a fine strainer into a bowl.

For the Fudge Sauce: In a medium saucepan, combine the chocolate, butter, sugar, and half-and-half, mixing well. Cook, stirring constantly, over medium heat until mixture boils. Reduce heat to low. Cook 5 minutes, stirring constantly. Remove from heat and whisk in vanilla.

When ready to serve the cheesecake, run a knife around the inside edge of pan and carefully remove the springform sides.

For the Topping: Using a pastry bag, pipe rosettes of whipped cream around the edge of the cheesecake, spacing ¼" apart. Place sugared cranberries between each rosette.

Serve each slice with a drizzle of Cranberry Sauce down one side and a drizzle of Fudge Sauce down the other. Serves 12-14.

Chocolate Chip Cookie Dough Cheesecake

For all of you who love chocolate chip cookie dough, this is the perfect dessert surprise—a simplified cookie dough batter in a smooth cheesecake.

1½ cups finely crushed chocolate wafers
1 cup granulated sugar
¼ cup plus 1 tbsp. unsalted butter, melted

COOKIE DOUGH

¼ cup unsalted butter, room temperature
¼ cup firmly packed light brown sugar
¼ cup granulated sugar
2 tbsp. water
1 tsp. vanilla extract
½ cup unbleached, all-purpose flour
1 cup semisweet chocolate chips

CHEESECAKE FILLING

16 oz. cream cheese, room temperature, cut into pieces
1 cup sour cream
3 large eggs
1 tsp. vanilla extract

Heat oven to 350 degrees.

In a medium bowl, mix together the crumbs, sugar, and melted butter. Press over bottom and ½" up sides of a 9" inch springform pan. Bake for 8 minutes. Cool on a wire rack. Leave oven on.

For the Cookie Dough: In a large bowl of an electric mixer, beat together the butter and sugars until light and fluffy. Scrape down sides and bottom of bowl. Stir in the water and vanilla until combined.

Beat in the flour until blended, and then stir in the chocolate chips. Set aside.

For the Cheesecake Filling: In a large bowl of an electric mixer, beat the cream cheese until creamy. With mixer on medium speed, stir in the sour cream, eggs, and vanilla until light and well blended. Scrape bowl. Spread batter onto prepared crust.

Drop 2 tbsp. cookie dough onto cake batter. Repeat with remaining cookie dough over entire cake. Push dough beneath the surface. Bake for 40 minutes or until center appears nearly set. (Center will still jiggle but not be liquidy.) Cool in pan on a wire rack. Cover loosely with waxed paper and refrigerate cheesecake overnight.

When ready to serve, run a knife around the inside edge of pan and carefully remove the springform sides. Serves 12-14.

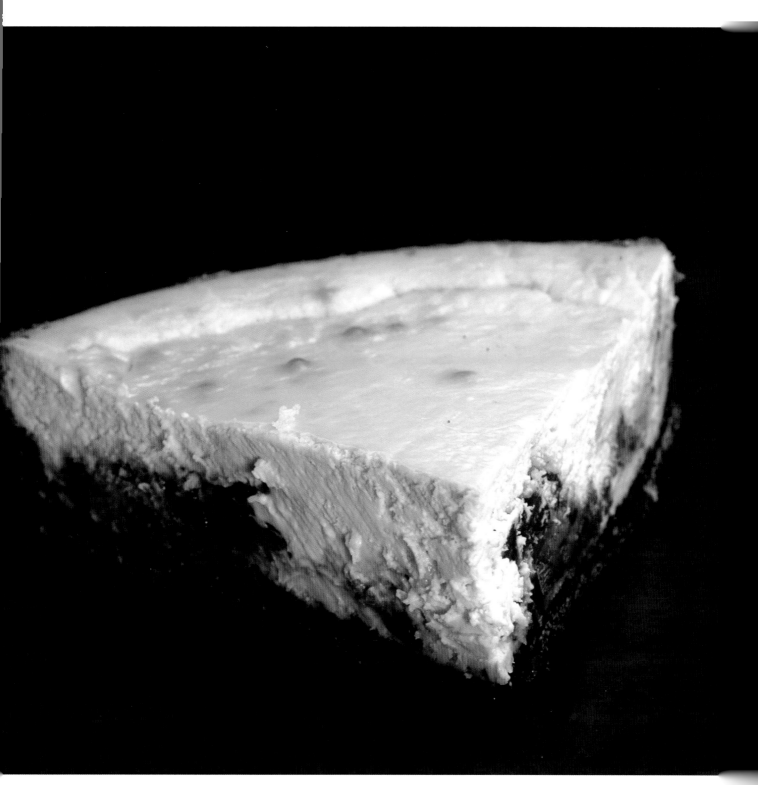

This Chocolate Chip Cookie Dough Cheesecake should be my reward for being extra good. (Well, okay, at least good.)

White Chocolate Cranberry Cheesecake

Dried cranberries are cooked and turned into a "jam" of sorts then combined with white chocolate and yogurt cheese. The result? A delicious, sweet-tart cheesecake.

32 oz. plain, nonfat yogurt

CRANBERRY "JAM"

1 cup dried cranberries
½ cup granulated sugar
½ cup water

CRUST

24 vanilla wafers
1 tbsp. unsalted butter, melted and
   cooled

CHEESECAKE

4 oz. white chocolate, coarsely chopped
2 tbsp. milk
1 tbsp. vanilla extract
8 oz. Neufchatel cheese, room
   temperature, cut into pieces
1 cup sour cream
1 cup granulated sugar
¼ cup cornstarch or arrowroot
¼ tsp. salt
3 large eggs

The day before you are planning to bake: Line a large strainer or colander with cheesecloth and set atop a bowl. Spoon yogurt into cheesecloth in strainer and cover with plastic wrap. Refrigerate overnight to allow yogurt to drain thoroughly and form the "cheese." When ready to use, discard the liquid and spoon the yogurt cheese into a small bowl.

For the Cranberry "Jam": In a small saucepan, combine the cranberries, sugar, and water. Bring to a boil over high heat. Cover saucepan and reduce to medium low, simmering until the dried cranberries are plump and soft. Remove saucepan from heat and let cool, covered, just until mixture is warm. Pulse in food processor to puree. Remove "jam" to a small bowl and set aside.

Heat oven to 350 degrees. Lightly grease a 9" springform pan.

For the Crust: In a sealed zip-top bag, crush the vanilla wafers to fine crumbs. Transfer crumbs to a small bowl. Quickly stir in the melted butter to combine.

Press crumb mixture onto bottom of the pan. Bake for 8 to 10 minutes or until lightly golden in color. Remove from the oven and cool on a wire rack.

Reduce oven to 300 degrees.

For the Cheesecake: Melt the chocolate with the milk in a double boiler set over barely simmering water, whisking until mixture is smooth. Remove from the heat and whisk in the vanilla. Set aside.

In a large bowl of an electric mixer, beat the yogurt cheese, Neufchatel, sour cream, sugar, cornstarch or arrowroot, and salt just until blended. Scrape bowl. Beat in the chocolate mixture until combined.

With mixer on low, beat in the eggs, one at a time, only until incorporated. Scrape bowl.

Fold the Cranberry "Jam" into the batter with a large rubber spatula until mixture is streaked and not completely combined.

CAKES TO DIE FOR!

A SLICE OF ADVICE FROM BEV

Feel free to make the "jam" a day ahead. Cool, cover, refrigerate, and bring to room temperature before using.

Spread batter onto crust-lined pan and quickly smooth the top. Cover the pan loosely with foil and bake for 65 minutes.

After 65 minutes, remove the foil and turn the oven off. Let the cheesecake cool in the oven with the door closed for 75 minutes. Remove from the oven and cool completely on a wire rack. Cover loosely with waxed paper and refrigerate cheesecake overnight.

When ready to serve, run a knife around the inside edge of pan and carefully remove the springform sides. Serves 8-12.

Triple Almond Cheesecake

This cheesecake is always a favorite . . . sophisticated flavors meet simple combinations!

2 cups graham cracker crumbs
¼ cup finely chopped almonds
⅓ cup unsalted butter, melted

AMARETTO CHEESECAKE
   FILLING

16 oz. cream cheese, room temperature,
   cut into pieces
1 cup granulated sugar
3 large eggs
1 cup sour cream
½ cup heavy cream
¼ cup Amaretto liqueur
½ tsp. almond extract

GLAZED ALMOND TOPPING

½ cup granulated sugar
¼ cup water
1 cup sliced almonds
1 tsp. Amaretto liqueur

A SLICE OF ADVICE FROM
   BEV

To minimize cracking, place a shallow pan half-full of hot water on lower oven rack during baking.

Heat oven to 350 degrees.

In a medium bowl, combine the crumbs, almonds, and melted butter, stirring just to blend. Press onto bottom and 1" up sides of a 10" springform pan.

For the Amaretto Cheesecake Filling: In a large bowl of an electric mixer, beat the cream cheese and sugar until mixture is light and fluffy. Scrape bowl.

Add eggs, one at a time, beating well after each addition. With mixer on low, stir in sour cream, heavy cream, Amaretto, and almond extract, mixing just to combine.

Spread batter onto prepared crust. Bake for 58 to 75 minutes or until center is set. Cool in pan on a wire rack. Cover loosely with waxed paper and refrigerate cheesecake overnight.

For the Glazed Almond Topping: In a small saucepan, combine the sugar and water. Bring to a boil and boil for 2 minutes. Remove from heat. Stir in almonds and Amaretto, tossing to combine.

With a slotted spoon, remove almonds to waxed paper, separating with a fork. Cool completely.

When ready to serve, run a knife around the inside edge of pan and carefully remove the springform sides. Arrange Glazed Almond Topping in a 2"-wide circle around outer edge of cheesecake. Serves 14-16.

 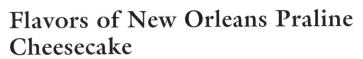

Flavors of New Orleans Praline Cheesecake

A beautiful presentation and a fine substitute for pecan pie.

¾ cup graham cracker crumbs
½ cup finely ground pecans
¼ cup firmly packed dark brown sugar
¼ cup unsalted butter, melted

CHEESECAKE FILLING

24 oz. cream cheese, room temperature,
    cut into pieces
1⅓ cups sweetened condensed milk
6 large eggs
2 tbsp. vanilla extract

PECAN PRALINE TOPPING

½ cup firmly packed light brown sugar
⅓ cup heavy cream
½ cup chopped pecans, lightly toasted

Heat oven to 300 degrees.

In a medium bowl, combine the crumbs, pecans, sugar, and melted butter; mix well. Press crumb mixture on bottom of 9" springform pan.

For the Cheesecake Filling: In a large bowl of an electric mixer, beat cream cheese until creamy. With mixer on low, beat in sweetened condensed milk until combined. Scrape bowl.

Add eggs, one at a time, beating just to combine. Stir in vanilla. Spread batter onto prepared crust.

Bake for 55 to 60 minutes or just until center is set. Cool in pan on a wire rack. Cover loosely with waxed paper and refrigerate cheesecake overnight.

For the Pecan Praline Topping: In a medium saucepan, combine the sugar and heavy cream. Cook and stir over medium high heat for 5 to 10 minutes or until mixture begins to thicken. Remove from heat and stir in pecan pieces. Gently spoon and spread atop cheesecake. Allow to set for 30 minutes at room temperature.

When ready to serve, run a knife around the inside edge of pan and carefully remove the springform sides. Serves 10-12.

 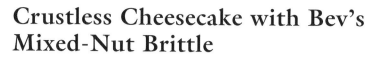

Crustless Cheesecake with Bev's Mixed-Nut Brittle

A tangy, silky, crustless cheesecake with the crunch and crackle of candy brittle.

24 oz. plain, whole-milk Greek yogurt
1½ cups mascarpone
¾ cup granulated sugar
3 tbsp. confectioners' sugar, sifted
3 large eggs
6 large egg yolks
½ tsp. salt
1½ tsp. vanilla extract

BEV'S MIXED-NUT BRITTLE

1½ cups granulated sugar
½ cup light corn syrup
Pinch of salt
¼ cup cold water
2½ cups mixed nuts (such as cashews, peanuts, and pecans)
1 tsp. vanilla extract
1 tsp. baking soda

Heat oven to 350 degrees. Grease a 10" springform pan and sprinkle with some additional granulated sugar, tapping out any excess sugar. Wrap the outside of the pan with foil, being sure bottom and sides of pan are completely covered (to prevent water from seeping into the pan).

In a large bowl of an electric mixer, beat together the yogurt, mascarpone, granulated sugar, and confectioners' sugar just until very smooth and creamy. Scrape bowl.

Add the eggs and egg yolks, one at a time, beating after each addition just until blended. Scrape bowl. Stir in the salt and vanilla. Spread the batter into the prepared pan, quickly and gently smoothing the top.

Place the springform into a larger pan and carefully pour boiling water in the second pan until it comes halfway up the sides of the springform.

Cover both pans with a single piece of foil, tenting the foil so it doesn't touch the top of the springform pan. Bake for 42 minutes, and then carefully remove the foil. The center of the cake should appear nearly set. (Center will still jiggle but not be liquidy.) Remove from oven.

Continue to cool in the water bath for 1 hour on a wire rack. Remove from the water bath, then cover loosely with waxed paper and refrigerate cheesecake overnight.

For Bev's Mixed-Nut Brittle: Brush a 13" by 9" rimmed baking sheet with melted butter. Oil an offset spatula; set aside.

Place the sugar, corn syrup, salt, and cold water in a medium saucepan. Bring to a boil over medium-high heat, stirring until sugar has dissolved. Wash down sides of the pan with a wet pastry brush to prevent crystals from forming.

Cook, swirling pan occasionally, until the mixture registers 238 degrees on a candy thermometer (soft-ball stage). Stir in the nuts and continue to cook, stirring often so they do not burn, until the mixture is a medium amber in color (about 10 to 15 minutes).

Carefully stir in vanilla and baking soda (the mixture will foam up). Pour onto prepared baking sheet and, using oiled spatula, *quickly* spread into a ½"-thick (or less) layer. Let cool completely. Break brittle into pieces; store in an airtight container at room temperature.

When ready to serve, run a knife around the inside edge of pan and carefully remove the springform sides. Sprinkle the top of the cheesecake with some of the brittle. Serve each slice with additional brittle pieces on the side. Serves 10-12.

This Crustless Cheesecake stands alone, but when combined with Bev's Mixed-Nut Brittle, it's in a (cheesecake) class by itself.

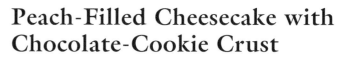

Peach-Filled Cheesecake with Chocolate-Cookie Crust

A surprise layer of peach filling sits between two creamy layers . . . atop a chocolate crust. A fruit lover's dream combination!

12 oz. frozen peaches, partially thawed, chopped
2 tbsp. cornstarch or arrowroot
½ cup sour cream

CHOCOLATE CRUST

9 oz. pkg. chocolate wafers
⅓ cup unsalted butter, melted

CHEESECAKE

8 oz. cream cheese, room temperature, cut into pieces
8 oz. Neufchatel cheese, room temperature, cut into pieces
1½ cups granulated sugar
4 large eggs
1½ cups sour cream
3 tbsp. cornstarch or arrowroot
1 tsp. vanilla extract

TOPPING

Fresh red raspberries
Grated chocolate

Heat oven to 325 degrees.

In a medium saucepan, combine the peach pieces and cornstarch or arrowroot. Cook over medium heat, stirring constantly, until mixture comes to a boil. Continue to boil for 1 minute, then remove saucepan from heat. Cool 10 minutes in saucepan, then cover and refrigerate.

For the Chocolate Crust: In a food processor, pulse the chocolate wafers until very finely chopped. Add the melted butter and process just until combined.

Press crumb mixture onto bottom of 9" springform pan.

For the Cheesecake: In a large bowl of an electric mixer, beat the cream cheese and Neufchatel cheese until creamy. Beat in the sugar. Scrape bowl.

Add the eggs, one at a time, beating just to combine. With mixer on low, stir in the sour cream, cornstarch, and vanilla to blend.

Remove saucepan of peaches from refrigerator and blend in the sour cream.

Spread *half* of the cheesecake batter into prepared crust. Spoon peaches evenly over cheesecake batter in pan, then top with remaining batter.

Bake for 62 to 75 minutes or until center appears nearly set. (Center will still jiggle but not be liquidy.) Let the cheesecake cool in the oven with the door closed for 1½ hours. Remove from the oven and cool pan completely on a wire rack. Cover loosely with waxed paper and refrigerate cheesecake overnight.

When ready to serve, run a knife around the inside edge of pan and carefully remove the springform sides. Garnish each slice with some red raspberries and grated chocolate. Serves 12-14.

CAKES TO DIE FOR!

Yo! Yogurt (Lower-Fat) Raspberry-Topped Cheesecake

Who's to know? Great flavors come in all calorie counts!

56 oz. plain, nonfat yogurt

CRUST

1 cup graham cracker crumbs
1 cup vanilla wafer crumbs
1 tbsp. unbleached, all-purpose flour
¼ cup unsalted butter, melted and
    cooled

CHEESECAKE FILLING

6 oz. Neufchatel cheese, room
    temperature, cut into pieces
1 cup granulated sugar
1 tbsp. fresh orange juice
3 large eggs
2 tsp. freshly grated orange zest

TOPPING

⅓ cup seedless raspberry preserves
3 cups fresh red raspberries, gently
    washed and dried

The day before you are planning to bake: Line a large strainer or colander with cheesecloth and set atop a bowl. Spoon yogurt into cheesecloth in strainer and cover with plastic wrap. Refrigerate overnight to allow yogurt to drain thoroughly and form the "cheese." When ready to use, discard the liquid and spoon the yogurt cheese into a small bowl.

Heat oven to 350 degrees.

For the Crust: In a medium bowl, combine the crumbs and flour. Drizzle with the melted butter, tossing to mix well. Press the mixture onto the bottom and 1" up the sides of an 8" springform pan. Bake for 5 minutes. Leave oven on.

For the Cheesecake Filling: In a large bowl of an electric mixer, combine the yogurt cheese, Neufchatel, sugar, and orange juice, beating until mixture is smooth.

With mixer on low, beat in the eggs just until combined. Stir in the orange zest. Spread batter onto prepared crust.

Bake for 45 to 50 minutes or until center appears nearly set. (Center will still jiggle but not be liquidy.) Cool in pan on a wire rack. Cover loosely with waxed paper and refrigerate cheesecake overnight.

For the Topping: Melt the raspberry preserves in a small saucepan over low heat. Cool slightly.

When ready to serve, run a knife around the inside edge of pan and carefully remove the springform sides. Top each slice with some raspberries and a drizzle of the warm preserves. Serves 8-10.

Sorry, but a two-orange slice of this Light Orange Vanilla Yogurt Cheesecake is too much!

Light Orange Vanilla Yogurt Cheesecake

The perfect summer cheesecake—refreshing and light. It has a thin crust and the filling is silky smooth.

1 cup vanilla wafer crumbs
2 tbsp. unsalted butter, melted

VANILLA YOGURT CHEESECAKE FILLING

2 envelopes unflavored gelatin
⅓ cup granulated sugar
¾ cup orange juice
15 oz. ricotta
16 oz. vanilla yogurt, nonfat or low fat, drained
2 tbsp. Grand Marnier liqueur
2 10-oz. cans mandarin oranges, well drained, plus additional for garnish

A SLICE OF ADVICE FROM BEV

No Grand Marnier in the house? Fresh orange juice will work, too!

Heat oven to 375 degrees.

In a small bowl, combine the wafer crumbs and melted butter. Press onto the bottom of a 10" springform pan.

Bake for 8 to 10 minutes. Cool on a wire rack.

For the Vanilla Yogurt Cheesecake Filling: In a small saucepan, combine the gelatin, sugar, and orange juice. Let stand 1 minute to soften gelatin.

Stir over medium heat until gelatin and sugar are dissolved.

In a food processor, process the ricotta until smooth. Remove to a medium bowl. Stir in the yogurt, gelatin mixture, and Grand Marnier; blend well.

Gently stir in drained mandarin oranges. Spread batter onto prepared crust.

Cover loosely with waxed paper and refrigerate cheesecake overnight.

When ready to serve, run a knife around the inside edge of pan and carefully remove the springform sides.

Garnish with additional mandarin orange slices. Serves 10-12.

Bev's Whipped Cheesecake with Blueberry Topping

This is a simply decadent, no-bake, light-as-air cheesecake that's a prizewinner of mine.

1⅔ cups graham cracker crumbs
¼ cup granulated sugar
⅓ cup unsalted butter, melted

WHIPPED CHEESECAKE FILLING

16 oz. cream cheese, room temperature, cut into pieces
2 cups confectioners' sugar, sifted
2 tsp. vanilla extract
2 cups heavy cream, whipped

BLUEBERRY TOPPING

2 tbsp. cornstarch or arrowroot
⅓ cup granulated sugar
½ cup water
1 tbsp. fresh lemon juice
1 cup blueberries, fresh or frozen

A SLICE OF ADVICE FROM BEV

It's important that the cream-cheese mixture and whipped cream are folded and blended together well, so no lumps remain in the final cheesecake.

If blueberries are frozen, thaw only slightly before using.

Heat oven to 350 degrees.

In a small bowl, stir together the crumbs, sugar, and melted butter. Press onto bottom and ¾" up sides of a 9" springform pan. Bake for 8 minutes, then cool completely on a wire rack.

For the Whipped Cheesecake Filling: In a large bowl of an electric mixer, beat together the cream cheese, confectioners' sugar, and vanilla until well combined. Scrape bowl. Beat again on low speed to ensure all is well mixed. Fold in the whipped cream carefully and thoroughly. Spread onto prepared crust. Refrigerate several hours to allow mixture to set.

For the Blueberry Topping: In a medium saucepan, mix together the cornstarch and sugar until well blended. Add the water and cook over medium heat, stirring constantly, until mixture is thickened. Remove from heat and add lemon juice; blend well.

Gently toss in the blueberries, mixing well to coat. Set aside to cool for 30 to 45 minutes before spreading atop cheesecake.

When ready to serve, run a knife around the inside edge of pan and carefully remove the springform sides. Garnish top of cheesecake with Blueberry Topping. Serves 10-12.

Sour Cherry Sour Cream Cheesecake

The sour cream and sour cherries are just the right complement to each other and to the smooth, dreamy texture of this cheesecake.

2 cups graham cracker crumbs
2 tbsp. unsalted butter, melted
2 tbsp. granulated sugar

CHEESECAKE FILLING

16 oz. cream cheese, room temperature, cut into pieces
1½ cups vanilla sugar or 1½ cups granulated sugar and 1 tsp. vanilla bean paste
2 cups sour cream
¼ cup half-and-half
3 large eggs
3 large egg yolks

TOPPING

1 cup dried sour or sweet cherries
2 cups sour cherry preserves or fruit spread

A SLICE OF ADVICE FROM BEV

This cheesecake is baked in a bain-marie (water bath), providing gentle heat that helps keep the outer edge of the cheesecake from overbaking and makes for a smooth cheesecake throughout.

Heat oven to 350 degrees. Wrap the outside of a greased 10" springform pan with foil, being sure bottom and sides of pan are completely covered (to prevent water from seeping into the pan).

Mix the crumbs, melted butter, and sugar in a small bowl. Pack the crumb mixture onto the bottom and partially up the sides of the pan.

For the Cheesecake Filling: In a large bowl of an electric mixer, beat the cream cheese until creamy. Add the sugar and beat until mixture is well blended. Scrape bowl.

With mixer on low, add the sour cream and half-and-half, beating until incorporated. Add the eggs and the yolks and beat to blend.

Spread batter onto prepared crust. Place the springform into a larger pan and carefully pour boiling water in the second pan until it comes halfway up the sides of the springform.

Place on the middle shelf in the oven and bake 70 minutes. After 70 minutes, turn the oven off. Let the cheesecake cool in the oven with the door closed for 45 minutes. Remove from the oven. Continue to cool in the water bath on a wire rack for 1 hour.

Remove from the water bath, cover loosely with waxed paper, and refrigerate cheesecake overnight.

When ready to serve, run a knife around the inside edge of pan and carefully remove the springform sides. Place the dried cherries around the outside edge of the cheesecake, then spread the sour cherry preserves in the center. Serves 8-10.

Oh! You Sweet Potato Cheesecake

Gingersnaps make a refreshing crust for this smooth and creamy cheesecake, and these flavor combinations will become a welcome addition to your fall and winter celebrations.

2 cups gingersnap crumbs
6 tbsp. unsalted butter, melted

SWEET POTATO CHEESECAKE FILLING

24 oz. cream cheese, room temperature, cut into pieces
½ cup unsalted butter, room temperature, cut into pieces
1⅓ cups granulated sugar
1 cup cooked, peeled, and mashed sweet potatoes
¾ tsp. freshly grated nutmeg
1 tsp. ground cinnamon
3 tbsp. bourbon
1 tsp. vanilla extract
4 large eggs

TOPPING

1½ cups sour cream
2 tbsp. granulated sugar
1 tbsp. vanilla extract
Gingersnap cookies, coarsely chopped

Heat oven to 350 degrees. Grease a 10½" springform pan.

In a medium bowl, stir together the crumbs and melted butter. Press mixture onto bottom and 1" up sides of prepared pan.

Bake for 8 to 10 minutes or just until color begins to deepen. Cool on a wire rack. Leave oven on.

For the Sweet Potato Cheesecake Filling: In a large bowl of an electric mixer, beat the cream cheese and butter until creamy. With mixer on medium speed, beat in the sugar. Scrape bowl.

Mix in the mashed sweet potatoes, nutmeg, and cinnamon, beating to combine. Add the bourbon and vanilla, thoroughly combining. Scrape bowl.

Add the eggs, one at a time, mixing just until combined.

Spread batter onto prepared crust. Bake for 20 minutes.

Reduce oven temperature to 300 degrees and continue baking for 35 minutes. Reduce oven temperature again to 250 degrees and continue baking for 20 minutes or until center appears nearly set. (Center will still jiggle but not be liquidy.) Remove from oven and increase oven temperature to 350 degrees.

For the Topping: In a medium bowl, whisk together the sour cream, sugar, and vanilla. Quickly and carefully spread topping evenly over cheesecake. Bake for 5 minutes to just set the topping.

Cool in pan on a wire rack. Cover loosely with waxed paper and refrigerate cheesecake overnight.

When ready to serve, run a knife around the inside edge of pan and carefully remove the springform sides. Sprinkle cheesecake with some chopped gingersnap cookies. Serves 12-14.

A gingersnap crust? Oh! You Sweet Potato Cheesecake, am I ever ready for you.

Laura's Surprise (Cheddar) Cheesecake

I was more than a little skeptical when friend and professional baker Laura Ruggles shared this recipe with me. Knowing her extensive experience and love of baking, I gave this cheesecake a try, and I'm glad. It's truly unique and delicious!

1½ cups zwieback crumbs
¼ cup finely ground, toasted almonds
3 tbsp. firmly packed light brown sugar
1 tsp. freshly grated lemon zest
1 tsp. freshly grated orange zest
½ tsp. ground cinnamon
6 tbsp. unsalted butter, melted

(CHEDDAR) CHEESECAKE FILLING

32 oz. cream cheese, room temperature, cut into pieces
8 oz. sharp cheddar cheese, grated then finely chopped
½ cup heavy cream
5 large eggs, lightly beaten
2 cups granulated sugar
2 tsp. vanilla extract
1 tsp. lemon extract
½ tsp. orange extract
1 tsp. freshly grated lemon zest
1 tsp. freshly grated orange zest

Heat oven to 300 degrees. Lightly grease a 9" springform pan and place a baking sheet under it.

In a large bowl, mix together the crumbs, almonds, sugar, zests, cinnamon, and melted butter until combined. Press onto bottom and ½" up the sides of the prepared pan.

For the (Cheddar) Cheesecake Filling: In a food processor in *4 or 5 batches,* combine the cream cheese and cheddar cheese, pulsing to blend each batch until thoroughly combined. (When combining the last batch, add the heavy cream and the eggs to blend well.) Transfer mixture to a large bowl.

Stir in the sugar, extracts, and zests until all are thoroughly combined. Spread batter onto prepared crust.

Bake for 2 hours and 15 minutes or until cheesecake appears set. Cool in pan on a wire rack. Cover loosely with waxed paper and refrigerate cheesecake overnight.

When ready to serve, run a knife around the inside edge of pan and carefully remove the springform sides. Serves 12-14.

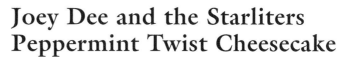

Joey Dee and the Starliters
Peppermint Twist Cheesecake

That oldie but goodie, "The Peppermint Twist," will be playing in your head as you bite into this pepperminty cheesecake. I like it like this. . . .

9 oz. chocolate wafers
¼ cup granulated sugar
½ cup unsalted butter, melted

PEPPERMINT TWIST CHEESECAKE
   FILLING

32 oz. cream cheese, room temperature,
   cut into pieces
1 cup granulated sugar
4 large eggs
¼ cup half-and-half
1 tsp. vanilla extract
1 tsp. peppermint extract
⅓ cup crushed hard peppermint candies

PEPPERMINT TOPPING

1½ cups sour cream
3 tbsp. granulated sugar
½ tsp. vanilla extract
¼ tsp. peppermint extract
Additional crushed peppermint candies

Heat oven to 350 degrees. Wrap the outside of a 9" springform pan with foil, being sure bottom and sides of pan are completely covered (to prevent water from seeping into the pan).

In a food processor, pulse the chocolate wafers with sugar until finely ground. Add the melted butter, processing just until blended. Press crumb mixture onto bottom and ½" up sides of pan, then refrigerate until ready to use.

For the Peppermint Twist Cheesecake Filling: In a large bowl of an electric mixer, beat the cream cheese until creamy. Add the sugar and beat until well blended.

With mixer on low, add the eggs, one at a time, beating just until blended. Stir in half-and-half and extracts. Stir in crushed peppermint candies. Spread filling onto prepared crust.

Bake cheesecake just until filling is set in the center, 45 to 55 minutes. Cool in pan 10 minutes on a wire rack. Leave oven on.

For the Peppermint Topping: In a small bowl, whisk together the sour cream, sugar, and extracts. Pour topping over hot cheesecake, quickly spreading with a metal spatula to cover completely.

Return cheesecake to oven. Continue to bake about 9 to 12 minutes or just until top begins to set. Cool in pan on a wire rack. Cover loosely with waxed paper and refrigerate cheesecake overnight.

When ready to serve, run a knife around the inside edge of pan and carefully remove the springform sides. Sprinkle top with additional crushed peppermint candies. Serves 12-14.

This Poppy Seed Cheesecake with Lemon Crust is easy to make and ready to serve a crowd.

Poppy Seed Cheesecake with Lemon Crust

Easy to cut and serve, with crowd-pleasing flavor and texture.

1 cup unbleached, all-purpose flour
½ cup unsalted butter, room temperature, cut into pieces
¼ cup granulated sugar
2 tsp. freshly grated lemon zest
1 large egg yolk

POPPY SEED CHEESECAKE FILLING

40 oz. cream cheese, room temperature, cut into pieces
1¾ cups granulated sugar
¼ cup poppy seeds
3 tbsp. unbleached, all-purpose flour
3 tbsp. freshly grated lemon zest
¼ tsp. salt
5 large eggs
2 large egg yolks
¼ cup heavy cream

1 cup lemon curd

Heat oven to 400 degrees. Lightly grease a 13″ x 9″ baking pan.

In a large bowl with a pastry blender, mix together the flour, butter, sugar, zest, and egg yolk until a dough forms. Press evenly onto bottom of pan.

Lightly prick crust with a fork. Bake for 12 to 15 minutes or until crust is a light golden brown. Cool on a wire rack.

Increase oven temperature to 475 degrees.

For the Poppy Seed Cheesecake Filling: In a large bowl of an electric mixer, beat the cream cheese, sugar, poppy seeds, flour, zest, and salt until combined. Scrape bowl.

With mixer on low, beat in eggs, egg yolks, and heavy cream until well blended. Spread batter onto prepared crust.

Bake 15 minutes. *Turn oven off* and let the cheesecake cool in the oven with the door closed for 20 minutes. Cool in pan on wire rack, then cover loosely with waxed paper and refrigerate cheesecake overnight.

Spread lemon curd over top of cheesecake. Serves 16-20.

No-Bake Lemon Berry Cheesecake

This delectable no-bake treat will travel well to your next party or picnic.

8 oz. cream cheese, room temperature,
  cut into pieces
½ cup sour cream
1½ tsp. lemon extract
¼ cup confectioners' sugar, sifted
9" graham cracker crust

TOPPING

1 qt. fresh, seasonal berries
  (strawberries, black raspberries,
  blackberries)

In a large bowl of an electric mixer, beat the cream cheese until creamy. With mixer on low, stir in the sour cream, lemon extract, and confectioners' sugar just until blended. Scrape bowl.

Spread batter in crust. Refrigerate, lightly covered with waxed paper, until cheesecake is set, at least 2 hours. When ready to serve, arrange sliced strawberries or other berries atop cheesecake. Serves 6-8.

Lemon Cheesecake in Cornmeal Crust

A refreshing change-of-pace cheesecake that would be perfect topped with fresh blueberries, red raspberries, or juicy, ripe, in-season peaches.

½ cup unsalted butter, room temperature, cut into pieces
¼ cup granulated sugar
½ cup unbleached, all-purpose flour
½ cup yellow cornmeal

LEMON CHEESECAKE FILLING

32 oz. cream cheese, room temperature, cut into pieces
1 cup mascarpone, room temperature
1½ cups granulated sugar
2 large eggs
2 tsp. freshly grated lemon zest
3 tbsp. fresh lemon juice

Heat oven to 350 degrees. Wrap the outside of a 10" springform pan with foil, being sure bottom and sides of pan are completely covered (to prevent water from seeping into the pan).

In a large bowl of an electric mixer, beat the butter and sugar until mixture is smooth. Scrape bowl. With mixer on low, blend in the flour and cornmeal until crumbly. Press onto bottom of pan. Lightly prick crust with a fork, then bake for 15 to 20 minutes or until crust is a light golden brown. Cool pan on a wire rack.

Decrease oven temperature to 325 degrees.

For the Lemon Cheesecake Filling: In a large bowl of an electric mixer, beat the cream cheese and mascarpone until creamy. With mixer on low, blend in the sugar until combined. Scrape bowl.

Stir in the eggs, one at a time, mixing until blended. With mixer on low, blend in the zest and lemon juice until combined. Spread batter onto prepared crust.

Place springform pan in a large rectangular baking pan. Fill baking pan with hot water a third of the way up the sides of the springform pan.

Bake in the water bath until center appears nearly set, about 65 to 70 minutes. (Center will still jiggle but not be liquidy.) Remove from the water bath and cool completely on a wire rack. Cover loosely with waxed paper and refrigerate cheesecake overnight.

When ready to serve, run a knife around the inside edge of pan and carefully remove the springform sides. Serve topped with fresh fruit as desired. Serves 12-14.

A Burst of Orange Cheesecake with Marmalade-Cranberry Sauce

Who doesn't love their dessert served with flair and flavor?!

1¼ cups graham cracker crumbs
¼ cup granulated sugar
1 tsp. ground cinnamon
⅓ cup unsalted butter, melted

BURST OF ORANGE CHEESECAKE FILLING

16 oz. cream cheese, room temperature, cut into pieces
⅔ cup granulated sugar
2 large eggs
⅓ cup sour cream
2 tbsp. freshly grated orange zest

MARMALADE-CRANBERRY SAUCE

1 cup cranberries, fresh or frozen
⅔ cup orange marmalade
⅓ cup granulated sugar
1 tsp. ground cinnamon
¼ cup fresh orange juice

TOPPING

¾ cup heavy cream, whipped
Fresh cranberries, wetted, rolled in sugar, and frozen

Heat oven to 325 degrees.

In a medium bowl, combine the crumbs, sugar, and cinnamon. Stir in the melted butter, and then press mixture onto bottom of a 9" springform pan. Bake for 6 to 8 minutes or just until set. Cool in pan on wire rack. Leave oven on.

For the Burst of Orange Cheesecake Filling: In a large bowl of an electric mixer, beat the cream cheese until creamy. With mixer on low, beat in the sugar. Scrape bowl.

With mixer still on low, beat in eggs, one at a time, just until blended. Stir in the sour cream and zest. Spread batter atop prepared crust.

Bake for 38 to 48 minutes or until center is set. Remove from the oven and cool pan completely on a wire rack. Cover pan loosely with waxed paper and refrigerate cheesecake overnight.

For the Marmalade-Cranberry Sauce: In a medium saucepan, combine the cranberries, marmalade, sugar, cinnamon, and orange juice. Bring to a boil. Reduce heat and simmer mixture about 10 minutes or until cranberries burst and mixture is syrupy, stirring occasionally. Set aside.

When ready to serve, run a knife around the inside edge of pan and carefully remove the springform sides.

For the Topping: Using a pastry bag or spoon, pipe or dollop whipped cream around top edge of cheesecake. Garnish with sugared cranberries. Cut into slices. Serve with Marmalade-Cranberry Sauce. Serves 12-14.

CAKES TO DIE FOR!

Tangerine Cheesecake with Mango Sauce

I love to make this cheesecake when tangerines are in season, and when they're not, you can substitute frozen tangerine juice and fresh orange zest to maintain the same deliciously clean flavor profile!

1 cup shortbread cookie crumbs
2 tbsp. unsalted butter, melted

CHEESECAKE FILLING

24 oz. cream cheese, room temperature, cut into pieces
1 cup granulated sugar
3 large eggs
1 tbsp. freshly grated tangerine zest or orange zest
¼ cup tangerine juice

MANGO SAUCE

16 oz. frozen mango pieces, thawed
Mango nectar as needed
1 tbsp. cornstarch or arrowroot
½ cup mango jam or preserves

A SLICE OF ADVICE FROM BEV

To minimize cracking with this cheesecake, place a shallow pan half-full of hot water on the lower oven rack during baking.

Heat oven to 325 degrees.

In a small bowl, stir together the crumbs and melted butter. Press onto bottom of a 9" springform pan. Refrigerate until ready to use.

For the Cheesecake Filling: In a large bowl of an electric mixer, beat the cream cheese until smooth. Gradually beat in the sugar; scrape bowl. With mixer on low, beat in the eggs, one at a time, just until combined. Stir in the zest and tangerine juice.

Spread batter onto prepared crust. Bake for 55 to 65 minutes or until set. Turn the oven off. Let the cheesecake cool in the oven with the door slightly open for 30 minutes. Remove from the oven and cool completely on a wire rack. Cover loosely with waxed paper and refrigerate cheesecake overnight.

For the Mango Sauce: Drain mangoes, reserving any liquid. Add mango nectar to syrup to make ¾ cup. In a small saucepan, combine the syrup mixture and cornstarch; mix well. Add jam. Cook and stir over medium heat until thickened and somewhat clear. Stir in mango pieces. Refrigerate until cold.

When ready to serve, run a knife around the inside edge of pan and carefully remove the springform sides. Serve each slice with Mango Sauce. Serves 12-14.

Café au Lait Cheesecake

When you need more than a cup of your favorite specialty coffee.

1¾ cups finely crushed chocolate wafers
⅓ cup unsalted butter, melted

CAFE AU LAIT CHEESECAKE
   FILLING

2 oz. semisweet chocolate, coarsely
   chopped
2 tbsp. water
1 tbsp. instant espresso powder
2 tbsp. coffee liqueur
24 oz. cream cheese, room temperature,
   cut into pieces
1 cup granulated sugar
2 tbsp. unbleached, all-purpose flour
1 tsp. vanilla extract
4 large eggs

Heat oven to 350 degrees.

In a small bowl, combine the wafer crumbs with the melted butter. Press mixture evenly onto bottom and 1" up the sides of an 8½" springform pan. Place pan on a baking sheet and refrigerate until needed.

For the Café au Lait Cheesecake Filling: In a small saucepan, combine the chocolate, water, and instant espresso powder. Cook and stir over low heat until chocolate begins to melt. Remove from heat and whisk until mixture is smooth. Stir in liqueur and set aside to cool.

In a large bowl of an electric mixer, beat the cream cheese until creamy. With mixer on medium, stir in the sugar, flour, and vanilla until smooth. Scrape bowl.

With mixer on low, add eggs, one at a time, beating just until combined.

Reserve 2 cups of this cream-cheese mixture; cover and chill.

Stir the melted and cooled chocolate mixture into the remaining cream-cheese mixture, stirring just until combined. Spread onto prepared crust.

Bake for 30 minutes or just until the center appears nearly set. (Center will still jiggle but not be liquidy.)

Remove the reserved cream-cheese mixture from the refrigerator 15 minutes before cheesecake is set.

Remove cheesecake from oven and place pan atop a hot pad. Quickly and carefully pour the reserved mixture over the outside edge of the chocolate mixture (not atop the center), then gently spread the mixture with a thin metal spatula over the entire top.

Return cheesecake to oven and continue to bake for 21 to 28 minutes or until the center appears nearly set. Let the cheesecake cool in the oven with the door closed for 20 minutes. Remove from the oven and cool pan completely on a wire rack. Cover loosely with waxed paper and refrigerate cheesecake overnight.

When ready to serve, run a knife around the inside edge of pan and carefully remove the springform sides. Serves 8-10.

CAKES TO DIE FOR!

Torta di Ricotta Revisited

My favorite version of a ricotta cheesecake . . . a combination of flavors from an East Coast bakery and a childhood Italian recipe.

¾ cup sliced blanched almonds, toasted
¼ cup unbleached, all-purpose flour
3 tbsp. granulated sugar
1 large egg yolk
2 tbsp. unsalted butter, melted and
  cooled
½ tsp. vanilla extract

FILLING

8 oz. cream cheese, room temperature,
  cut into pieces
¾ cup granulated sugar
¼ tsp. salt
30 oz. fresh whole-milk ricotta
3 large eggs
1 tsp. vanilla extract
1 tbsp. Amaretto liqueur
1 tbsp. cornstarch or arrowroot
2 tbsp. finely chopped dried cherries,
  tart or sweet
2 tbsp. finely chopped dried apricots

Heat oven to 325 degrees. Grease and flour a 9" springform pan, tapping out excess flour.

Place the almonds, flour, and sugar in a food processor and pulse until the nuts are finely chopped.

In a small bowl, whisk together the egg yolk, melted butter, and vanilla. Add the liquid to the nut mixture. Pulse to moisten and thoroughly combine the ingredients.

Press the mixture onto the bottom and ¾" up the sides of the prepared pan. Refrigerate for 30 minutes to firm up the crust. Bake for 12 to 16 minutes or until the crust is a light golden brown. Remove the pan from the oven and cool completely on a wire rack. Leave oven on.

For the Filling: In a large bowl of an electric mixer, beat the cream cheese until creamy. Add the sugar and salt and beat until blended. Scrape bowl.

With mixer on low, add the ricotta cheese and beat until mixture is well combined. Beat in the eggs, one at a time, until combined. Add the vanilla, Amaretto, and cornstarch. Scrape bowl.

Fold in the dried cherry and apricot pieces. Spread batter onto crust-lined pan, gently smoothing top. Bake for 48 to 52 minutes or until the center is set. (Center will still jiggle but not be liquidy.) Cool in pan on a wire rack.

Cover loosely with waxed paper and refrigerate cheesecake overnight. When ready to serve, run a knife around the inside edge of pan and carefully remove the springform sides. Serves 10-12.

COFFEECAKES AND "FLIPPED OVER" CAKES

*The fall flavors of this Pear-Filled Streusel Coffeecake make it a
perfect brunch or breakfast treat.*

My coffeecake selections in this book are (and don't say I didn't warn you) to die for. They're loaded with flavor and texture and crumbs and fruit enrobed in moist cake. They're perfect for brunch or breakfast or a potluck or a bake sale or just because. They're tasty, and making them doesn't require too big of a production.

And as for "flipped over" cakes, aren't you just tired of calling them "upside-down cakes"? Doesn't it sound as if you slipped and fell, and all that effort went to waste? Let's just say, "Yes, I made this fabulous cake, and then I flipped it over, and voila! It became an entirely different cake."

Pear-Filled Streusel Coffeecake

Once you serve this coffeecake, you'll tag the page and make it often (at your request and anyone who has the pleasure to taste it!).

1½ cups pecans, toasted
⅓ cup firmly packed light brown sugar
2 tbsp. unbleached, all-purpose flour
1 tsp. ground cinnamon
2 tbsp. unsalted butter, cold, cut into pieces

COFFEECAKE

2¾ cups unbleached, all-purpose flour
2 tsp. baking powder
½ tsp. salt
½ tsp. baking soda
½ cup sour cream
½ cup milk, whole
1 cup unsalted butter, room temperature, cut into pieces
1 cup granulated sugar
½ cup firmly packed light brown sugar
¼ cup dark brown sugar
3 large eggs
1 tsp. freshly grated lemon zest
1 tsp. vanilla extract
1½ cups peeled, thinly sliced pears

Heat oven to 350 degrees. Grease and flour a 13" by 9" baking pan, tapping out excess flour.

In a food processor, pulse to chop and combine the pecans, brown sugar, flour, and cinnamon. Add the butter and pulse on and off *just* until coarse crumbs form. Remove to a bowl and set aside.

For the Coffeecake: In a medium bowl, whisk together the flour, baking powder, salt, and baking soda.

In a small bowl, whisk together the sour cream and milk.

In a large bowl of an electric mixer, beat the butter and sugars until light and fluffy. Scrape bowl.

Beat in eggs, one at a time, beating well after each addition. Stir in lemon zest and vanilla.

With mixer on low, alternately add the flour mixture and the sour cream mixture to the butter mixture until blended. Scrape bowl.

Using *half* of the batter, drop spoonfuls into prepared pan (batter will be thick). Sprinkle *half* of the streusel atop batter in pan. Cover with pear slices.

Spoon remaining batter over, and sprinkle with remaining streusel. Bake for 40 to 50 minutes or until top is golden brown and a tester inserted in the center comes out clean.

Cool in pan on a wire rack. Serves 12-16.

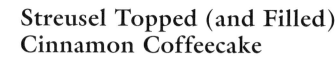

Streusel Topped (and Filled) Cinnamon Coffeecake

This streusel-infused coffeecake always garners the same comment: "It's the best coffeecake I've ever had." Give it your own kitchen litmus test!

3¾ cups unbleached, all-purpose flour
1 tsp. salt
2½ tsp. baking powder
¾ cup sour cream
1¼ cups milk, whole
¾ cup unsalted butter, room
    temperature, cut into pieces
1½ cups granulated sugar
⅓ cup firmly packed light brown sugar
2 tsp. vanilla extract
3 large eggs

STREUSEL FILLING

1 cup firmly packed light brown sugar
1½ tbsp. ground cinnamon

STREUSEL TOPPING

1¼ cups granulated sugar
¼ tsp. salt
1½ cups unbleached, all-purpose flour
1 tbsp. ground cinnamon
¼ cup unsalted butter, melted

A SLICE OF ADVICE FROM BEV ———

Don't combine the filling and batter thoroughly; just swirl the filling throughout the batter.

Heat oven to 350 degrees. Grease a 9" springform pan.

In a large bowl, whisk together the flour, salt, and baking powder.

In a small bowl, whisk together the sour cream and milk.

In a large bowl of an electric mixer, beat the butter and sugars until light and fluffy. Scrape bowl.

Mix in vanilla. Add eggs, one at a time, beating well after each addition.

With mixer on low, alternately add the flour mixture and the sour cream mixture to the butter mixture, beating just until combined. Do not overbeat.

For the Streusel Filling: In a small bowl, whisk together the brown sugar and cinnamon.

Spread *half* of the batter into prepared pan, smoothing to edges of pan. Sprinkle the Streusel Filling atop batter.

Spread the remaining batter atop the filling. Using a knife, gently swirl the filling into the batter.

For the Streusel Topping: In a medium bowl, whisk together the sugar, salt, flour, and cinnamon. Stir in the melted butter just until crumbs form.

Sprinkle the Streusel Topping evenly over the batter in the pan. Bake for 41 to 52 minutes or until a toothpick inserted in the center comes out clean. The cake should spring back when lightly touched in the middle.

Cool on a wire rack for 25 minutes. Then run a knife around the inside edge of pan and carefully remove the springform sides. Serves 10-14.

While You Were Sleeping Coffeecake

This stress-free cake will be ready when you are. Simply prepare, spread in the pan, bake 24 hours later, then serve!

3 cups unbleached, all-purpose flour
1½ tsp. baking powder
1½ tsp. baking soda
1 tsp. salt
1 cup unsalted butter, room
    temperature, cut into pieces
1¼ cups granulated sugar
3 large eggs
15 oz. ricotta cheese

STREUSEL TOP

¾ cup coarsely chopped pecans, toasted
½ cup firmly packed light brown sugar
2 tbsp. toasted wheat germ
1 tbsp. ground cinnamon
1 tsp. freshly grated nutmeg

Up to 24 hours before baking: Grease the bottom and sides of a 13" by 9" baking pan.

In a medium bowl, whisk together the flour, baking powder, baking soda, and salt.

In a large bowl of an electric mixer, beat the butter and the sugar until light and fluffy. Scrape bowl.

Add the eggs, one at a time, beating well after each addition. With mixer on low, alternately beat in the ricotta cheese and flour mixture just until combined. Batter will be very thick.

Spread batter into prepared pan.

For the Streusel Top: In a small bowl, stir together the nuts, brown sugar, wheat germ, cinnamon, and nutmeg until combined. Sprinkle evenly over batter. Cover and refrigerate for up to 24 hours.

When ready to bake: Heat oven to 350 degrees. Uncover coffeecake and bake for 32 to 42 minutes or until a toothpick inserted near the center comes out clean.

Cool for 15 minutes on a wire rack. Serve warm. Serves 12-16.

"Blueberry Muffin" Anytime Cake with Streusel

Honestly, this is my favorite way to use fresh blueberries . . . when they're abundant and we're picking them by the pint off our bushes or when they're in season at my local farmer's market.

2 cups unbleached, all-purpose flour
2 tsp. baking powder
¾ tsp. salt
10 tbsp. unsalted butter, room temperature, cut into pieces
1½ cups granulated sugar
1½ tsp. vanilla extract
2 large eggs
¾ cup milk, whole
2 cups fresh blueberries, gently washed and dried

STREUSEL

½ cup unsalted butter, cold, cut into pieces
¼ cup unbleached, all-purpose flour
½ cup granulated sugar
½ cup firmly packed light brown sugar
½ tsp. ground cinnamon

Heat oven to 350 degrees. Grease a 10" springform pan.

In a medium bowl, whisk together the flour, baking powder, and salt.

In a large bowl of an electric mixer, beat the butter and sugar until light and fluffy. Stir in the vanilla. Scrape bowl.

Add the eggs, one at a time, beating well after each addition.

With mixer on low, alternately add the flour mixture and the milk to the butter mixture, just until blended. Scrape bowl. Quickly and gently stir in the blueberries.

Spread batter into prepared pan. Bake just until top is set, 24 to 29 minutes. When the top of the cake is set, remove the pan to a wire rack. Leave oven on.

For the Streusel: In a medium bowl with a pastry blender, combine the butter, flour, sugars, and cinnamon until crumbly.

Quickly cover the surface of the cake with the streusel and return pan to the oven. Bake until streusel spreads and begins to get crunchy, 14 to 21 minutes.

Cool on wire rack 20 minutes. Then run a knife around the inside edge of pan and carefully remove the springform sides. Serve cake warm. Serves 8-12.

CAKES TO DIE FOR!

Dried Cherry Streusel Coffeecake with Silky Cherry Butter Sauce

An easy-to-make coffeecake with a wonderfully complementary, silky sauce.

2¼ cups cake flour, sifted
1½ cups granulated sugar
¾ cup unsalted butter, room
    temperature, cut into pieces
¾ cup milk, whole
3 large eggs
2½ tsp. baking powder
1 tsp. salt
1 tsp. vanilla extract
1½ cups coarsely chopped dried cherries

STREUSEL

½ cup unbleached, all-purpose flour
½ cup firmly packed light brown sugar
¼ cup unsalted butter, room
    temperature, cut into pieces
½ cup chopped walnuts, pecans, or
    hazelnuts, toasted

CHERRY BUTTER SAUCE

1 cup granulated sugar
½ cup tart cherry juice
½ cup unsalted butter, room
    temperature, cut into pieces
1 tbsp. freshly grated lemon zest

Heat oven to 350 degrees. Grease a 13" by 9" baking pan.

In a large bowl of an electric mixer, combine the flour, sugar, butter, milk, eggs, baking powder, salt, and vanilla. With mixer on low, beat until well mixed. Scrape bowl. With mixer on medium high, beat for 4 minutes. Scrape bowl.

Stir in the dried cherries. Spread batter into prepared pan.

For the Streusel: In a small bowl with a pastry blender, combine the flour, brown sugar, and butter until crumbly. Stir in the nuts. Sprinkle evenly over batter. Bake for 31 to 49 minutes or until a toothpick inserted in the center comes out clean. Cool in pan on a wire rack for 15 minutes.

For the Cherry Butter Sauce: In a small saucepan over medium heat, combine the sugar, cherry juice, and butter. Bring to a boil, whisking constantly. Reduce to a simmer and cook for 1 minute. Remove from heat and stir in zest.

Serve warm slices of coffeecake with a spoonful of warm Cherry Butter Sauce. Serves 12-16.

Almond Crunch Pear Coffeecake

A coffeecake enrobing pears and topped with a great almond crunch. Perfect warm!

1 cup unbleached, all-purpose flour
½ tsp. baking powder
¼ tsp. salt
½ cup unsalted butter, room temperature, cut into pieces
½ cup granulated sugar
1 tsp. vanilla extract
3 large eggs
3 medium, firm-ripe pears, peeled and cut into 8 slices each

ALMOND CRUNCH

½ cup unbleached, all-purpose flour
½ cup finely chopped toasted almonds
½ cup firmly packed light brown sugar
1 tsp. ground cinnamon
¼ cup unsalted butter, room temperature, cut into pieces

Heat oven to 375 degrees. Grease and flour a 10" springform pan, tapping out excess flour.

In a small bowl, whisk together the flour, baking powder, and salt.

In a large bowl of an electric mixer, beat the butter and sugar until light and fluffy. Add vanilla and eggs, beating well. Scrape bowl.

Add the flour mixture, stirring until well combined.

Spread batter into prepared pan. Press pear slices, on their sides, into batter.

For the Almond Crunch: In a medium bowl with a pastry blender, combine the flour, almonds, brown sugar, cinnamon, and butter until crumbly. Sprinkle evenly over batter.

Bake for 28 to 36 minutes or until center of cake springs back when lightly touched. Cool 15 minutes on wire rack. Then run a knife around the inside edge of pan and carefully remove the springform sides. Serves 12-16.

This pear didn't make the cut. We've already baked (and tasted)
this Almond Crunch Pear Coffeecake.

Raspberry Lime Sour Cream Coffeecake

Fresh juicy raspberries and tart hints of lime are the perfect complements to this moist, light, and fluffy coffeecake.

2 cups unbleached, all-purpose flour
1 tsp. baking powder
½ tsp. baking soda
1 cup unsalted butter, room temperature, cut into pieces
1½ cups granulated sugar
2 large eggs
2 tsp. freshly grated lime zest
1 cup sour cream

RASPBERRY LIME FILLING

1½ cups fresh red raspberries, gently washed and dried
½ cup coarsely chopped almonds, toasted
2 tbsp. granulated sugar
1½ tsp. freshly grated lime zest
1 tsp. ground cinnamon

NUT "TOPPING"

½ cup coarsely chopped almonds, toasted
¼ cup granulated sugar
1 tsp. ground cinnamon

Heat oven to 350 degrees. Grease and flour a 12-cup tube pan, tapping out excess flour.

In a medium bowl, whisk together the flour, baking powder, and baking soda.

In a large bowl of an electric mixer, cream the butter and sugar until light and fluffy. Scrape bowl.

Add eggs, one at a time, beating well after each addition.

Add the lime zest to the sour cream. With mixer on low, alternately add the sour cream and the flour mixture to the butter mixture, mixing until smooth. Scrape bowl.

For the Raspberry Lime Filling: In a medium bowl, gently stir together the raspberries, almonds, sugar, lime zest, and cinnamon.

Spread *half* of the batter into prepared pan. Gently spread filling atop batter, pressing gently into batter. Top with remaining batter, smoothing so batter reaches all edges of the pan.

For the Nut "Topping": In a small bowl, stir together the almonds, sugar, and cinnamon. Sprinkle on batter. Bake for 62 to 86 minutes or until a toothpick inserted in the center comes out clean.

Cool in pan 35 minutes, then run a knife around inside edge of pan to loosen cake. Cover pan with a large, lint-free towel-covered plate and invert pan. Remove pan from cake. Re-invert cake from plate onto cooling rack. Allow to cool completely on wire rack. Serves 12-16.

Coffee Coffeecake

Truly a caffeine lover's cake . . . with coffee in the cake batter and the frosting!

2¼ cups cake flour, sifted
1½ cups granulated sugar, divided
1 tbsp. baking powder
1 tsp. salt
¼ cup strong brewed coffee
½ cup water
½ cup light olive oil
6 large eggs, separated
2 tsp. freshly grated lemon zest
1 tbsp. vanilla extract

FROSTING

1½ cups heavy cream
¼ cup strong brewed coffee
1 tsp. instant espresso powder
3 tbsp. confectioners' sugar, sifted

Heat oven to 325 degrees. Grease and flour a 10" tube pan, tapping out excess flour.

In a large bowl of an electric mixer, mix together the flour, ¾ cup sugar, baking powder, and salt. Scrape bowl.

Add the coffee, water, oil, egg yolks, zest, and vanilla, beating until smooth. Scrape bowl.

In another large bowl of an electric mixer, beat egg whites until foamy. With mixer on medium high, add remaining ¾ cup sugar, 1 tbsp. at a time, until stiff peaks form. Do not underbeat.

Quickly and gently fold beaten egg whites into batter in 2 additions.

Bake until a cake tester inserted in the center comes out clean, about 48 to 60 minutes.

Cool in pan 45 minutes, then run a knife around inside edge of pan to loosen cake. Cover pan with a large, lint-free towel-covered plate and invert pan. Remove pan from cake. Re-invert cake from plate onto cooling rack. Allow to cool completely on wire rack.

For the Frosting: In a large bowl of an electric mixer, whip the heavy cream, coffee, espresso powder, and sugar until stiff peaks form. Use immediately to frost cake. Serves 12-16.

A Tribute to the Queen of Spices Coffeecake

Widely used in Scandinavian and East Indian cooking, cardamom (known as the queen of spices and a member of the ginger family) should be used frugally. A little goes a long way in adding a distinct flavor to baked goods.

2½ cups unbleached, all-purpose flour
2 tsp. baking powder
1 tsp. baking soda
½ tsp. salt
¼ cup unsalted butter, room temperature, cut into pieces
¾ cup granulated sugar
¾ cup sour cream
2 large eggs
1 tsp. vanilla extract
½ cup milk, whole

FILLING

⅓ cup firmly packed light brown sugar
⅓ cup chopped, skinned hazelnuts
1 tsp. ground cardamom

GLAZE

¾ cup confectioners' sugar, sifted
½ tsp. vanilla extract
1½ tbsp. milk, whole

Heat oven to 350 degrees. Grease and flour a 12-cup Bundt pan, tapping out excess flour.

In a medium bowl, whisk together the flour, baking powder, baking soda, and salt.

In a large bowl of an electric mixer, beat the butter, sugar, and sour cream until mixture is light and fluffy.

Add the eggs, one at a time, beating well after each addition. Stir in the vanilla. Scrape bowl.

With mixer on low, alternately add the flour mixture and the milk to the butter mixture, stirring just until combined. Scrape bowl.

For the Filling: In a small bowl, combine the brown sugar, hazelnuts, and cardamom, stirring to blend well.

Spoon *half* of the batter into prepared pan. Sprinkle filling over batter, then spoon remaining coffeecake batter over filling.

Bake for 30 to 41 minutes or until a toothpick inserted in the center comes out clean.

Cool 15 minutes on wire rack. Remove from pan and place cake on rack atop large piece of waxed paper.

For the Glaze: In a small bowl, whisk together the confectioners' sugar, vanilla extract, and milk. Drizzle over warm cake. Allow glaze to set, at least 30 minutes, before serving. Serves 12-16.

Cranberry "Flipped Over" Cake with Cinnamon-Infused Whipped Cream

Sugared cranberries atop a spongelike cake make for a sure-to-become-your-next-fall-favorite dessert.

¼ cup unsalted butter, cut into pieces
⅔ cup firmly packed light brown sugar
2 cups fresh or frozen, unthawed, cranberries, gently rinsed and dried

CAKE

¾ cup unbleached, all-purpose flour
¼ cup cornstarch
1 tsp. baking powder
⅛ tsp. salt
4 large eggs
¾ cup granulated sugar
1½ tsp. freshly grated orange zest
1 tbsp. unsalted butter, melted
½ tsp. vanilla extract

CINNAMON-INFUSED WHIPPED CREAM

1¼ cups heavy cream
1 tsp. ground cinnamon
2 tbsp. granulated sugar

Heat oven to 350 degrees.

In a medium saucepan, melt the butter over medium heat. Add the brown sugar and stir just until it begins to dissolve.

Spread the mixture into a 9" square cake pan. Add the cranberries in an even layer.

For the Cake: In a medium bowl, whisk together the flour, cornstarch, baking powder, and salt.

In a large bowl of an electric mixer, beat the eggs, sugar, and zest until very pale and thick and mixture has doubled in volume.

With mixer on low, alternately mix the flour mixture and the butter and vanilla into the egg mixture, working quickly just until mixture is combined.

Scoop batter into cranberry-lined pan. Quickly and gently spread batter to smooth. Bake for 28 to 37 minutes or until the center springs back when lightly touched.

Let stand 5 minutes on a wire rack, then run a knife around the inside edge of pan. Place a large platter atop cake pan and, using potholders and both hands, hold platter and cake firmly together and invert. Shake gently, which should allow cake to settle on platter.

Gently remove pan, reapplying to the cake any fruit that remains in the pan. Cool 30 minutes.

For the Cinnamon-Infused Whipped Cream: In a large bowl of an electric mixer, whip together the heavy cream, cinnamon, and sugar until soft peaks form. Serve atop slices of the cake. Serves 8-10.

This "Flipped Over" Gingerbread cake is a real "showoff." It shows off a topping of baked pineapple, cranberries, and walnuts and, for a grand finale, a Swirl of Lemon Cream.

CAKES TO DIE FOR!

"Flipped Over" Gingerbread with a Swirl of Lemon Cream

This is a comfort-food cake at its finest . . . with a "what's next" assortment of flavors and textures in every bite!

½ cup firmly packed dark brown sugar
¼ cup unsalted butter, melted
8-oz. can pineapple chunks in
    unsweetened juice, well drained
¾ cup frozen cranberries
¼ cup coarsely chopped walnuts, toasted

GINGERBREAD

1⅓ cups unbleached, all-purpose flour
½ tsp. baking powder
½ tsp. baking soda
¼ tsp. salt
¾ tsp. ground cinnamon
¾ tsp. ground ginger
½ tsp. ground allspice
½ cup firmly packed light brown sugar
½ cup unsalted butter, room
    temperature, cut into pieces
½ cup boiling water
½ cup molasses, preferably Barbados
1 large egg, lightly beaten

LEMON CREAM

1 cup heavy cream
4 tbsp. confectioners' sugar, sifted
1 tbsp. finely grated lemon zest

A SLICE OF ADVICE FROM BEV

Frozen cranberries have less of a tendency to float to the top of the cake. If you're using fresh, freeze the cranberries for 1 hour prior to using, and then measure them directly from the freezer.

Heat oven to 350 degrees.

In a small bowl, combine the brown sugar and butter; blend well. Spread in the bottom of an ungreased 8" square cake pan.

Arrange pineapple pieces in 3 diagonal rows over the sugar mixture. Sprinkle cranberries and walnuts around pineapple.

For the Gingerbread: In a large bowl of an electric mixer, combine the flour, baking powder, baking soda, salt, cinnamon, ginger, and allspice, mixing well to combine.

With mixer on medium, add the brown sugar, butter, boiling water, molasses, and egg, stirring until blended. Scrape bowl.

Scoop batter into fruit-lined pan. Quickly and gently spread batter to smooth.

Bake for 44 to 55 minutes or until a toothpick inserted in the center comes out clean.

Let stand 5 minutes on a wire rack, then run a knife around the inside edge of pan. Place a large platter atop cake pan and, using potholders and both hands, hold platter and cake firmly together and invert. Shake gently, which should allow cake to settle on platter.

Gently remove pan, reapplying to the cake any fruit that remains in the pan. Cool 30 minutes.

For the Lemon Cream: In a large bowl of an electric mixer, whip the heavy cream, confectioners' sugar, and zest until soft peaks form.

Serve cake warm with a generous swirl of Lemon Cream. Serves 8-10.

Pumpkin Patch Cranberry "Flipped Over" Cake

Pumpkin and cranberries are a perfect marriage of fall flavors, and this cake provides a bright, unexpected change of pace.

10 oz. cranberry preserves
1 cup dried cranberries
⅓ cup unsalted butter, cut into pieces

CAKE

2 cups unbleached, all-purpose flour
1½ tsp. baking powder
¾ tsp. ground cinnamon
¼ tsp. freshly grated nutmeg
¼ tsp. ground allspice
⅛ tsp. ground ginger
⅛ tsp. ground cloves
½ tsp. baking soda
½ cup unsalted butter, room
    temperature, cut into pieces
1¼ cups granulated sugar
1 tsp. vanilla extract
2 large eggs
½ cup pumpkin puree
¾ cup buttermilk

A SLICE OF ADVICE FROM BEV

Can't find cranberry preserves? Pomegranate jelly is a perfect substitute.

Heat oven to 350 degrees.

In a small saucepan, combine the cranberry preserves, dried cranberries, and butter. Bring to a boil, stirring constantly. Remove from heat. Pour mixture into a 13" by 9" baking pan, spreading evenly.

For the Cake: In a medium bowl, whisk together the flour, baking powder, cinnamon, nutmeg, allspice, ginger, cloves, and baking soda.

In a large bowl of an electric mixer, beat the butter, sugar, and vanilla until light and fluffy. Scrape bowl.

With mixer on low, add eggs one at a time, beating well after each addition. Beat in pumpkin.

Alternately add the flour mixture and the buttermilk to the butter mixture, beating just until combined. Scoop batter into cranberry-lined pan; quickly and gently spread batter to smooth.

Bake for 28 to 34 minutes or until a toothpick inserted near the center comes out clean.

Let stand 5 minutes on a wire rack, then run a knife around the inside edge of pan. Place a large tray or cake platter atop cake pan and, using potholders and both hands, hold tray and cake firmly together and invert. Shake gently, which should allow cake to settle on tray.

Gently remove pan, reapplying to the cake any fruit that remains in the pan. Cool 15 minutes. Serve warm. Serves 12-16.

A rich pumpkin cake with a tart, sweet cranberry bottom . . . that soon becomes the top.

Luscious Blueberry-Orange "Flipped Over" Cake with Orange-Infused Whipped Cream

A tender almond cake with a blueberry topping and orange whipped cream. . . aromatic and delicious!

¾ cup firmly packed light brown sugar
½ cup unsalted butter, room temperature, cut into pieces
1½ cups fresh blueberries, gently washed and dried

ORANGE ALMOND CAKE

¾ cup cake flour, sifted
¼ tsp. baking powder
¼ tsp. salt
4 oz. almond paste, broken into small pieces
½ cup granulated sugar
3 tbsp. freshly grated orange zest
½ cup unsalted butter, room temperature, cut into pieces
3 large eggs, room temperature

ORANGE-INFUSED WHIPPED CREAM

1½ cups heavy cream
4 tbsp. granulated sugar
1 tbsp. freshly grated orange zest
1 tsp. orange extract

Heat oven to 350 degrees.

In an 8" by 2" round cake pan, combine the brown sugar and butter. Place pan over medium heat and stir until butter is melted and mixture is smooth and bubbling.

Carefully remove pan from heat; cool 10 minutes on a wire rack. Sprinkle blueberries evenly over butter/sugar mixture.

For the Orange Almond Cake: In a medium bowl, whisk together the cake flour, baking powder, and salt.

In a large bowl of an electric mixer, combine the almond paste, sugar, and orange zest. Scrape bowl.

With mixer on low, add butter, mixing until smooth. Scrape bowl. Add eggs, one at a time, beating well after each addition.

With mixer on low, add the flour mixture, beating just until combined. Scoop batter into blueberry-lined pan; quickly and gently spread batter to smooth.

Bake for 35 to 46 minutes or until cake is a deep golden color and a toothpick inserted in the center comes out clean.

Let stand 5 minutes on a wire rack, then run a knife around the inside edge of pan. Place a large platter atop cake pan and, using potholders and both hands, hold platter and cake firmly together and invert. Shake gently, which should allow cake to settle on platter.

Gently remove pan, reapplying to the cake any fruit that remains in the pan. Cool 30 minutes.

For the Orange-Infused Whipped Cream: In a large bowl of an electric mixer, combine the heavy cream, sugar, orange zest, and orange extract. Whip on high speed just until stiff peaks form.

Serve each slice of "flipped over" cake with a generous dollop of the Orange-Infused Whipped Cream. Serves 8-10.

CAKES TO DIE FOR!

Caramel Apple "Flipped Over" Cake

If fall reminds you of crisp apples, caramel flavors, and raking leaves, take some time to enjoy the flavors of caramel apple cake. (Rake the leaves later!)

½ cup firmly packed light brown sugar
3 tbsp. unsalted butter, cut into pieces
2 tbsp. chopped walnuts, toasted
2 large tart-crisp apples, peeled, cored, and thinly sliced

CAKE

1½ cups unbleached, all-purpose flour
1 tsp. baking powder
½ tsp. salt
⅔ cup firmly packed dark brown sugar
⅓ cup unsalted butter, room temperature, cut into pieces
1 large egg
1 tsp. vanilla extract
½ cup milk, whole

Heat oven to 350 degrees. Grease a 9" round cake pan.

In a small bowl with a pastry blender, combine the brown sugar and butter until crumbly. Stir in the walnuts. Press onto bottom of prepared pan.

Arrange apple slices atop sugar/butter mixture.

For the Cake: In a medium bowl, whisk together the flour, baking powder, and salt.

In a large bowl of an electric mixer, beat the brown sugar and butter until light and fluffy. Scrape bowl. Add the egg and vanilla, beating until well combined. Scrape bowl.

With mixer on low, alternately add the flour mixture and the milk to the sugar mixture, beating until mixture is combined. Scoop batter into apple-lined pan; quickly and gently spread batter to smooth.

Bake for 34 to 46 minutes or until a toothpick inserted in the center comes out clean. Let stand 5 minutes on a wire rack, then run a knife around the inside edge of pan. Place a large platter atop cake pan and, using potholders and both hands, hold platter and cake firmly together and invert. Shake gently, which should allow cake to settle on platter.

Gently remove pan, reapplying to the cake any fruit that remains in the pan. Cool 20 minutes. Serve warm. Serves 8-10.

This Fresh Peach "Flipped Over" Cake is worth every minute of peeling fresh, seasonal peaches at their ripest and juiciest. The most difficult part of this cake? Letting go when it's all gone.

Fresh Peach "Flipped Over" Cake

Ripe, juicy, in-season peaches atop a rich, moist cake . . . I doubt that one piece will be enough.

½ cup unsalted butter, cut into pieces
¾ cup firmly packed light brown sugar
6 to 8 fresh, ripe peaches, peeled, halved, and pitted

CAKE

1¾ cups unbleached, all-purpose flour
1½ tsp. baking powder
½ tsp. baking soda
½ tsp. salt
½ cup unsalted butter, room temperature, cut into pieces
¾ cup granulated sugar
1¾ tsp. vanilla extract
2 large eggs
¾ cup buttermilk

A SLICE OF ADVICE FROM BEV

If any peach halves remain, enjoy eating them while the cake is baking!

Heat oven to 375 degrees.

Place the butter in an ovenproof 10" nonstick sauté pan with 2" sides. Heat over medium heat until melted.

With heat on low, sprinkle brown sugar evenly over butter, cooking without stirring for 3 minutes. Remove from heat and carefully arrange peach halves, cut side down, as close together as possible on top of the brown sugar.

For the Cake: In a medium bowl, whisk together the flour, baking powder, baking soda, and salt.

In a large bowl of an electric mixer, beat the butter and sugar until light and fluffy. Scrape bowl. Stir in vanilla.

Add eggs, one at a time, beating well after each addition.

With mixer on low, alternately add the buttermilk and the flour mixture to the butter mixture, mixing just until combined. Scrape bowl.

Quickly and gently spread atop peaches in pan, smoothing batter to the sides of the pan.

Bake for 38 to 49 minutes or until a toothpick inserted in the center comes out clean. (Timing will depend a lot on the juiciness of your peaches.)

Let stand 5 minutes on a wire rack, then run a knife around the inside edge of pan. Place a large platter atop cake pan and, using potholders and both hands, hold platter and cake firmly together and invert. Shake gently, which should allow cake to settle on platter.

Gently remove pan, reapplying to the cake any fruit that remains in the pan. Cool 20 minutes. Serve cake warm. Serves 8-10.

Star Fruit "Flipped Over" Cake

Let's rethink our upside-downs and take full advantage of the abundance of tropical fruits available to us today. Carambola, or star fruit, that is grown in Florida is often smaller and more tart in flavor than imported varieties. Wash and then slice the fruit horizontally to make star shapes.

14 to 18 star fruit slices, depending on size of fruit
½ cup turbinado sugar
¼ cup unsalted butter, room temperature, cut into pieces

CAKE

3 large egg yolks
½ cup sour cream
1 tsp. vanilla extract
1½ cups cake flour, sifted
¾ cup granulated sugar
¾ tsp. baking powder
¼ tsp. baking soda
¼ tsp. salt
½ cup plus 1 tbsp. unsalted butter, melted

14 to 18 blackberries

Heat oven to 350 degrees.

Place the star fruit slices on paper towels to absorb any excess moisture.

In a 10" by 2" round cake pan, combine the sugar and butter. Place pan over medium heat and stir until butter is melted and mixture is smooth and bubbling.

Carefully remove pan from heat; cool 10 minutes on a wire rack. Carefully space star fruit slices evenly over butter/sugar mixture.

For the Cake: In a large bowl of an electric mixer, beat the egg yolks, sour cream, and vanilla until blended.

With mixer on low, beat in the flour, sugar, baking powder, baking soda, and salt. Scrape bowl. Beat the melted butter into the batter until combined.

Scoop batter into star fruit lined pan; quickly and gently spread batter to smooth. Bake for 39 to 54 minutes or until golden brown and a toothpick inserted near the center comes out clean.

Let stand 5 minutes on a wire rack, then run a knife around the inside edge of pan. Place a large platter atop cake pan and, using potholders and both hands, hold platter and cake firmly together and invert. Shake gently, which should allow cake to settle on platter.

Gently remove pan, reapplying to the cake any fruit that remains in the pan. Cool 30 minutes.

When ready to serve, place blackberries decoratively atop star fruit slices on cake. Serves 8-10.

Frosting-on-the-Bottom German Chocolate Cake

Everything is baked at once, with the frosting on the bottom, then "flipped over" when done.

¼ cup unsalted butter, cut into pieces
1¼ cups water
1 cup firmly packed dark brown sugar
1 cup unsweetened coconut flakes
2 cups mini marshmallows
1 cup coarsely chopped pecans, toasted

CHOCOLATE CAKE

4 oz. semisweet chocolate, coarsely
   chopped
½ cup water
2½ cups unbleached, all-purpose flour
1½ cups granulated sugar
1 tsp. baking soda
½ tsp. salt
1 cup sour cream
½ cup unsalted butter, room
   temperature, cut into pieces
1 tsp. vanilla extract
3 large eggs

Heat oven to 350 degrees.

In a medium saucepan, heat the butter with the water until the butter is melted and the mixture is smooth.

Pour mixture into an ungreased 13" by 9" baking pan. Stir in the brown sugar and coconut. Sprinkle marshmallows and nuts evenly over the top.

For the Chocolate Cake: In a small saucepan over low heat, heat the chocolate with the water until the chocolate is melted and the mixture is smooth.

In a large bowl of an electric mixer, combine the flour, sugar, baking soda, salt, sour cream, butter, vanilla, and eggs. With mixer on low, beat until well mixed. Scrape bowl.

Stir in the chocolate mixture. With mixer on medium high, beat mixture for 2 minutes. Scrape bowl.

Scoop batter into pan. Quickly and gently spread batter to smooth.

Place pan atop large baking sheet. Bake for 41 to 58 minutes or until a toothpick inserted in the center comes out clean.

Let stand 5 minutes on a wire rack, then run a knife around the inside edge of pan. Place a serving tray atop cake pan and, using potholders and both hands, hold tray and cake firmly together and invert. Shake gently, which should allow cake to settle on tray.

Gently remove pan, reapplying to the cake any frosting that remains in the pan. Cool 30 minutes. Serves 12-16.

FANCY-SCHMANCY CAKES

Once you taste this Ginger Peach Cake Roll, you'll be a fan of the flavor combinations. Serve with a few slices of fresh peaches when they're in season to take the cake roll over the top.

Oh yes! You definitely want all your friends to say, upon being served these cakes, "Well, la-di-da!"

"Fancy schmancy" is the caviar on the cracker and the icing on the cake. This chapter will satisfy your craving for those "it was time-consuming but well worth it!" cakes, those *pièces de résistance* when only something extra special will do.

Ginger Peach Cake Roll

A firm cake with a peach filling that really jumps out, and the crystallized ginger is a perfect complement.

3 large eggs
1 cup granulated sugar
1 cup unbleached, all-purpose flour
1 tsp. baking powder
½ tsp. salt
½ tsp. ground ginger
5 tbsp. water

Confectioners' sugar, sifted

FILLING

¼ cup finely chopped crystallized ginger
10 oz. peach preserves

TOPPING

1 cup heavy cream, whipped and
    sweetened
¼ cup finely chopped crystallized ginger

Heat oven to 375 degrees. Grease a 15" by 10" jelly-roll pan. Line with waxed paper; grease paper.

In a large bowl of an electric mixer, beat eggs on high speed until thick and lemon colored. Gradually add sugar, beating until blended.

With mixer at medium speed, blend in the flour, baking powder, salt, ginger, and water. Spread batter into prepared pan.

Bake for 10 to 14 minutes or until light golden brown and top springs back when lightly touched in the center.

Place a lint-free, clean kitchen towel atop a wire rack, and sprinkle with sifted confectioners' sugar. Loosen cake from sides of pan; invert onto towel. Carefully remove paper.

While hot, roll cake and towel from shorter side. Cool rolled cake in towel on wire rack for 30 minutes.

For the Filling: In a small bowl, combine the crystallized ginger and peach preserves until well blended.

Unroll cake. Spread cake with filling; reroll (*without towel!*). Place cake roll on a serving plate with seam side down.

When ready to serve, top with sweetened whipped cream and garnish with additional crystallized ginger pieces. Serves 10-12.

Citrusy Lemon Roulade Sprinkled with Coconut

Perfect for a bridal or baby shower, this flavorful and fancy roulade will take some effort, but the accolades will be worth it.

3 large egg yolks
¼ cup granulated sugar
¼ cup fresh lemon juice

SUGARED COCONUT FLAKES

2⅓ cups unsweetened coconut flakes
2 tbsp. granulated sugar
1 tbsp. boiling water

SPONGE CAKE

⅔ cup unbleached, all-purpose flour
½ tsp. baking powder
4 large eggs
1 large egg yolk
¾ cup granulated sugar
2 tbsp. unsalted butter, cut into small
    pieces
¼ cup milk, whole
Confectioners' sugar, sifted

LEMON FROSTING

½ cup unsalted butter, room
    temperature, cut into pieces
4 cups confectioners' sugar, sifted,
    divided
¼ cup milk, whole
1 tsp. lemon extract

In a small saucepan, whisk the egg yolks with the sugar and lemon juice. Cook over low heat, stirring constantly, until the mixture just begins to thicken—*do not boil!*

Immediately strain the curd into a bowl, then place plastic wrap directly on the surface of the curd and refrigerate until cold.

Return to saucepan and cook over medium heat until thickened to a pudding-like consistency. (*Watch carefully, as this happens quickly!*) Remove saucepan from heat. When cool, cover surface of curd with a piece of waxed paper.

For the Sugared Coconut Flakes: Heat oven to 350 degrees. Line a baking sheet with parchment paper.

Place the coconut in a medium bowl. In a large measuring cup, combine the sugar and boiling water, stirring to dissolve sugar. Add the sugared water to the coconut and toss until thoroughly coated.

Spread the coconut evenly on the baking sheet. Toast it in the oven for 6 to 10 minutes, stirring occasionally, until golden. (*Watch carefully so it doesn't burn!*) Transfer to a plate to cool.

For the Sponge Cake: Heat oven to 375 degrees. Grease a 15" by 10" jelly-roll pan and line it with waxed paper. Grease paper.

In a small bowl, whisk together the flour and baking powder.

In a large heatproof bowl, whisk together the eggs, yolk, and sugar. Set the bowl over a pot of simmering water and whisk constantly until the mixture is warm to the touch. Remove the bowl from the heat and beat the mixture at high speed until it is pale in color and as thick as whipped cream.

In a small saucepan, melt the butter in the milk over low heat. Turn off the heat but leave the pan on the stove to keep warm.

Sift a third of the flour mixture over the egg mixture and gently fold it in with a spatula, repeating twice.

Drizzle half of the milk mixture over the batter and fold it in. Repeat with the remaining milk mixture, folding gently to incorporate.

Spread the batter into the prepared pan and gently smooth the surface. Bake for 9 to 12 minutes or until the cake springs back when lightly touched.

Cool on a wire rack for 5 minutes. Run a knife around edge of pan, then flip the cake over atop a clean, lint-free kitchen towel dusted with sifted confectioners' sugar. Gently remove the waxed paper and, starting with the long end, roll the cake in the towel. Allow to cool (as a roll in the towel) on a wire rack.

For the Lemon Frosting: In a large bowl of an electric mixer, beat the butter until smooth. With the mixer on low, add *half* of the confectioners' sugar, beating to combine. Scrape bowl.

With mixer on low, blend in the milk and lemon extract, beating to combine. Mix in the remaining confectioners' sugar. Scrape bowl.

With mixer on medium, beat frosting until mixture is light and fluffy and of desired spreading consistency.

Unroll the cake. Evenly spread the curd over the cake. Reroll the cake (*without the towel!*) and let stand at room temperature for 5 minutes, seam side down.

Transfer to a serving platter. Spread the frosting in a thick layer over the top, sides, and ends of the rolled cake. Scatter the toasted coconut over the log, pressing with your clean hands to help the coconut adhere to the frosting. Serve the cake at room temperature. Serves 10-12.

Roll with me, baby, and enjoy a slice of this Citrusy Lemon Roulade Sprinkled with Coconut.

A chestnut festival poster from our trip to Tuscany stands tall behind a slice of Chef Roger Thomas's Tuscan Chestnut Cake.

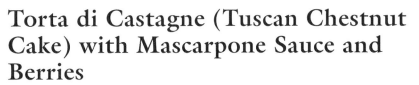

Torta di Castagne (Tuscan Chestnut Cake) with Mascarpone Sauce and Berries

Chef Roger Thomas grew up in the Midwest, but his work in France, Italy, and Great Britain has given him a very broad range of culinary experiences. This torta is his twist on a traditional Tuscan recipe, making it more suited to his little gastronomic Mecca of Akron, Ohio!

6 large eggs, separated
½ cup granulated sugar, divided
½ tsp. freshly grated lemon zest
½ cup unsalted butter, room
  temperature, cut into pieces
17 oz. can sweetened chestnut paste
  with vanilla

MASCARPONE SAUCE

8 oz. mascarpone, room temperature
¼ cup milk, whole
3 tbsp. confectioners' sugar, sifted
3 tbsp. Vin Santo, brandy, or sherry

TOPPING

Confectioners' sugar, sifted
Fresh berries

A SLICE OF ADVICE FROM BEV

Sweetened chestnut paste is available at Italian specialty markets.

Vin Santo, originating in Tuscany, is a strong Italian dessert wine.

Heat oven to 350 degrees. Grease and flour a 10" springform pan, tapping out excess flour.

In a large bowl of an electric mixer, beat the egg yolks with ¼ cup sugar until slightly thickened. Scrape down sides and bottom of bowl.

Add the zest and butter, and mix well. Add the chestnut paste, mixing well. Scrape bowl.

In a medium mixing bowl, beat the egg whites until foamy. Gradually beat in the remaining ¼ cup sugar, a little at a time, until whites are stiff but not dry.

Fold a third of the whites into the chestnut mixture to lighten it. Then gently but thoroughly fold remaining whites into the mixture.

Spread batter into prepared pan, smoothing the top with a spatula. Bake in the center of the oven for 36 to 44 minutes or until a toothpick inserted in the center comes out clean.

Cool for 20 minutes on a wire rack. Run a knife around the inside edge of pan and carefully remove the springform sides.

For the Mascarpone Sauce: In a medium bowl, whisk together the mascarpone and milk until smooth. Whisk in the confectioners' sugar and Vin Santo, mixing well.

Place cake on a serving plate and dust the top with confectioners' sugar. Cut into serving pieces, spoon sauce over each slice, and garnish with berries to serve. Serves 12.

Baby Cakes in Waffle Bowls with Simply Fresh Raspberry Topping

These cakes are perfect for a kid's birthday or young-at-heart older adults!

6 waffle ice-cream bowls, 3½" in diameter
¾ cup unbleached, all-purpose flour
½ cup granulated sugar
¼ cup unsalted butter, room temperature, cut into pieces
¼ cup milk
½ tsp. baking powder
½ tsp. vanilla extract
1 large egg

TOPPING

1 qt. fresh raspberries, gently washed and dried
1 tbsp. granulated sugar
½ tsp. vanilla extract

A SLICE OF ADVICE FROM BEV

Surprisingly, these keep well for several days without the waffle bowl going soggy!

Heat oven to 325 degrees.

Place waffle bowls in 6-oz. custard cups or a jumbo muffin pan (for support while baking). If using custard cups, place them on a jelly-roll pan.

In a large bowl of an electric mixer, beat the flour, sugar, butter, milk, baking powder, vanilla, and egg until blended. Scrape bowl.

With mixer on high, beat for 2 additional minutes or until ingredients are blended. Scrape bowl. Spoon about ¼ cup batter into each waffle bowl. Bake for 38 to 45 minutes or until a toothpick inserted in the center comes out clean.

Cool for 2 minutes. Then with a thin metal spatula, gently loosen the waffle bowls from the cups or pan. Immediately remove bowls from cups or pan to a wire rack to cool completely.

For the Topping: While cakes are baking, macerate raspberries. In a large bowl, combine the raspberries, sugar, and vanilla, tossing gently to combine. Cover and allow to sit at room temperature for at least 30 minutes or up to 2 hours.

Serve each Baby Cake in Waffle Bowl with a generous spoonful of Simply Fresh Raspberry Topping. Serves 6.

These Baby Cakes in Waffle Bowls are just plain fun to make and eat. Kids of all ages will love them!

Beyond the Campfire S'Mores Cakes

Kids of all ages will adore this cake. The chocolate cake base is simply sensational, and the marshmallow topping with "stuff" just makes you want to gather the wood and light a campfire!

2 cups unbleached, all-purpose flour
2 cups granulated sugar
⅔ cup unsweetened cocoa powder, sifted
1 tsp. baking powder
1 tsp. baking soda
1 tsp. salt
1½ cups milk
½ cup light olive oil
2 large eggs
1 large egg white, room temperature
2 tbsp. vanilla extract

MARSHMALLOW TOPPING

1½ tsp. unflavored gelatin
2 tbsp. cold water
1 cup granulated sugar, divided
¾ cup light corn syrup
3 large egg whites, room temperature
½ tsp. vanilla bean paste
6 whole graham crackers, broken
2 oz. semisweet chocolate, melted

A SLICE OF ADVICE FROM BEV

Don't be discouraged if the topping seems really "sticky" when beating—it is! Some will stick to the beater . . . just try to get as much hot syrup into the bowl as you can!

Want to do some of this ahead? Bake the cake layers, cool completely, then wrap and keep refrigerated for up to 4 days. Bring the cake layers to room temperature before continuing on your adventure. . . .

Heat oven to 325 degrees. Grease 2 8" square baking pans and cover each pan bottom with a square of parchment paper. Grease the paper and flour the pans, tapping out excess flour.

In a large bowl, whisk together the flour, sugar, cocoa powder, baking powder, baking soda, and salt.

In a medium bowl, whisk the milk with the oil, eggs, egg white, and vanilla. Add the liquid to the dry ingredients, whisking just until smooth.

Spread the batter into prepared pans. Bake for 24 to 32 minutes or until a toothpick inserted in the center comes out with a few moist crumbs attached.

Cool in pans for 10 minutes. Then run a knife around inside edge of pans to loosen cakes. Cover a pan with a large, lint-free towel-covered plate and invert pan. Remove pan from cake. Peel off parchment and re-invert cake from plate onto cooling rack. Repeat with remaining cake.

Place the cakes, right side up, on 2 baking sheets.

For the Marshmallow Topping: In a small bowl, sprinkle the gelatin over the cold water and let stand until softened (about 5 minutes).

In a medium saucepan, combine ½ cup sugar with the corn syrup. Stir over medium heat until sugar is thoroughly dissolved.

Bring the corn syrup mixture to a boil, wiping down any sugar crystals on the side of the pan with a wet pastry brush.

Cook over medium heat, *without stirring*, until the mixture reaches 250 degrees on a candy thermometer. Remove from the heat and stir in the softened gelatin (*careful: mixture will foam up!*).

In a large bowl of an electric mixer, beat the egg whites and vanilla paste at medium speed until soft peaks form. Add the remaining ½ cup sugar, a little at a time, beating well after each addition. Beat until the whites are stiff and glossy, about 5 minutes.

CAKES TO DIE FOR!

With the mixer at medium, *carefully* pour the hot corn syrup mixture in a thin stream into the egg whites, aiming for the area between the whisk and the side of the bowl. Beat the topping until very thick and opaque, about 8 minutes.

Heat the broiler and position a rack 8" from the heat. Using an offset spatula, spread the marshmallow topping over the tops of the cakes. Let stand for about 1 minute, until slightly set.

Broil the cakes (*watch carefully—this doesn't take long at all!*), one at a time, shifting the pan as necessary for even browning, 1 to 2 minutes. Immediately insert the broken graham cracker pieces into the marshmallow topping and drizzle with the melted chocolate. Serve the same day. Serves 8-10 per cake.

See the glow of the campfire flickering on the Beyond the Campfire S'Mores Cake?
(That's just your imagination—the campfire is optional!)

Celebration Trifle with Holiday Custard Sauce

A trifle can be the perfect centerpiece for so many celebrations, and the variations are only limited by your imagination.

2 cups milk, whole only
1 vanilla bean, split lengthwise
6 tbsp. granulated sugar, divided
5 large egg yolks
1½ tbsp. Grand Marnier or Amaretto

CELEBRATION TRIFLE

Marmalade-Glazed "Not-So-Many-
    Pounds" Cake, unglazed (see index)
2 tbsp. sweet or dry sherry
2 tbsp. dark rum or brandy
1 pt. fresh red raspberries
½ cup raspberry jam
2 cups Holiday Custard Sauce (above)
1 cup heavy cream
2 tsp. confectioners' sugar
½ tsp. vanilla extract
⅓ cup slivered almonds, toasted

Additional red raspberries

In a medium saucepan, add the milk, vanilla bean, and 3 tbsp. sugar. Bring mixture just to a boil over medium heat. Remove saucepan from heat, cover, and allow to steep for 1 hour.

Return the milk to a simmer over low heat.

In a bowl, whisk together the egg yolks with the remaining sugar until blended. Gradually whisk about *half* of the warm milk mixture into the egg yolks. Pour all of the egg mixture back into the saucepan.

Cook, stirring constantly, until custard thickens. *Do not boil.*

Immediately pour custard through a fine sieve into a bowl. Scrape the seeds from the split vanilla bean into the sauce. Stir in the Grand Marnier. Cool in the refrigerator, stirring once or twice. Cover when chilled.

For the Celebration Trifle: Cut the cake into 1" triangular wedges or slices. Fit the pieces on their sides, as close together as possible, into the bottom of a 1½-qt. glass trifle bowl or soufflé dish. (Save leftover cake scraps for another use, or eat immediately!)

Sprinkle the sherry and rum over the cake. In a medium bowl, gently mix together the berries and the jam. Spread the berry mixture over the soaked cake, reaching to the sides of the dish.

Pour the Holiday Custard Sauce over the berries. Cover with waxed paper and refrigerate for 2 hours or longer to allow flavors to meld.

Whip the heavy cream with the sugar and vanilla until soft peaks form. With a spatula, spread the cream over the trifle. Chill for at least 2 hours.

Just before serving, sprinkle the almonds over the top and decorate with some red raspberries. Serve, spooning up from the bottom of the bowl. Serves 8-12.

Mango Buttercream Cake

One trip to Southeast Asia will have you craving mangoes, and this decadent buttercream cake will take your cravings over the top!

2½ cups unbleached, all-purpose flour
2 cups granulated sugar
1 tsp. baking powder
½ tsp. baking soda
⅛ tsp. salt
1⅓ cups buttermilk
½ cup unsalted butter, room temperature, cut into pieces
1 tsp. vanilla extract
4 large egg whites

MANGO BUTTERCREAM

4 ripe mangoes, peeled, pitted, and cut into pieces
1 cup granulated sugar
6 large egg yolks
3 tbsp. orange liqueur, Grand Marnier or Triple Sec preferred
2 cups unsalted butter, room temperature, cut into pieces

Heat oven to 350 degrees. Grease and flour 2 9" round cake pans.

In a large bowl of an electric mixer, combine the flour, sugar, baking powder, baking soda, and salt. Stir in the buttermilk, butter, and vanilla, mixing until combined. Scrape bowl.

Beat on medium-high speed for 2 minutes. Scrape bowl. Add egg whites and beat for another 2 minutes until well blended.

Spread batter into prepared pans. Bake for 22 to 29 minutes or until a toothpick inserted near the center comes out clean.

Cool in pans for 10 minutes. Then run a knife around inside edge of pans to loosen cakes. Cover a pan with a large, lint-free towel-covered plate and invert pan. Remove pan from cake. Re-invert cake from plate onto cooling rack. Repeat with remaining cake. Allow to cool completely on wire racks.

For the Mango Buttercream: In a food processor, puree about a third of the mango pieces until smooth. Remove and repeat with remaining mangoes. (You will need 1½ cups mango puree.)

In a large saucepan, simmer the mango puree over medium-low heat until reduced to 1 cup, stirring frequently to prevent scorching.

Raise heat to medium. Whisk the sugar into the saucepan, cooking and stirring until bubbly. Remove from heat. Leave burner on.

Place the egg yolks in a medium bowl and whisk to blend. Quickly stir about 1 cup hot mixture into the beaten egg yolks, then return all of the yolk mixture to the saucepan.

Bring to a boil, and then reduce to a simmer. Cook and stir for 2 minutes. Remove mixture from heat and whisk in the liqueur. Cool to room temperature.

In a large bowl of an electric mixer, beat the butter until fluffy. Scrape bowl. With mixer on medium high, add the cooled mango mixture to the butter mixture, beating until well blended and fluffy.

Place 1 cake layer on a cake stand or serving plate. Spread with a portion of the Mango Buttercream. Top with the other layer. Frost the sides and then the top of the cake with the remaining Mango Buttercream. Refrigerate for 1 hour to allow buttercream to set. Serves 12-14.

Mascarpone Mango Cheesecake with Raspberry Praline Mascarpone

Mascarpone adds a richness and a smoothness to this cheesecake, and the mango topping and mascarpone spread make it even more divine!

2½ cups graham cracker crumbs
½ cup shredded coconut
4 tbsp. granulated sugar
¾ cup unsalted butter, melted

MASCARPONE CHEESECAKE FILLING

16 oz. cream cheese, room temperature, cut into pieces
8 oz. mascarpone, room temperature
2 large eggs
¾ cup granulated sugar
1 tsp. vanilla extract

MANGO TOPPING

3 cups chopped, ripe mango, divided
3 tbsp. granulated sugar
3 tbsp. fresh lime juice
3 tbsp. water, divided
1 tbsp. cornstarch or arrowroot

RASPBERRY PRALINE MASCARPONE

⅓ cup finely chopped almonds
¼ cup granulated sugar
1 tbsp. unsalted butter
¼ tsp. vanilla extract
8 oz. mascarpone, room temperature
1 tbsp. freshly grated orange zest
1 tbsp. Grand Marnier or orange juice
¼ cup dried red raspberries
1 tbsp. milk

Heat oven to 350 degrees.

In a small bowl, combine the graham cracker crumbs, coconut, and sugar. Add the melted butter, stirring to combine. Press crust onto the bottom and 1" up the sides of a 10" springform pan

Refrigerate for 10 minutes, and then bake for 10 minutes. Cool on a wire rack. Leave oven on.

For the Mascarpone Cheesecake Filling: In a large bowl of an electric mixer, beat the cream cheese, mascarpone, eggs, sugar, and vanilla just until mixture is smooth.

Spread batter into crust-lined pan. Bake for 60 to 74 minutes or until a knife comes out clean when inserted into the center. Cool completely on a wire rack. Refrigerate, loosely covered, for at least 3 hours or overnight.

For the Mango Topping: Puree 2 cups mango with the sugar, lime juice, and 2 tbsp. water. Pour mixture into a medium saucepan and simmer, stirring, for a few minutes.

In a small bowl, dissolve the cornstarch or arrowroot in the remaining water. Pour into the mango mixture, heating for 1 or 2 minutes just until thick.

Spoon the topping over the cheesecake, and scatter the remaining mango pieces over the top.

For the Raspberry Praline Mascarpone: Line a baking sheet with foil and lightly grease the foil.

Cook the almonds, sugar, butter, and vanilla in a small skillet over medium heat (*do not stir*) until sugar begins to soften, shaking skillet occasionally. Reduce heat to low and cook just until sugar begins to turn golden, stirring frequently.

Immediately spread coated nuts on prepared baking sheet. Cool, then break into pieces and finely chop.

CAKES TO DIE FOR!

In a large bowl of an electric mixer, beat the mascarpone, zest, and Grand Marnier until combined. Stir in dried raspberries.

Mix in the finely chopped almond praline and the milk to make a spreading consistency.

When ready to serve, place a spoonful of the Raspberry Praline Mascarpone on a dessert plate next to a slice of the Mascarpone Mango Cheesecake. Serves 10-12.

Shade? In the tropics? Only if you're eating this Coconut Cream Cake with Mango-Infused Whipped Cream under a palm tree!

Shades of the Tropics Coconut Cream Cakes with Mango-Infused Whipped Cream

Two very moist cakes that even non-coconut lovers will enjoy . . . especially when served with a mango-infused whipped cream.

2¾ cups cake flour, sifted
4 tsp. baking powder
¾ tsp. salt
1 cup milk, whole
1 tsp. vanilla extract
1 tsp. coconut extract
¾ cup unsalted butter, room
   temperature, cut into pieces
1½ cups sugar, divided
4 large egg whites, room temperature
14 oz. can sweetened condensed milk
14 oz. can sweetened cream of coconut

**MANGO-INFUSED WHIPPED
  CREAM**

¼ cup mango nectar
1½ cups heavy cream

Sweetened flaked coconut

Heat oven to 350 degrees. Grease 2 8" cake pans and cover each pan bottom with a round of parchment paper. Grease and flour parchment rounds, tapping out excess flour.

In a medium bowl, whisk together the flour, baking powder, and salt.

In a small bowl, whisk together the milk, vanilla, and coconut extract.

In a large bowl of an electric mixer, beat together the butter and 1 cup sugar until light and fluffy.

Beat in the flour mixture alternately with the milk mixture in several batches, beating just to blend after each addition.

In another large bowl of an electric mixer, beat the egg whites until soft peaks form. Gradually add remaining ½ cup sugar and beat until stiff but not dry peaks form. Fold egg whites into cake batter in 3 additions.

Divide batter between prepared pans. Bake until a toothpick inserted into the center of the cakes comes out clean, about 32 to 36 minutes. Cool in pans on a wire rack for 10 minutes.

In a medium bowl, combine the condensed milk and cream of coconut. Poke holes all over top of each cake layer with a skewer. Pour coconut cream mixture evenly over cakes, allowing mixture to be absorbed before adding more. Cool completely in pans.

For the Mango-Infused Whipped Cream: In a large bowl of an electric mixer, combine the mango nectar and heavy cream. Beat until stiff peaks form.

Run a knife around inside edge of pans to loosen cakes. Cover a pan with a large, lint-free towel-covered plate and invert pan. Remove pan from cake. Peel off parchment and re-invert cake from plate onto cake platter. Repeat with remaining cake and place onto another cake platter.

Serve slices with a large dollop of Mango-Infused Whipped Cream and sprinkle generously with flaked coconut. Serves 8-10 per cake.

Sweet-Tart Cranberry Torte

Both the crust and the filling feature a tasty yet interesting combination of ingredients, and the cranberries make for a beautiful, intensely colored topping. A slice of this torte has a refreshing, tart flavor.

1½ cups unbleached, all-purpose flour
½ cup granulated sugar
½ tsp. ground cinnamon
1½ tsp. baking powder
¼ tsp. salt
¼ cup light olive oil or canola oil
2 large egg whites, lightly beaten, room temperature
1 tbsp. unsalted butter, melted
1 tsp. vanilla extract

TORTE

1 large egg
⅔ cup sweetened condensed milk
2 tbsp. cornstarch or arrowroot
1½ cups nonfat plain yogurt
1 tsp. freshly grated lemon zest
1 tsp. vanilla extract
3 cups cranberries, fresh or frozen (unthawed)

Confectioners' sugar, sifted

Heat oven to 300 degrees. Grease a 9" springform pan.

In a large bowl, stir together the flour, sugar, cinnamon, baking powder, and salt.

Add the oil, egg whites, butter, and vanilla, mixing until well blended. Press onto the bottom of the prepared pan.

For the Torte: In a clean large mixing bowl, whisk together the egg, condensed milk, and cornstarch until smooth. Add the yogurt, whisking until smooth.

Blend in the lemon zest and vanilla. Pour over the crust.

Sprinkle cranberries evenly over the top. Bake for 72 to 86 minutes or until the top is just set. (The center will quiver slightly when the pan is gently shaken.)

Cool in pan on wire rack for 15 minutes. Run a knife around the inside edge of pan and carefully remove the springform sides. Serve warm or chilled, dusted with confectioners' sugar. Serves 10-12.

CAKES TO DIE FOR!

A red artist's palette holds this Sweet-Tart Cranberry Torte.

Crunch of Praline Torte with Eggnog Cream

Eggnog lovers rejoice! This will be a holiday masterpiece at your next dinner party.

1½ cups pecan pieces, toasted
8 large eggs, separated
2 large egg whites, room temperature
1 cup granulated sugar
⅓ cup fresh breadcrumbs
1¼ tsp. baking powder
1 tsp. vanilla extract
½ tsp. freshly grated nutmeg
⅛ tsp. salt
Confectioners' sugar, sifted

PRALINE

¾ cup granulated sugar
¾ cup coarsely chopped pecans, toasted

EGGNOG CREAM

½ cup firmly packed light brown sugar
¼ cup eggnog
2 cups heavy cream

A SLICE OF ADVICE FROM BEV

Have all your ingredients ready before starting this recipe (remember, mise en place!), because once the egg whites are whipped, you'll want to proceed quickly.

A word of caution: The praline by itself can be extremely hard, so be careful and don't break a tooth!

Heat oven to 325 degrees. Grease a 15" by 10" jelly-roll pan. Line pan with waxed paper, extending about 1" over ends of pan; grease well.

Place pecans in a food processor and pulse until finely ground (being careful not to grind into pecan butter!). Remove to a bowl.

In a large bowl of an electric mixer, beat 10 egg whites at high speed until stiff peaks form. Transfer to another large bowl; set aside.

In the same large bowl of the electric mixer, beat 8 egg yolks at medium speed until thick and lemon colored. Add sugar and continue beating until very thick.

With mixer on low, add the ground pecans, breadcrumbs, baking powder, vanilla, nutmeg, and salt. Beat until well mixed.

Quickly and gently stir about 1 cup beaten egg whites into the pecan mixture by hand. Then gently fold in remaining beaten egg whites just until mixed.

Spread batter into prepared pan. Bake for 24 to 31 minutes or until golden brown and edges begin to pull away from sides of pan.

Lightly sprinkle top of cake with sifted confectioners' sugar. Invert cake onto a clean, lint-free kitchen towel; peel off waxed paper. Cool completely on a wire rack (atop towel).

For the Praline: Line baking sheet with foil. Place the sugar in a 10" skillet and cook over medium heat, stirring occasionally, until sugar melts and turns golden brown (being careful not to burn sugar).

Quickly stir in the chopped pecans until well coated. Spread nut mixture onto foil-lined baking sheet. Cool completely.

Break praline into small pieces, reserving several pieces to use as garnish. Place praline pieces in a food processor and pulse until coarsely ground.

For the Eggnog Cream: In a large bowl of an electric mixer, beat together the brown sugar and eggnog on high speed, gradually adding heavy cream until stiff peaks form.

To Assemble Torte: Cut cake crosswise into 4 equal strips (about 10" by 3½"). Place 1 cake strip onto serving plate. Frost with about ½ cup Eggnog Cream and sprinkle with ⅓ cup ground praline mixture.

Repeat stacking layers of cake, Eggnog Cream, and ground praline. Frost sides and top of cake with Eggnog Cream.

Refrigerate at least 2 hours or overnight. When ready to serve, garnish with reserved praline pieces. Serves 12-16.

Praline and eggnog and whipped cream and cake . . . oh my!

Luscious Layered Tiramisu Torte

This torte is simply amazing in so many ways. It's easy to make (amazing), has all the flavors of the perfect tiramisu (amazing), and when served with your best grated chocolate the layers taste even more, well, amazing!

4 large eggs, separated
¾ cup granulated sugar, divided
3 tbsp. water
½ tsp. vanilla extract
¾ cup unbleached, all-purpose flour
1 tsp. baking powder

SYRUP

½ cup granulated sugar
½ cup water
2 tbsp. instant espresso powder
2 tbsp. dark rum

FILLING

½ cup confectioners' sugar
16 oz. mascarpone cheese, room temperature
½ tsp. vanilla extract
3 oz. bittersweet chocolate, grated, divided

TOPPING

2 cups heavy cream
Chocolate-covered espresso beans

Heat oven to 375 degrees. Grease a 15" by 10" jelly-roll pan. Line with parchment paper, then grease paper.

In a large bowl of an electric mixer, beat egg whites at high speed until foamy. Continue beating, gradually adding ¼ cup sugar, until stiff peaks form.

Combine remaining ½ cup sugar, egg yolks, water, and vanilla in a smaller mixing bowl. Beat at high speed, scraping bowl often, until thick and lemon colored. Gently stir in flour and baking powder by hand.

Quickly and gently fold egg yolk mixture into beaten egg white mixture just until blended.

Spread batter into prepared pan. Bake for 12 to 15 minutes or until top springs back when lightly touched in center.

Run a knife around edge of pan to loosen cake. Cover pan with a large, lint-free towel-covered board or rack and invert pan. Remove pan from cake. Peel off parchment paper and re-invert cake onto cooling rack. Allow to cool completely on wire rack.

For the Syrup: In a small saucepan, combine the sugar, water, and espresso powder. Cook over medium heat until mixture comes to a full boil. Boil 1 minute, then stir in rum. Cool completely.

Cut cake crosswise into 3 (10" by 5") pieces. Brush top of each piece generously with syrup mixture, *reserving 2 tbsp. syrup mixture*.

For the Filling: In a medium bowl, whisk together the confectioners' sugar, mascarpone, vanilla, and 2 oz. grated chocolate.

Place 1 piece of cake, syrup side up, on a serving plate. Spread *half* of the filling on top of the cake on the serving plate. Repeat layering, topping with third cake layer.

For the Topping: In a large bowl of an electric mixer, beat heavy cream until soft peaks form. Continue beating, gradually adding the reserved 2 tbsp. syrup mixture, until stiff peaks form.

CAKES TO DIE FOR!

Spread whipped cream on sides and top of cake. Refrigerate at least 3 hours before serving.

When ready to serve, sprinkle with remaining grated chocolate. Cut into 8 slices, then cut each slice in half. Garnish each serving with a chocolate-covered espresso bean. Serves 16.

This Luscious Layered Tiramisu Torte is deserving of a special serving.

Deep Dark Chocolate Soufflé Cake with Roasted Pear Cream

An unusual but delicious marriage of flavors: deep dark chocolate soufflé cake with roasted and spiced pears in a flavorful cream.

1 cup unbleached, all-purpose flour
1½ tsp. baking powder
¼ tsp. salt
⅓ cup heavy cream
⅔ cup milk, divided
1⅓ cups granulated sugar, divided
4 large egg yolks
7 oz. bittersweet chocolate, coarsely
    chopped
2 oz. unsweetened chocolate, coarsely
    chopped
¾ cup unsalted butter, room
    temperature, cut into pieces
3 large eggs
1 tsp. vanilla extract

PEAR CREAM

5 medium, ripe pears, peeled, halved,
    and cored
2 tbsp. dark brown sugar
2 tbsp. dark rum
2 cups heavy cream

A SLICE OF ADVICE FROM BEV

When you draw your clean finger across the back of a metal spoon dipped in the custard mixture, and it leaves a path, it is ready.

As the cake cools, it may crack and fall. Not to worry!

Heat oven to 350 degrees. Grease a 9" springform pan and cover pan bottom with a round of parchment paper. Grease and flour paper and sides of pan, tapping out excess flour. Wrap outside bottom and sides of pan with foil to prevent leakage.

In a medium bowl, whisk together the flour, baking powder, and salt.

In a medium saucepan, bring the heavy cream, ⅓ cup milk, and ⅓ cup sugar to a simmer over medium heat, stirring until sugar is dissolved.

Place the egg yolks in a medium bowl and whisk to blend. Quickly stir a third of the hot mixture into the beaten egg yolks, then return all of the yolk mixture to the saucepan.

Stir over medium-low heat until custard mixture thickens, about 2 to 3 minutes; *do not boil*. Stir in chocolate pieces, whisking until melted and smooth.

In a large bowl of an electric mixer, beat the butter and remaining 1 cup sugar until light and fluffy. Add the eggs, one at a time, beating well after each addition. With mixer on medium, add the vanilla, beating until light and fluffy.

By hand, add the butter mixture to the chocolate mixture, folding until well incorporated. Alternately fold the flour mixture and the remaining ⅓ cup milk into the chocolate mixture.

Quickly and gently spread batter into prepared pan. Place springform pan in roasting pan and pour hot water into roasting pan to a depth of 1¼".

Bake cake for 40 minutes, then loosely cover top of cake with foil. Continue baking until cake forms a hard crust, is firm to the touch, and a toothpick inserted into the center comes out with a few moist crumbs attached, about 40 to 55 additional minutes.

Cool completely on a wire rack. Cover and refrigerate overnight.

CAKES TO DIE FOR!

For the Pear Cream: Heat oven to 350 degrees. Place pears cut side down on a lightly greased, foil-lined baking pan and roast for 20 minutes. Cool completely in the pan on a wire rack.

Place the pears, sugar, and rum in a food processor; puree until blended and smooth.

In a large bowl of an electric mixer, whip heavy cream until stiff peaks form. Quickly and gently fold pear puree into whipped cream to blend.

Serve a generous portion of pear cream with each slice of cake. Serves 8-10.

A Hint of Raspberry Celebration Cake

This cake, using all your decorating skills, would be perfect for a small wedding, a graduation, a shower, or a special birthday!

12 large egg whites, room temperature
3⅓ cups granulated sugar, divided
6¼ cups cake flour, sifted
3 tbsp. baking powder
2 tsp. salt
4 cups cold water, divided
1½ cups light olive oil
1 tbsp. freshly grated orange zest
1 tbsp. vanilla extract
1 tbsp. raspberry-flavored liqueur

FROSTING

¾ cup shortening
1 cup unsalted butter, room
    temperature, cut into pieces
12 cups confectioners' sugar, sifted
⅔ cup fresh orange juice
2 tbsp. freshly grated orange zest
1 to 2 tbsp. milk, as needed

RASPBERRY GLAZE

1¼-oz. envelope unflavored gelatin
½ cup plus 3 tbsp. water, divided
⅓ cup granulated sugar
2 tbsp. raspberry-flavored liqueur

A SLICE OF ADVICE FROM BEV

The cakes may be made, cooled, tightly wrapped in plastic wrap, and frozen for up to 5 days.

Heat oven to 350 degrees. Grease 2 10" round and 2 8" round cake pans. Cover pan bottoms with a round of parchment paper. Lightly grease and flour parchment paper rounds, tapping out excess flour.

In a large bowl of an electric mixer, beat the egg whites at high speed, scraping bowl often, until soft peaks form. Continue beating, gradually adding 1⅓ cups sugar, until stiff peaks form.

In a very large bowl, whisk together the remaining 2 cups sugar, cake flour, baking powder, and salt.

Stir in 3 cups water, oil, orange zest, vanilla, and raspberry liqueur. Beat at low speed, scraping bowl often, until smooth.

Gently fold in egg whites. Gradually and gently stir in remaining 1 cup water.

Spread about 6 cups batter into each 10" prepared pan and about 4 cups batter into each 8" prepared pan.

Tap pans on countertop 2 or 3 times to remove any excess air bubbles. Bake for 23 to 28 minutes or until cakes pull away from sides of pans. (If necessary, rotate pans in oven for even browning.)

Cool in pans for 10 minutes. Then run a knife around inside edge of pans to loosen cakes. Cover a pan with a large, lint-free towel-covered plate and invert pan. Remove pan from cake. Peel off parchment and re-invert cake from plate onto cooling rack. Repeat with remaining cakes. Allow to cool completely on wire racks.

Brush all browned crumbs from surfaces of cake with a soft pastry brush.

For the Frosting: In a large bowl of an electric mixer, beat the shortening and butter until light and fluffy. Scrape bowl. Continue beating, gradually adding confectioners' sugar alternately with orange juice and orange zest, until fluffy. Scrape bowl. Add milk, as needed, to reach a desired spreading consistency.

For the Glaze: In a small bowl, soften gelatin in 3 tbsp. water. Stir together softened gelatin, ½ cup water, and sugar in a small saucepan. Cook over medium-high heat until gelatin is dissolved. Stir in the raspberry liqueur. Refrigerate, stirring occasionally, until gelatin mounds on a spoon (about 10 minutes).

CAKES TO DIE FOR!

When ready to assemble, place 1 10" layer on a 10" cake cardboard round, bottom side up. Spread with a thin, smooth layer of the frosting. Top with a thin layer of the raspberry glaze to within ½" of the edge of the cake. Refrigerate until slightly set (30 minutes).

Place 1 8" layer on an 8" cake cardboard round, bottom side up. Spread with a thin, smooth layer of frosting. Top with a thin layer of raspberry glaze. Refrigerate until set (30 minutes). Place remaining cake layers, top side up, on matching bottom layers. Frost sides and top of each cake. Spread so frosting is smooth.

If desired, place some of the remaining frosting in a pastry bag with ribbon tip. Pipe ½"-wide ribbons around outer edge of cake and across top of cake to form decorative lines. Change decorating tip and pipe tiny dots on decorative frosting ribbons.

To assemble, remove cakes from cake rounds. Place 10" cake on large platter or tiered cake stand. Center 8" cake on top of 10" cake. Place remaining frosting in pastry bags with choice of decorating tips. Decorate as desired. Serves 36.

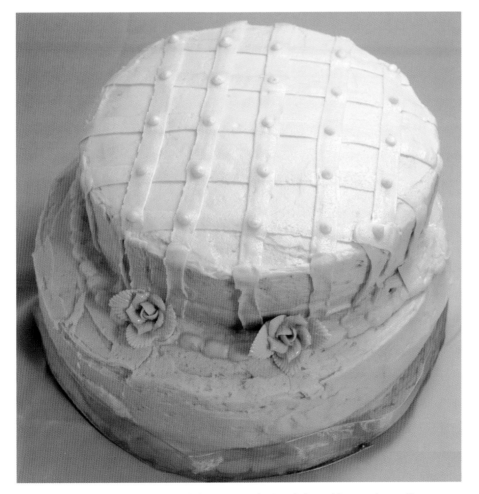

What are you ready to celebrate? Maybe just being able to enjoy a slice of homemade cake, beautifully decorated.

Simple, beautiful, delicious = Orange Crème Fraîche Cake.

Orange Crème Fraîche Cake

I adore the richness and simplicity of this cake . . . something you can enjoy as is or "gussie up" for company. Well wrapped, it freezes beautifully, too!

1¼ cups cake flour, sifted
½ tsp. baking powder
½ tsp. baking soda
⅛ tsp. salt
¾ cup unsalted butter, room temperature, cut into pieces
1 cup granulated sugar
2 large eggs
1 tbsp. freshly grated orange zest
1½ tsp. freshly grated lemon zest
1 tsp. vanilla extract
⅔ cup crème fraîche

GLAZE

3 tbsp. confectioners' sugar, sifted
2 tsp. fresh orange juice

Heat oven to 350 degrees. Grease and flour a 9" round cake pan, tapping out excess flour.

In a medium bowl, whisk together the flour, baking powder, baking soda, and salt.

In a large bowl of an electric mixer, beat the butter and sugar until light and fluffy. With mixer on low, add eggs, one at a time, beating well after each addition. Scrape bowl.

Beat in zests and vanilla. Scrape bowl. With mixer on low, add half of the dry ingredients a little at a time until blended. Add crème fraîche and beat just until smooth. Scrape bowl.

Add remaining dry ingredients and beat just until combined. Spread batter into prepared pan and smooth top. Bake for 34 to 41 minutes or until a toothpick inserted in the center comes out clean.

Cool in pan on a wire rack for 15 minutes. Then run a knife around the inside edge of pan and carefully remove the cake. Place cake on rack atop a large piece of waxed paper.

For the Glaze: In a medium bowl, whisk together the confectioners' sugar and orange juice until well combined. Drizzle atop warm cake and allow to set before serving. Serves 8-10.

ONE-PAN WONDERS

I remember Tuscany . . . and Italian bakeries on the East Coast as a child . . . and Panforte.

A little dressier than snack cakes, but not as "schmancy" as fancy cakes, these moist and marvelous one-pan cakes are perfect for *any* occasion.

They evoke smiles (Dark Chocolate Velvet Underground Cake with Sauces) and fond memories (East Coast Ultimate Crumb Cake), but most of all, they delight you with forkfuls of great tastes!

Panforte Remembrances

Weekly stops at Italian bakeries were a huge part of my childhood. Here is my (rich) adaptation of an Italian classic.

3 cups whole blanched almonds, toasted, coarsely chopped
1¾ cups whole hazelnuts, toasted, skinned, coarsely chopped
1 cup diced candied cherries
2 tbsp. freshly grated orange zest
8 oz. dried apricots, diced
8 oz. dried figs, diced
1⅓ cups unbleached, all-purpose flour
2 tbsp. ground cinnamon
1 tbsp. unsweetened cocoa powder
1 tsp. salt
1 tsp. freshly grated nutmeg
½ tsp. ground cloves
¼ tsp. freshly ground black pepper
1¾ cups granulated sugar
1¾ cups honey
6 tbsp. unsalted butter, room temperature, cut into pieces
Confectioners' sugar, sifted

A SLICE OF ADVICE FROM BEV

For a more traditional version, candied orange peel can be substituted for the candied cherries.

Heat oven to 325 degrees. Grease a 9" round cake pan and cover pan bottom with a round of parchment paper. Grease the parchment paper and flour the paper and sides of the pan, tapping out excess flour.

Place the chopped nuts, cherries, zest, apricots, and figs in a large bowl, tossing to combine.

In a medium bowl, whisk together the flour, cinnamon, cocoa powder, salt, nutmeg, cloves, and pepper, combining thoroughly. Add this mixture to the nut/fruit mixture, combining thoroughly.

In a medium saucepan, mix together the sugar, honey, and butter. Cook over medium heat until a candy thermometer registers 217 degrees. Remove the pan from the heat and quickly pour the sugar mixture over the dry ingredients. Stir to thoroughly combine the mixtures.

Spread batter into prepared pan. Bake for 18 to 24 minutes or until the entire surface is bubbling. Cool in pan completely on a wire rack.

When completely cool, run a knife around inside edge of pan. Carefully flip panforte and remove parchment paper. Wrap the panforte in waxed paper, then plastic wrap. Store in a cool, dry place for at least 1 week and up to 3 weeks.

When ready to serve, dust the panforte with confectioners' sugar and cut into *thin* wedges. Serves 16-20.

East Coast Ultimate Crumb Cake

A great crumb cake is my passion when I visit friends on the East Coast. My criteria include a small amount of moist cake topped, heavily, with incredible sweet crumb and dusted with confectioners' sugar. Enjoy this today, with all the East Coast attitude that goes with it! (You talkin' to me?)

5 cups unbleached, all-purpose flour
2 cups firmly packed light brown sugar
1 tbsp. plus 1½ tsp. ground cinnamon
2 cups unsalted butter, melted

CAKE

3 cups unbleached, all-purpose flour
1 cup granulated sugar
1 tbsp. baking powder
1½ tsp. baking soda
½ tsp. salt
2 large eggs
1¼ cups buttermilk
¼ cup canola oil or light olive oil
1 tbsp. plus 2 tsp. vanilla extract

½ cup or more confectioners' sugar, sifted

A SLICE OF ADVICE FROM BEV

Be careful not to overmix the sweet crumb mixture. Your ultimate goal is crumbs, not a batter.

Remember, a little cake goes a long way, so this batter will *just* cover the pan.

Heat oven to 325 degrees. Grease and flour a 12" by 17" by 1" baking sheet, tapping out excess flour.

In a large bowl, stir together the flour, brown sugar, and cinnamon until well blended. Using a flat whisk or a spoon, quickly stir in the butter until mixture is combined and crumbs are formed. Do not overmix.

For the Cake: In a large bowl, stir together the flour, sugar, baking powder, baking soda, and salt.

In a medium bowl, whisk together the eggs, buttermilk, oil, and vanilla until blended.

Stir the flour mixture into the egg mixture just until dry ingredients are moist and well blended. Do not overmix.

Spread batter into prepared pan.

Sprinkle all the sweet crumb mixture evenly over the cake batter, pressing *ever so lightly* into the batter.

Bake 25 to 32 minutes or until a toothpick inserted into the cake comes out clean.

Cool completely in pan on a wire rack. When ready to serve, dust generously with sifted confectioners' sugar and cut into pieces. Serves 18+.

My dear friend Hal would always take me to Manchokers Bakery for crumb cake when I would visit—and this East Coast Ultimate Crumb Cake is the perfect sweet remembrance. (Crumb this!)

Spice Is Nice Crumb Cake

This one-pan method is great fun to make with kids (of all ages).

2 cups unbleached, all-purpose flour
½ cup firmly packed dark brown sugar
½ cup firmly packed light brown sugar
½ cup unsalted butter, melted
1 tsp. baking powder
½ tsp. baking soda
¼ tsp. salt
1 tsp. ground cinnamon
¼ tsp. ground cloves
1 cup buttermilk
1 tsp. vanilla extract
1 large egg

Heat oven to 350 degrees.

In an 8" square cake pan, combine the flour, brown sugars, and melted butter.

Stir with a fork until mixture resembles coarse crumbs. Remove 1 cup crumb mixture and set aside.

To the pan, add baking powder, baking soda, salt, cinnamon, and cloves, stirring with a fork to blend well.

In a small bowl, blend together the buttermilk, vanilla, and egg. Pour atop the flour mixture in the pan, mixing until smooth. With a spatula, gently scrape the corners, sides, and bottom of pan to be sure all ingredients are moistened.

Sprinkle reserved crumb mixture evenly over top of batter. Bake for 34 to 49 minutes or until a toothpick inserted in the center comes out clean.

Cool in pan on a wire rack for 15 minutes. Serve warm. Serves 6-9.

Dark Chocolate Velvet Underground Cake with Sauces

"Paint" some sweet, rich sauces on a plate, and embellish with a deeply chocolate cake. Serve as your masterpiece!

5 oz. semisweet chocolate, coarsely chopped
1 oz. unsweetened chocolate, coarsely chopped
½ cup unsalted butter, room temperature, cut into pieces
3 large eggs
⅔ cup granulated sugar
¼ cup unbleached, all-purpose flour

WHITE CHOCOLATE SAUCE

1½ cups heavy cream
2 tbsp. confectioners' sugar, sifted
½ cup coarsely chopped white chocolate
¼ tsp. vanilla extract

RED RASPBERRY SAUCE

10 oz. frozen red raspberries, thawed
¼ cup seedless raspberry jam

Heat oven to 350 degrees. Grease a 9" springform pan.

In a medium saucepan over low heat, melt the chocolates and butter until mixture is smooth. Remove from heat.

In a large bowl of an electric mixer, beat the eggs and sugar on high speed until mixture is lemon colored. By hand with a spatula, fold flour into egg mixture until well blended.

Add the chocolate mixture, stirring just to combine. Do not overmix.

Spread batter into prepared pan. Bake for 22 to 36 minutes or until a toothpick inserted in the center comes out clean.

Cool in pan on a wire rack for 15 minutes. Then run a knife around the inside edge of pan and carefully remove the springform pan sides. Cool cake completely on wire rack.

For the White Chocolate Sauce: In a small saucepan, combine and stir over low heat the heavy cream, confectioners' sugar, and white chocolate pieces until chocolate is melted and mixture is smooth. Remove from heat and add the vanilla. Chill to thicken slightly.

For the Red Raspberry Sauce: Puree raspberries in a blender or food processor, then strain to remove seeds. Stir in seedless jam.

When ready to serve, "paint" each plate with sauces and add a slice of cake. Serves 12-14.

No-Bake Chocolate Cake

Somewhere between a tiramisu and a trifle, this no-bake cake is rich and easy and a decadent hit!

60 ladyfingers, sponge-cake type
2¾ cups heavy cream, divided
4 oz. unsweetened chocolate, coarsely chopped
¼ cup granulated sugar
1 cup plus 2 tbsp. confectioners' sugar, sifted, divided
½ cup unsalted butter, room temperature, cut into pieces
2 tsp. vanilla extract, divided
1 tsp. ground cinnamon
Semisweet chocolate, grated

Line the bottom of a 9" springform pan with ladyfingers, flat side down, cutting as necessary to fit. Line sides of pan with ladyfingers, standing ladyfingers side by side with rounded side out.

In a small saucepan over low heat, stir together ¾ cup heavy cream, the unsweetened chocolate, and the granulated sugar until chocolate melts and mixture is smooth. Remove from heat and cool to room temperature.

In a large bowl of an electric mixer, beat 1 cup confectioners' sugar, butter, 1 tsp. vanilla until mixture is light and fluffy. Stir in the cooled chocolate mixture. Scrape bowl.

In another large bowl of an electric mixer, beat the remaining 2 cups heavy cream, 2 tbsp. confectioners' sugar, 1 tsp. vanilla, and the cinnamon until stiff peaks form.

Fold *half* of the whipped cream mixture into the chocolate mixture.

Spread *half* of the chocolate filling in the prepared pan. Top with a layer of ladyfingers, flat side down. Top with the remaining chocolate filling.

With a pastry bag or spatula, pipe or spread remaining whipped cream mixture over filling. Sprinkle generously with the grated semisweet chocolate.

Refrigerate, uncovered, until firm (at least 3 hours). When ready to serve, run a knife around the inside edge of pan and carefully remove the sides of the springform pan. Serves 12-16.

CAKES TO DIE FOR!

Quick and Easy Fudge Cake with a Ganache (That's Worth Slowing You Down a Bit!)

Fast is one thing, but when you can make a silky ganache while the cake is cooling . . . well, that's another thing altogether.

1 cup unbleached, all-purpose flour
¼ cup plus 2 tbsp. unsweetened cocoa powder, sifted
½ tsp. baking soda
¼ tsp. salt
½ cup unsalted butter, melted
1 cup firmly packed light brown sugar
¼ cup firmly packed dark brown sugar
2 large eggs, lightly beaten
1 tsp. vanilla extract
½ cup hot water

GANACHE

4 oz. bittersweet chocolate, finely chopped
2 oz. milk chocolate, finely chopped
¾ cup heavy cream

Heat oven to 350 degrees. Grease an 8" round cake pan.

In a medium bowl, whisk together the flour, cocoa powder, baking soda, and salt.

In a large bowl, stir together the butter and brown sugars until blended. Mix in the eggs and vanilla.

Stir in the flour mixture just until combined. Pour the hot water over the batter and stir just until the batter is smooth.

Spread batter into prepared pan. Bake for 32 to 41 minutes or until a toothpick inserted in the center comes out with a few moist crumbs attached. Cool in pan for 15 minutes.

For the Ganache: While the cake is cooling, in a medium bowl, combine the chocolate pieces. In a small saucepan, bring the heavy cream to a simmer. Pour over chocolate and allow to steep for 5 minutes. Whisk until mixture is smooth.

Run a knife around edge of pan to loosen cake. Cover pan with a large, lint-free towel-covered plate and invert pan. Remove pan from cake. Re-invert cake from plate onto cooling rack atop a large piece of waxed paper.

Pour the warm ganache over the cake, spreading over the top and sides. Allow to set for 1 hour before serving. Serves 6-8.

Time it, then enjoy a slice of this Dark Chocolate Mousse Cake.

Dark Chocolate Mousse Cake

A flourless wonder: rich and moist and the perfect base for an abundance of fresh, seasonal fruits.

10½ oz. bittersweet chocolate, coarsely chopped
1½ cups granulated sugar
10 tbsp. unsalted butter, cut into pieces
5 large eggs, lightly beaten
1 tbsp. ground hazelnuts
⅛ tsp. sea salt
Confectioners' sugar, sifted

Heat oven to 350 degrees. Grease and flour a 9" tart pan with removable bottom, tapping out excess flour.

In a medium saucepan, melt and combine the chocolate, sugar, and butter, whisking until smooth. Remove saucepan from heat.

In a medium bowl, whisk together the eggs, hazelnuts, and salt. Quickly and gently fold into the chocolate mixture.

Pour the batter into the prepared pan. Set atop a rimmed baking sheet that has been lined with parchment paper, in case of leakage. Bake for 35 to 46 minutes or until a toothpick inserted near the center comes out clean.

Cool in pan on a wire rack for 25 minutes. Then run a knife around the inside edge of pan, and carefully remove the sides from the cake. Cool completely on wire rack.

When ready to serve, dust with sifted confectioners' sugar. Serves 10-12.

Ganache Mousse Torte

A twist on the classic ganache-on-the-outside theme, this decadent torte has a rich ganache as part of its batter.

12 oz. semisweet chocolate, coarsely
    chopped
1 cup heavy cream
1 tbsp. instant espresso powder
6 large eggs, room temperature
½ cup granulated sugar
¼ cup unbleached, all-purpose flour

TOPPING

2 tbsp. confectioners' sugar, sifted
1 tsp. unsweetened cocoa powder, sifted

Heat oven to 400 degrees. Grease a 10" springform pan and wrap the outside bottom and sides in foil to prevent leakage.

Place chocolate pieces in a medium bowl. In a small saucepan, bring the heavy cream to a simmer. Whisk in the espresso powder to blend. Pour the hot cream over chocolate pieces and allow to steep for 5 minutes. Whisk the ganache until smooth.

In a large bowl of an electric mixer, beat the eggs, sugar, and flour at medium-high speed until light and fluffy and doubled in volume.

Quickly and gently fold about a third of the egg mixture into the ganache, mixing until combined. Add the remaining egg mixture, folding just until combined and no streaks remain.

Spread the batter into the prepared pan. Set the pan inside a large roasting pan and fill the roasting pan with 1½" of very hot water.

Bake for 20 to 24 minutes or just until a dry crust forms on the top of the torte. The edges will seem set, but the center of the torte will still be a bit wobbly when jiggled!

Remove from the water bath and remove outer foil. Cool pan completely on a wire rack. Refrigerate torte in pan overnight to completely set.

Run a knife around inside edge of pan to loosen torte. Remove sides of springform pan. Cover top of torte with a large, lint-free towel-covered plate and invert. Remove bottom of pan, then re-invert cake from plate onto cake platter.

When ready to serve, mix the confectioners' sugar and cocoa powder, then sift over top. Serves 12-14.

Low-Fat but Still Delicious Mocha Cake

A favorite at our home as well as of my culinary students, this cake always gets a "wow" whenever I teach and serve it as part of a low-fat menu.

⅓ cup unsweetened cocoa powder, sifted, plus additional for dusting pan
1 cup unbleached, all-purpose flour
1½ tsp. instant espresso powder
1 tsp. baking powder
1 tsp. baking soda
6 large egg whites, room temperature
1½ cups firmly packed light brown sugar
1 cup coffee yogurt, nonfat or low fat
1 tsp. vanilla extract

TOPPING

1½ tsp. confectioners' sugar, sifted
1 tsp. ground cinnamon
1 tsp. unsweetened cocoa powder, sifted

Heat oven to 350 degrees. Grease a 9" round cake pan and cover pan bottom with a round of parchment paper. Grease parchment paper and sides of pan, then dust with sifted cocoa powder, tapping out excess cocoa.

In a large bowl, sift together the cocoa powder, flour, espresso powder, baking powder, and baking soda.

In another large bowl, whisk together the egg whites, brown sugar, yogurt, and vanilla until blended. Mix into flour mixture until smooth.

Spread batter into prepared pan. Bake for 32 to 38 minutes or until a toothpick inserted in the center comes out clean.

Cool in pan on a wire rack for 15 minutes. Then run a knife around the inside edge of pan. Cover pan with a large, lint-free towel-covered plate and invert pan. Remove pan from cake. Peel off parchment and re-invert cake from plate onto cooling rack. Allow to cool completely on wire rack.

For the Topping: In a small bowl, whisk together the confectioners' sugar, cinnamon, and cocoa powder.

When ready to serve, sprinkle topping over cake. Serves 6-8.

Caribbean Coconut Cake

We eat first with our eyes, but just one bite will knock their tropical socks off!

1¼ cups unbleached, all-purpose flour
1½ tsp. baking powder
¼ tsp. salt
4 large eggs
3 large egg yolks
1½ cups granulated sugar
1 tsp. vanilla extract
¾ cup unsalted butter, melted
½ cup sweetened cream of coconut
2 cups large coconut flakes, lightly toasted *just* until golden
2 tsp. confectioners' sugar, sifted

RUM FROSTING

6 oz. cream cheese, room temperature, cut into pieces
6 tbsp. sweetened cream of coconut
1½ tbsp. dark rum
½ tsp. vanilla extract
4 to 6 tbsp. heavy cream, divided
1 cup confectioners' sugar, sifted

A SLICE OF ADVICE FROM BEV

Cream of coconut can usually be found in Asian markets, Spanish markets, and liquor stores. It's *not* the same as coconut milk.

Heat oven to 350 degrees. Grease a 9" round cake pan and cover pan bottom with a round of parchment paper. Grease parchment, then flour pan, tapping out excess flour.

In a small bowl, whisk together the flour, baking powder, and salt.

In a large bowl, whisk together the eggs, egg yolks, sugar, and vanilla. Gradually whisk in the flour mixture until combined. Scrape bowl.

Whisk in the butter, mixing just until combined.

Spread batter into prepared pan, tapping on counter once or twice to release any air bubbles.

Bake for 35 to 40 minutes until cake is golden brown and a toothpick inserted in the center comes out clean.

Cool in pan for 10 minutes. Then run a knife around inside edge of pan to loosen cake. Cover pan with a large, lint-free towel-covered plate and invert pan. Remove pan from cake. Peel off parchment and re-invert cake from plate onto cooling rack.

Generously (and carefully) brush top of warm cake with some cream of coconut, allowing it to soak in before brushing on more. Cool completely.

Carefully transfer cake to a cake stand when cool.

In a medium bowl, toss together the toasted coconut flakes and confectioners' sugar.

For the Rum Frosting: In a large bowl of an electric mixer, beat together the cream cheese, cream of coconut, rum, vanilla, and 4 tbsp. heavy cream until smooth. Scrape bowl.

Beat in the confectioners' sugar until desired consistency is reached. Add more heavy cream only if necessary.

Smooth frosting over top of cooled cake, allowing some to drip over side. Top with coconut flakes. Serves 10-12.

CAKES TO DIE FOR!

Lightly toasted coconut flakes top this "for company" Caribbean Coconut Cake.

Lots of Spice Cake with Maple-Syrup Poached Apples

Realtors often tell people if they want to sell their home, have an apple pie baking when prospective buyers come around. The aroma of this cake baking might even up the offer!

1½ cups unbleached, all-purpose flour
1 tsp. baking powder
1 tsp. baking soda
1 tsp. ground cinnamon
¼ tsp. salt
¼ tsp. freshly grated nutmeg
¼ tsp. freshly ground black pepper
⅛ tsp. ground cloves
1¼ cups chopped walnuts, toasted, divided
⅓ cup firmly packed dark brown sugar
⅓ cup firmly packed light brown sugar
⅓ cup granulated sugar
½ cup unsalted butter, room temperature, cut into pieces
2 large eggs
1 cup milk, whole
1 tsp. vanilla extract

POACHED APPLES

2½ cups maple syrup
⅓ cup firmly packed dark brown sugar
¼ tsp. salt
3 whole cloves
2 cinnamon sticks
1 tbsp. unsalted butter
2 tsp. fresh lemon juice
¼ cup apple cider
4 crisp, tart apples, halved, cored, and quartered

Heat oven to 350 degrees. Grease a 9" round cake pan.

In a medium bowl, whisk together the flour, baking powder, baking soda, cinnamon, salt, nutmeg, pepper, and cloves. In a food processor or grinder, finely grind ¾ cup toasted walnuts. Stir these walnuts into the flour mixture.

In a large bowl of an electric mixer, beat the sugars and butter until light and fluffy. Scrape bowl.

Beat eggs into the sugar mixture. With mixer on low, alternately add the flour mixture and the milk to the sugar mixture, mixing until blended. Scrape bowl. Stir in the vanilla and the remaining ½ cup chopped walnuts.

Spread batter into prepared pan, tapping pan once or twice to remove any air bubbles. Bake for 28 to 34 minutes or until a toothpick inserted in the center comes out clean. Cool in pan on a wire rack for 15 minutes.

For the Poached Apples: In a large skillet, combine the maple syrup, brown sugar, salt, cloves, cinnamon sticks, butter, lemon juice, and cider. Bring mixture to a boil, and then reduce to a simmer.

Add the apples, carefully submerging them in the liquid. Cut a piece of waxed paper to fit atop the skillet, and then place over the apples. Top paper with a pie plate or other heatproof flat item that will keep the apples submerged.

Cook for 20 to 26 minutes or just until tender when pierced with the tip of a small knife. Drain, *reserving the liquid*, and allow to cool. Return the liquid to the skillet and simmer until reduced by half. Pour the "syrup" over the apples and allow to cool.

When ready to serve, run a knife around the inside edge of cake pan and carefully remove the cake. Serve each cake slice with some apple slices and "syrup." Serves 6-8.

The Simplest Cornmeal Cake

I love this cake served in the dead of winter, with segments of fresh pink grapefruit, blood oranges, tangerines, and navel oranges. A warm blazing fire in the fireplace and a good book to read are optional!

1 cup cornmeal, sifted, divided
½ cup unbleached, all-purpose flour
1½ tsp. baking powder
¼ tsp. salt
1 cup unsalted butter, room
   temperature, cut into pieces
1 cup granulated sugar
4 large eggs
¼ cup plain, low-fat or Greek yogurt
4 tsp. freshly grated lemon zest
1 tbsp. fresh lemon juice
¾ tsp. vanilla extract

Heat oven to 350 degrees. Grease a 10" round cake pan and cover pan bottom with a round of parchment paper. Grease parchment and sides of pan. Dust pan with 2 tbsp. cornmeal, tapping out excess cornmeal.

In a medium bowl, whisk together the remaining cornmeal, flour, baking powder, and salt.

In a large bowl of an electric mixer, beat the butter and sugar until light and fluffy. Scrape bowl.

Beat in the eggs, one at a time, just until combined. Mix in the yogurt, zest, lemon juice, and vanilla.

With mixer on low, stir in the flour mixture, blending just until combined. Scrape bowl.

Spread batter in prepared pan. Bake for 25 to 39 minutes or until cake is golden in color and springs back when lightly touched.

Cool in pan for 15 minutes. Then run a knife around inside edge of pan to loosen cake. Cover pan with a large, lint-free towel-covered plate and invert pan. Remove pan from cake. Peel off parchment and re-invert cake from plate onto cooling rack. Allow to cool completely on wire rack. Serves 12-16.

This Italian Heritage Orange Cake is a flashback to Bev's childhood.

Italian Heritage Orange Cake

This orange delight reminds me of my childhood and eating anisette sponge cookies from Italian bakeries. I created this recipe with these memories in mind. The cornmeal adds a decidedly different mouthfeel to this simple but flavorful cake.

1⅓ cups unbleached, all-purpose flour
½ cup fine yellow cornmeal
1 cup granulated sugar
2 tsp. baking powder
Pinch of salt
5 large eggs
2 tbsp. freshly grated orange zest
½ cup fresh orange juice
⅓ cup light olive oil
½ tsp. almond extract

TOPPING

Confectioners' sugar, sifted
Orange segments, diced

Heat oven to 350 degrees. Grease a 9" springform pan.

In a medium bowl, whisk together the flour, cornmeal, sugar, baking powder, and salt.

In a large bowl of an electric mixer, beat the eggs, zest, juice, oil, and almond extract until well mixed. With mixer on low, add the flour mixture, a third at a time, until well combined. Scrape bowl.

Spread batter into prepared pan. Bake for 38 to 45 minutes or until a toothpick inserted in the center comes out clean.

Cool pan completely on a wire rack. When cool, run a knife around the inside edge and remove the spingform pan sides.

When ready to serve, dust with confectioners' sugar and top with diced orange pieces. Serves 10-12.

Bev's Orange-Carrot Cake with Cinnamon Cream-Cheese Frosting

Everyone will enjoy this moist version of carrot cake with a hint of orange and the crunch of brown sugar added to the frosting.

3 cups unbleached, all-purpose flour
2 cups granulated sugar
2½ tsp. baking soda
1 tsp. salt
2 tsp. ground cinnamon
2 cups shredded carrots
1¼ cups light olive oil or canola oil
1½ tsp. vanilla extract
1 tsp. freshly grated orange zest
3 large eggs, lightly beaten
11-oz. can mandarin orange segments,
   undrained

FROSTING

8 oz. cream cheese, room temperature,
   cut into pieces
3 cups confectioners' sugar, sifted
2 tbsp. unsalted butter, melted
1 tsp. vanilla extract
2 tbsp. firmly packed light brown sugar
1 tsp. ground cinnamon

Heat oven to 350 degrees. Grease a 13" by 9" baking pan.

In a large bowl of an electric mixer, combine the flour, sugar, baking soda, salt, cinnamon, carrots, oil, vanilla, zest, eggs, and undrained mandarin orange segments. With mixer on low, beat until all ingredients are moistened.

With mixer on high, beat 2 minutes until well combined. Scrape bowl. Spread batter into prepared pan.

Bake for 40 to 45 minutes or until a toothpick inserted in the center comes out clean. Cool pan completely on a wire rack.

For the Frosting: In a large bowl of an electric mixer, combine the cream cheese, confectioners' sugar, butter, vanilla, brown sugar, and cinnamon. With mixer on low, beat until ingredients are blended. With mixer on high, beat until smooth.

Spread over cooled cake. Store cake in refrigerator or cut into pieces and serve immediately! Serves 14-18.

Don't be scared of these carrots. They're only there (temporarily) to protect your slice of Bev's Orange-Carrot Cake with Cinnamon Cream-Cheese Frosting.

Fresh Raspberry Streusel Cake

Adapted from a friend's German heritage, this streusel-topped cake was always a childhood favorite of mine.

1¾ cups unbleached, all-purpose flour
1 cup granulated sugar
2 tsp. baking powder
¼ tsp. baking soda
¼ tsp. salt
3 large eggs
1 cup sour cream
1 tsp. vanilla extract
2½ cups fresh red raspberries, gently
    washed and dried well

STREUSEL TOPPING

1 cup unbleached, all-purpose flour
⅔ cup firmly packed light brown sugar
2 tsp. freshly grated orange zest
½ cup unsalted butter, melted

Confectioners' sugar, sifted

Heat oven to 350 degrees. Grease and flour a 10" springform pan, tapping out excess flour.

In a large bowl, whisk together the flour, sugar, baking powder, baking soda, and salt.

In another medium bowl, whisk together the eggs, sour cream, and vanilla. Stir the egg mixture into the flour mixture, beating by hand until mixture is very smooth.

Spread batter into prepared pan. Cover evenly with the fresh raspberries.

For the Streusel Topping: In a small bowl, stir together the flour, sugar, and orange zest. Stir in the melted butter just until mixture forms coarse crumbs. Sprinkle over the berries.

Bake for 34 to 48 minutes or until a toothpick inserted in the center comes out clean. Cool in pan on a wire rack for 25 minutes. Then run a knife around the inside edge of pan and carefully remove the springform pan sides. Serve warm, dusted with confectioners' sugar. Serves 9-12.

CAKES TO DIE FOR!

Juicy Plum Streusel Cake

If you don't use fresh plums for much more than eating out of hand, you're in for a treat. This plum streusel goodie with a tart, juicy burst of freshness will soon become one of your seasonal favorites.

¾ cup granulated sugar
¼ cup unsalted butter, room
 temperature, cut into pieces
2 large eggs
½ tsp. vanilla extract
1¾ cups unbleached, all-purpose flour
1 tsp. baking soda
1 tsp. baking powder
½ tsp. ground cinnamon
¼ tsp. salt
⅔ cup buttermilk
2 cups halved, pitted fresh plums

STREUSEL TOPPING

⅓ cup unbleached, all-purpose flour
¼ cup granulated sugar
¼ tsp. lemon extract
2 tbsp. unsalted butter, cold, cut into
 pieces

Confectioners' sugar, sifted

Heat oven to 350 degrees. Grease and flour a 13" by 9" baking pan, tapping out excess flour.

In a large bowl of an electric mixer, beat the sugar and butter until light and fluffy. Beat in the eggs and vanilla until combined.

In a medium bowl, whisk together the flour, baking soda, baking powder, cinnamon, and salt.

Alternately add the flour mixture and the buttermilk to the sugar mixture, beating to blend. Scrape bowl.

Spread batter into prepared pan. Arrange the plums, cut side up, on batter.

For the Streusel Topping: In a small bowl, combine the flour, sugar, and lemon extract. Cut in the butter until mixture resembles crumbs.

Sprinkle the Streusel Topping atop the fruit and cake batter. Bake for 22 to 34 minutes or until a toothpick inserted near the center comes out clean. Cool completely on a wire rack. When ready to serve, dust cake with confectioners' sugar. Serves 12-16.

Classic Strawberry Rhubarb Cake

This is a down-home dessert, perfect for one of my favorite pairings . . . strawberries and rhubarb.

¼ cup water
1½ tsp. cornstarch or arrowroot
⅓ cup firmly packed light brown sugar
2 cups chopped fresh rhubarb stalks
1 cup chopped fresh strawberries
½ cup granulated sugar
1 cup unbleached, all-purpose flour
1¾ tsp. baking powder
½ tsp. salt
1 large egg
½ cup half-and-half
½ cup unsalted butter, melted
1 tsp. vanilla extract

A SLICE OF ADVICE FROM BEV

Rhubarb freezes well. When it's growing in our backyard, I remove the leaves, wash and cut the stalks into pieces, and freeze (labeled) in portions needed for my recipes.

Heat oven to 400 degrees. Grease an 8" square cake pan.

In a small saucepan, stir together the water, cornstarch or arrowroot, and brown sugar. Bring to a simmer and stir in rhubarb pieces, cooking and gently stirring for 3 minutes. Remove from heat; add strawberries. Remove and reserve ½ cup fruit mixture.

In a medium bowl, whisk together the granulated sugar, flour, baking powder, and salt.

In a large bowl, whisk together the egg, half-and-half, butter, and vanilla just until combined.

In a large bowl of an electric mixer, beat together the flour mixture with the egg mixture until combined. Scrape bowl.

Add the fruit mixture from the saucepan to the prepared pan. Spread batter over fruit mixture. Spoon reserved fruit mixture over batter.

Bake for 22 to 35 minutes or until a toothpick inserted in the center comes out clean. Cool in pan on a wire rack for 15 minutes. Serve warm. Serves 6-9.

Fresh Picked Blueberry Pudding Cake

I can't wait for local blueberries in the heat of the summer, so I can pop a few in my mouth and pop a few in this treat of a pudding cake!

⅓ cup firmly packed light brown sugar
¼ cup water
1 tbsp. fresh lemon juice
1 tsp. cornstarch or arrowroot
2 cups fresh blueberries, gently washed and dried well
½ cup granulated sugar
1 cup unbleached, all-purpose flour
1¾ tsp. baking powder
½ tsp. salt
1 large egg
½ cup half-and-half
½ cup unsalted butter, melted
½ tsp. freshly grated lemon zest
1 tsp. vanilla extract

A SLICE OF ADVICE FROM BEV

If you've not had a pudding cake before, you're in for a real treat. Spoon it into your best dessert bowls and savor every bite of its cakey top and dreamy pudding on the bottom.

Heat oven to 375 degrees. Grease a 9" round cake pan.

In a medium saucepan, mix together the brown sugar, water, lemon juice, and cornstarch. Bring to a simmer and stir in the blueberries, cooking and gently stirring for 3 minutes. Remove from heat.

In a medium bowl, whisk together the granulated sugar, flour, baking powder, and salt.

In a large bowl, whisk together the egg, half-and-half, butter, lemon zest, and vanilla just until combined.

In a large bowl of an electric mixer, beat together the sugar mixture with the egg mixture until combined. Scrape bowl.

Spread batter into prepared pan. Pour blueberry mixture evenly over batter.

Bake for 24 to 35 minutes or until a toothpick inserted in the center comes out clean. Cool in pan on a wire rack for 15 minutes. Serve warm. Serves 9.

Pudding or cake? Can't decide? You'll enjoy a treat of both when you make this Luscious Lemon Pudding Cake.

Luscious Lemon Pudding Cake

Halfway between a soufflé and a cake, this pudding cake features bright flavors and a silky texture that will make it a year-round favorite. In the summer, it's divine served with an abundance of juicy, just-picked berries, and in the winter, it's flavorful and citrusy.

3 large eggs, separated
1 cup granulated sugar, divided
⅓ cup unsalted butter, room temperature, cut into pieces
¼ cup lemon juice
1 tbsp. freshly grated lemon zest
¼ cup unbleached, all-purpose flour
⅛ tsp. salt
½ cup milk, whole
½ cup half-and-half
¼ tsp. vanilla extract
Confectioners' sugar, sifted

Heat oven to 350 degrees. Set aside a 1½-qt. soufflé dish.

In a small bowl of an electric mixer, beat egg whites at high speed until foamy. Continue beating, gradually adding ¼ cup sugar, until glossy and stiff peaks form. Set aside.

In a large bowl of an electric mixer, combine the remaining ¾ cup sugar and butter, beating until creamy. Scrape down bowl. Add the egg yolks, lemon juice, and zest; continue beating until well mixed.

With mixer on low, add the flour and salt and beat until well mixed. Stir in the milk, half-and-half, and vanilla by hand. Gently fold in the beaten egg whites.

Pour mixture into ungreased 1½-qt. round soufflé dish. Place in a large baking pan. Place pan on oven rack; pour boiling water into baking pan to ½" depth.

Bake for 38 to 52 minutes or until golden brown. Remove from water bath; cool 10 minutes. Sprinkle with confectioners' sugar and serve warm. Serves 8-10.

Fruit-on-the-Bottom Peach Pudding Cake

Fresh peaches and a moist, light cake batter are a match made in cake heaven. You'll adore this cake, still warm from the oven, served with cinnamon-spiked freshly whipped cream.

1¾ cups plus 2 tbsp. unbleached, all-purpose flour
2¼ tsp. baking powder
1 tsp. salt
¾ cup unsalted butter, room temperature, cut into pieces, plus additional for foil cover
1¾ cups granulated sugar
2 tbsp. vanilla extract
2 large eggs
1 cup half-and-half
4 cups peeled, sliced fresh peaches

WHIPPED CREAM

1½ cups heavy cream
2 tbsp. granulated sugar
1½ tsp. ground cinnamon

A SLICE OF ADVICE FROM BEV

As this cake bakes, the peaches will sink to the bottom.

Heat oven to 350 degrees. Grease a 13" by 9" baking pan.

In a medium bowl, whisk together the flour, baking powder, and salt.

In a large bowl of an electric mixer, beat the butter and sugar until light and fluffy.

With mixer on low, beat in the vanilla and eggs, mixing well after each addition. Scrape bowl.

Alternately add flour mixture and half-and-half into butter mixture, beating well to combine. Scrape bowl.

Spread batter into prepared pan. Quickly arrange peach slices over batter, overlapping slices only as needed.

Tear a large sheet of foil to cover pan. Lightly butter foil, then place atop cake pan (buttered side down), sealing edges.

Bake for 40 minutes. Gently remove foil, and continue to bake for 36 to 42 minutes or until cake is golden brown and a toothpick inserted in the center comes out clean.

Cool in pan on a wire rack for 15 minutes.

For the Whipped Cream: In a large bowl of an electric mixer, combine the heavy cream, sugar, and cinnamon. Beat on high speed until soft peaks form.

Serve cake in wide bowls, each with a large dollop of whipped cream. Serves 9-12.

Fresh Cranberry Cake with Dried Cranberries and Silky Butter Sauce

This festive tart-sweet cake would make a perfect new holiday tradition.

2¾ cups unbleached, all-purpose flour
1¼ cups granulated sugar
2 tsp. baking powder
1 tsp. baking soda
¼ tsp. salt
3½ cups fresh cranberries
1 cup dried cranberries
2 cups sour cream
½ cup milk, whole
¼ cup canola oil or light olive oil
½ tsp. vanilla extract
2 large eggs

SILKY BUTTER SAUCE

1½ cups granulated sugar
¾ cup unsalted butter, cut into pieces
¾ cup heavy cream
1½ tsp. vanilla extract

Heat oven to 375 degrees. Grease and flour the bottom only of a 13" by 9" baking pan, tapping out excess flour.

In a medium bowl, whisk together the flour, sugar, baking powder, baking soda, and salt.

In another medium bowl, toss 2 tbsp. flour mixture with the fresh and dried cranberries.

In yet another medium bowl, whisk together the sour cream, milk, oil, vanilla, and eggs until well blended.

Add the sour cream mixture to the flour mixture, stirring just until the dry ingredients are moistened. Quickly and gently fold in the cranberries.

Spread batter into prepared pan. Bake for 38 to 54 minutes or until a toothpick inserted in the center comes out clean. Cool in pan on a wire rack for 15 minutes.

For the Silky Butter Sauce: In a medium saucepan, combine the sugar, butter, and heavy cream. Bring mixture to a boil, then reduce to a simmer. Stir constantly until sugar is dissolved and mixture is smooth. Whisk in vanilla.

Serve Fresh Cranberry Cake warm with a generous drizzle of the Silky Butter Sauce. Serves 9-12.

Everyone Loves My Pumpkin-Gingerbread Cake with an Assortment of Sauces

The surprise crumb bottom and rich pumpkin flavor will have you falling in love with this recipe, and the sauces—each and every one of them—add their own uniqueness to the dessert.

2½ cups unbleached, all-purpose flour
½ cup granulated sugar
⅔ cup unsalted butter, cut into pieces, cold
¾ cup coarsely chopped pecans, toasted
1½ tsp. ground ginger
1 tsp. baking soda
½ tsp. ground cinnamon
¼ tsp. salt
¼ tsp. ground cloves
¾ cup buttermilk
½ cup molasses, preferably Barbados
½ cup cooked, mashed pumpkin
1 large egg, lightly beaten

A SLICE OF ADVICE FROM BEV

It's important that the butter pieces are very cold to ensure that you create a crumb and not a blend.

Heat oven to 350 degrees. Have ready an ungreased 9" square cake pan.

In a food processor, combine the flour and sugar and pulse once or twice to blend.

Add the cold butter pieces, pulsing *just* until mixture resembles fine crumbs. Add the pecans and pulse once or twice to incorporate.

Remove mixture to a large mixing bowl. Measure 1¼ cups crumb mixture and gently press onto the bottom of the pan.

To the mixing bowl, add the ginger, baking soda, cinnamon, salt, and cloves. Stir to blend.

Add the buttermilk, molasses, pumpkin, and egg; mix well to combine.

Gently spread batter into pan, being careful not to disturb the crumb bottom.

Bake for 42 to 52 minutes or until a toothpick inserted in the center comes out clean. Cool on a wire rack. Serves 9-12.

An Assortment of Sauces

Why not serve a "sauce buffet" to go with the gingerbread cake? Yum!

CREAMY CARAMEL SAUCE

½ cup unsalted butter, cut into pieces
1¼ cups firmly packed light brown sugar
2 tbsp. brown rice syrup
½ cup heavy cream

For the Creamy Caramel Sauce: In a medium saucepan, melt the butter. Then stir in the brown sugar and syrup. Bring mixture to a boil and cook, stirring, until sugar dissolves.

Whisk in heavy cream and return mixture to a boil. Remove from heat; cool slightly and serve warm. Make about 2 cups.

DRIED CRANBERRY SAUCE

1½ cups dried cranberries, coarsely
    chopped
1 cup 100 percent cranberry juice
¼ tsp. vanilla extract

For the Dried Cranberry Sauce: Combine the dried cranberries and juice in a small saucepan. Bring mixture to a boil and cook, stirring, for 3 minutes. Remove from heat and cover saucepan.

Let mixture sit for 45 minutes to allow cranberries to absorb most of the juice. Stir in vanilla. Serve warm or cold. Makes about 1½ cups.

PRALINE SAUCE

½ cup firmly packed dark brown sugar
¼ cup water
¼ cup unsalted butter, cut into pieces
1 large egg, lightly beaten
⅓ cup coarsely chopped pecans, toasted
½ tsp. vanilla extract

For the Praline Sauce: In a small saucepan, combine the sugar, water, and butter. Bring mixture to a boil and cook, stirring, for 3 minutes.

Gradually blend a small amount of the hot syrup into the beaten egg. Return egg mixture to the saucepan and cook over low heat for 1 minute, stirring constantly.

Remove from heat and stir in the pecans and vanilla. Cool slightly and serve warm. Makes about 1 cup.

LEMON SAUCE

½ cup granulated sugar
1 tbsp. cornstarch or arrowroot
⅛ tsp. salt
1 cup boiling water
2 tbsp. unsalted butter
1½ tsp. freshly grated lemon zest
3 tbsp. fresh lemon juice

For the Lemon Sauce: In a medium saucepan, combine the sugar, cornstarch or arrowroot, and salt; mix well. Gradually whisk in the boiling water. Return mixture to a boil.

Cook over medium heat, whisking often, until thickened. Remove from heat and blend in the butter, zest, and lemon juice until smooth. Cool slightly and serve warm. Makes about 1 cup.

Lemon Meringue Cake with Mango-Raspberry Sauce

All the luxury of a lemon meringue pie without the fuss of a crust! As with all meringues, it's best to eat this cake the same day it's made.

1 cup granulated sugar
¼ cup unsalted butter, room
    temperature, cut into pieces
1¼ cups unbleached, all-purpose flour
¼ tsp. salt
1½ tsp. baking powder
1 tsp. lemon extract
1 large egg, lightly beaten
½ cup milk, whole
2 tsp. freshly grated lemon zest

MERINGUE

3 large egg whites, room temperature
¼ tsp. plus ⅛ tsp. cream of tartar
¾ cup granulated sugar

MANGO-RASPBERRY SAUCE

2 cups mango pieces, divided
3 tbsp. granulated sugar
2 tbsp. water
1 cup fresh red raspberries

Heat oven to 350 degrees. Grease and flour a 9" square cake pan, tapping out excess flour.

In a large bowl of an electric mixer, beat together the sugar and butter until mixture is light and fluffy. Scrape bowl.

In a small bowl, whisk together the flour, salt, and baking powder. In another small bowl, whisk together the lemon extract, egg, and milk.

With mixer on low, alternately add the flour mixture and the milk mixture to the sugar mixture. Stir in lemon zest. Scrape bowl. With mixer on medium, beat until well combined.

Spread batter into prepared pan. Bake 23 to 28 minutes or until a toothpick inserted in the center comes out clean.

Increase oven temperature to 400 degrees.

For the Meringue: In a large bowl of an electric mixer, beat egg whites and cream of tartar on high speed, until foamy. Beat in sugar, 1 tbsp. at a time, until whites are stiff and glossy. Do not underbeat!

Quickly and gently spread meringue over cake, sealing meringue to edge of pan.

Bake for 8 to 10 minutes or until meringue is light golden brown. Cool on a wire rack.

For the Mango-Raspberry Sauce: Place 1 cup mango pieces in a small saucepan with the sugar and the water. Quickly heat to boiling. Reduce heat to low and simmer, uncovered, just until the mango has softened slightly.

Remove saucepan from heat. Add the remaining mango pieces, stirring gently to combine. Cool for 15 minutes. Then gently toss in the red raspberries.

Serve cake the same day it is baked, with the Mango-Raspberry Sauce. Serves 9.

*Cut me a piece of that Lemon Meringue Cake . . . and bring on the
Mango-Raspberry Sauce.*

You're such a doll for making Pounds of Pineapple Cake.

Pounds of Pineapple Cake

This no-fuss recipe comes from friend and pastry chef Sarah Warnke. Everyone is always surprised by its abundance of pineapple and not-too-sweet flavors.

2 lb. crushed pineapple with juice
2 tsp. baking soda
2 cups granulated sugar
2 large eggs
2 cups unbleached, all-purpose flour
½ tsp. salt

PINEAPPLE CREAM-CHEESE FROSTING

½ cup unsalted butter, room
    temperature, cut into pieces
8 oz. cream cheese, room temperature,
    cut into pieces
1½ cups confectioners' sugar, sifted
1 tsp. vanilla extract
2 oz. *well-drained* crushed pineapple

A SLICE OF ADVICE FROM BEV

This is reminiscent of an upside-down cake that's . . . well . . . not flipped over. It's loaded with pineapple and great flavors! For a tropical treat, serve with coconut ice cream.

Heat oven to 350 degrees. Grease a 13" by 9" baking pan.

In a large bowl, mix together the pineapple and baking soda.

In a medium bowl, mix together the sugar, eggs, flour, and salt. Stir the sugar mixture into the pineapple mixture until blended.

Spread batter into prepared pan. Bake for 30 to 35 minutes or until a toothpick inserted in the center comes out clean. Cool completely on a wire rack.

For the Pineapple Cream-Cheese Frosting: In a large bowl of an electric mixer, beat together the butter and cream cheese until light and fluffy. Scrape bowl.

Beat in the confectioners' sugar and vanilla until fluffy and frosting consistency is reached. Quickly and gently fold in the crushed pineapple.

Spread atop cooled cake. Serves 12-15.

LOAF CAKES AND SNACK CAKES

A slice of this Ricotta Vanilla-Bean Pound Cake, toasted, would be the perfect base for sorbet and fresh fruit . . . or whipped cream and strawberries for your own version of strawberry "shortcake."

Cakes to turn into surprise treats, toasted and served with tea or coffee or a big glass of ice-cold organic milk, warm from the oven with some sugared fresh seasonal berries, a simple but caring finish to a perfect meal with friends, or your contribution to a bake sale—that's what this chapter is all about.

Heat the oven, get out the mixing bowls, grease those pans, and work some powerfully sweet magic!

Ricotta Vanilla-Bean Pound Cake

With a burst of vanilla, this pound cake is perfect alone or with fresh seasonal sliced peaches or apricots and a dollop of freshly whipped, vanilla-infused cream.

1½ cups cake flour, sifted
2½ tsp. baking powder
1 tsp. salt
¾ cup unsalted butter, room temperature, cut into pieces
1½ cups fresh whole-milk ricotta
1½ cups granulated sugar
3 large eggs
1 tsp. vanilla-bean paste
1 tsp. vanilla extract
Confectioners' sugar

Heat oven to 350 degrees. Grease and flour a 9" loaf pan, tapping out excess flour.

In a medium bowl, whisk together the flour, baking powder, and salt.

In a large bowl of an electric mixer, beat the butter, ricotta, and sugar until smooth and light. Scrape bowl.

Beat in the eggs, one at a time, just until blended.

With mixer on low, beat the vanilla-bean paste and extract into the cake batter.

Add the flour mixture, a little at a time, until blended. Scrape bowl.

Spread batter into prepared pan, then "cut" through (about halfway down into batter) from end to end with a thin metal spatula to rid batter of any large air pockets.

Bake for 25 minutes. Reduce oven temperature to 325 degrees. Continue baking for 30 to 45 minutes or until the cake springs back when lightly touched and a toothpick inserted in the center comes out clean.

Cool in pan on a wire rack for 15 minutes. Then run a knife around the inside edge of pan and carefully remove the pound cake. Cool completely on wire rack.

When ready to serve, dust with sifted confectioners' sugar. Serves 8-10.

Moist and flavorful, John's pound cake is the perfect treat.

John's Perfect Pound Cakes

This recipe makes a perfect pound cake: flavorful, soft and tender, and a "springboard" for fresh berries (think strawberry pound cake) or vanilla ice cream and Jane's Butterscotch Sauce (see index). Or, secretly sliced and nibbled for breakfast . . .

3 cups cake flour, sifted
½ tsp. salt
2 tsp. baking powder
2 cups unsalted butter, room
   temperature, cut into pieces
2 cups granulated sugar
1 tbsp. vanilla extract
6 large eggs

A SLICE OF ADVICE FROM JOHN

Before spreading the batter in the pans, pinch some between your finger and thumb to be sure the sugar has dissolved. If it hasn't, beat on medium just until the batter is ready. Do not overbeat.

Heat oven to 350 degrees. Grease 2 9" by 5" loaf pans.

In a medium bowl, whisk together the cake flour, salt, and baking powder.

In a large bowl of an electric mixer, beat the butter and sugar until light and fluffy. Stir in the vanilla extract. Scrape bowl.

Add the eggs, one at a time, beating well after each addition. With mixer on low, beat in the flour mixture, ½ cup at a time, until combined. Scrape bowl. Beat at medium speed for 30 seconds.

Spread batter in prepared pans, then "cut" through (about halfway down into batter) from end to end with a thin metal spatula to rid batter of any large air pockets. Bake for 50 to 65 minutes or until a toothpick inserted in the centers comes out with a few moist crumbs attached.

Cool in pans on a wire rack for 35 minutes. Then run a knife around the inside edge of pans and carefully remove the pound cakes. Cool completely on wire rack. Serves 8-10 per cake.

The toffee chips soften and melt ever so slightly in this Tantalizing Toffee Pound Cake,
and the Hot Butterscotch Sauce pairs perfectly with the cake.

Tantalizing Toffee Pound Cake with Hot Butterscotch Sauce

The toffee chips add a butterscotch flavor to a great pound-cake flavor. Drizzle with a hot butterscotch sauce and . . . oh my!

1 cup unsalted butter, room
    temperature, cut into pieces
½ cup granulated sugar
½ cup firmly packed light brown sugar
5 large eggs
2 tsp. vanilla extract
2 cups unbleached, all-purpose flour
½ tsp. baking powder
½ tsp. salt
½ cup English toffee chips

SAUCE

1 cup firmly packed light brown sugar
⅔ cup light corn syrup
¼ cup unsalted butter, cut into pieces
⅔ cup evaporated milk
⅛ tsp. baking soda
1 tsp. vanilla extract

A SLICE OF ADVICE FROM BEV

Leftover sauce? Place in a covered jar and refrigerate for later use atop ice cream or fresh apple or pear slices. To reheat the sauce, place the jar in a pan of warm water until the sauce is fluid.

Heat oven to 325 degrees. Grease and flour a 9" by 5" loaf pan, tapping out excess flour.

In a large bowl of an electric mixer, beat the butter, sugar, and brown sugar until light and fluffy. Scrape down sides and bottom of bowl. With mixer on low, add the eggs, one at a time, beating well after each addition. Add vanilla and beat well. Scrape bowl.

In a small bowl, whisk together the flour, baking powder, and salt. Add flour mixture to butter mixture, beating just until smooth. Scrape bowl.

Quickly and gently stir in the toffee chips. Spread batter into prepared pan, then "cut" through (about halfway down into batter) from end to end with a thin metal spatula to rid batter of any large air pockets.

Bake for 52 to 62 minutes or until a toothpick inserted in the center comes out clean. Cool in pan on a wire rack for 15 minutes. Then run a knife around the inside edge of pan and carefully remove the pound cake. Cool completely on wire rack.

For the Sauce: In a medium saucepan, combine the sugar, syrup, and butter. Cook, stirring constantly, over medium heat until sugar has dissolved and mixture comes to a full rolling boil. Turn heat down and allow mixture to cook on a low boil, without stirring, for 1 minute.

Remove from heat and let stand for 5 minutes.

In a large measuring cup, whisk together the evaporated milk, baking soda, and vanilla. Stir into the sauce. Makes 2 cups.

When ready to serve, drizzle some of the Hot Butterscotch Sauce atop each slice of cake on a plate. Serves 8-10.

Full-Flavored Fudge Pound Cake

Deep, dark, and chocolaty—this pound cake is a chocoholic's delight.

½ cup unsalted butter, room temperature, cut into pieces
1 tsp. baking powder
½ tsp. baking soda
¾ tsp. salt
1¼ cups granulated sugar
2 tsp. vanilla extract
½ cup unsweetened cocoa powder, sifted
4 large eggs
1¼ cups unbleached, all-purpose flour
¼ cup buttermilk

A SLICE OF ADVICE FROM BEV

In the mood for a chocolate sensation? Toast slices of this Full-Flavored Fudge Pound Cake and serve with fudge swirl ice cream and fudge sauce! You can *never* have too much chocolate.

Heat oven to 350 degrees. Lightly grease a 9" by 5" loaf pan.

In a large bowl of an electric mixer, beat the butter, baking powder, baking soda, salt, and sugar.

With mixer on low, stir in the vanilla and cocoa powder. Scrape bowl.

Add the eggs, one at a time, beating just until combined. With mixer on low, alternately add the flour and the buttermilk until combined.

Spread batter into prepared pan, then "cut" through (about halfway down into batter) from end to end with a thin metal spatula to rid batter of any large air pockets.

Bake for 44 to 58 minutes or until a toothpick inserted in the center comes out with moist crumbs attached.

Cool in pan on a wire rack for 35 minutes. Then run a knife around the inside edge of pan and carefully remove the pound cake. Cool completely on a wire rack. Serves 8-10.

CAKES TO DIE FOR!

Full flavored? Fudge pound cake? Bring on the ice cream and fudge sauce!

Marmalade-Glazed "Not-So-Many-Pounds" Cake

Fellow baker and tester Darlene commented that this even "smelled delicious baking." And the taste? It's one of the best "pound" cakes she's ever made.

1½ cups unbleached, all-purpose flour
2 tsp. baking powder
¼ tsp. salt
1⅛ cups plain, low-fat yogurt, well drained
1 cup granulated sugar
3 large eggs
1 tsp. freshly grated orange zest
¼ tsp. vanilla extract
½ cup light olive oil

GLAZE

⅓ cup orange marmalade
1 tsp. water

A SLICE OF ADVICE FROM BEV

This cake may be made 1 day ahead, unglazed, then wrapped well and stored at room temperature.

Light olive oil, with its delicate flavor, is perfect for baking. (Don't be fooled, however, into thinking it's lighter in calories!)

Heat oven to 350 degrees. Grease an 8½" by 4½" loaf pan.

In a medium bowl, whisk together the flour, baking powder, and salt.

In a large bowl, stir together the yogurt, sugar, eggs, zest, and vanilla, just until blended.

Whisk in the flour mixture. Using a rubber spatula, quickly and gently fold in the oil.

Spread batter into prepared pan. Place pan atop a baking sheet. Bake for 48 to 52 minutes or until a toothpick inserted in the center comes out clean.

Cool in pan on a wire rack for 15 minutes. Then run a knife around the inside edge of pan and carefully remove the pound cake. Cool completely on wire rack.

For the Glaze: In a small saucepan, stir together the marmalade and water over medium heat until the marmalade "melts." Brush hot mixture over top of cake. Let glaze cool and set. Serves 8-10.

Oh! That Orange Poppy-Seed Cake with Orange Glaze

My dear friend, Lili, says, "I love this cake. I could take it to my room and eat the whole thing!" Fortunately for her husband, Bob, she does share.

2 cups unbleached, all-purpose flour
1 tbsp. poppy seeds
1 tsp. baking soda
½ tsp. baking powder
½ tsp. salt
1 cup granulated sugar
½ cup unsalted butter, room temperature, cut into pieces
1 cup sour cream
1 large egg
2 tsp. freshly grated orange zest
⅓ cup fresh orange juice

ORANGE GLAZE

12 tbsp. confectioners' sugar, sifted
2 tbsp. fresh orange juice

Heat oven to 350 degrees. Grease an 8" square baking pan.

In a medium bowl, whisk together the flour, poppy seeds, baking soda, baking powder, and salt.

In a large bowl of an electric mixer, beat the sugar and butter until light and fluffy. Scrape bowl.

With mixer on low, add the sour cream, egg, and orange zest, beating until well combined.

With mixer on low, alternately beat the flour mixture and the orange juice into the sugar mixture until blended. Scrape bowl.

Spread batter into prepared pan. Bake for 40 to 46 minutes or until a toothpick inserted in the center comes out clean.

For the Orange Glaze: In a small bowl, whisk together the confectioners' sugar and orange juice until smooth. Spread or drizzle over warm cake.

Cake may be served warm or at room temperature. Serves 2-9 (depending on whether you're at Lili's home or making this yourself!).

Cookies 'n Cream Cake

This cake is delicious, fun, and, without the topping (which makes it a little more "la-di-da"), will make you the envy of the lunchbox crowd.

2 cups unbleached, all-purpose flour
1½ cups granulated sugar
1 cup sour cream
½ cup unsalted butter, room temperature, cut into pieces
½ cup water
1 tsp. baking soda
1 tsp. baking powder
2 large eggs
18 cream-filled chocolate sandwich cookies, coarsely chopped

TOPPING

1 cup heavy cream
3 tbsp. granulated sugar

Filled chocolate sandwich cookies, coarsely chopped

Heat oven to 350 degrees. Grease and flour a 13" by 9" baking pan, tapping out excess flour.

In a large bowl of an electric mixer, beat together the flour, sugar, sour cream, butter, water, baking soda, baking powder, and eggs on low speed to combine. Scrape bowl. With mixer on high, beat ingredients until well combined. Scrape bowl.

Gently and quickly stir the chopped cookies into the batter. Spread into prepared pan.

Bake for 36 to 40 minutes or until cake springs back when lightly touched or a toothpick inserted in the center comes out clean. Cool completely on a wire rack.

For the Topping: In a small bowl of an electric mixer, beat together the heavy cream and sugar on high speed until stiff. Spread atop cake and garnish with additional chopped cookies. Serves 12-16. (Leftovers? Store covered in the refrigerator.)

This is the "la-di-da" version of a simple yet sensational Cookies 'n Cream Cake.

A Chip Off the Old Whipped-Cream Loaf

Heavy cream in the batter adds a rich decadence to this not-too-sweet, tender loaf cake.

1½ cups unbleached, all-purpose flour
1 cup granulated sugar
2 tsp. baking powder
½ tsp. salt
1 cup heavy cream, cold
2 large eggs, lightly beaten
1 tsp. vanilla
½ cup mini chocolate chips

Heat oven to 350 degrees. Grease and flour a 9" by 5" loaf pan, tapping out excess flour.

In a medium bowl, whisk together the flour, sugar, baking powder, and salt.

In a large bowl of an electric mixer, beat the heavy cream until soft peaks form. Add the eggs and vanilla, and continue beating just until blended.

Quickly and gently stir in the flour mixture and chocolate chips just until blended.

Spread batter into prepared pan. Bake for 42 to 60 minutes or until a toothpick inserted in the center comes out clean.

Cool in pan on a wire rack for 15 minutes. Then run a knife around the inside edge of pan and carefully remove the loaf cake. Cool completely on wire rack. Serves 8-10.

"Packed to Go" Apple Cake

A picnic? Office lunch? After-school snack? This cake is perfect for any of these.

½ cup unsalted butter, room temperature, cut into pieces
¾ cup granulated sugar
½ cup firmly packed light brown sugar
¼ cup firmly packed dark brown sugar
1 cup buttermilk
2 tsp. baking soda
2 large eggs
2¼ cups unbleached, all-purpose flour
1 tsp. ground cinnamon
1 tsp. freshly grated nutmeg
½ tsp. salt
2 cups peeled, chopped tart apples

CRUMB TOPPING

½ cup chopped pecans, toasted
¼ cup granulated sugar
¼ cup firmly packed dark brown sugar
½ tsp. ground cinnamon

Heat oven to 350 degrees. Grease and flour a 13" by 9" baking pan, tapping out excess flour.

In a large bowl of an electric mixer, beat butter until creamy. Beat in the granulated sugar and brown sugars until mixture is fluffy. Scrape bowl.

In a small bowl, whisk together the buttermilk and baking soda. With mixer on low, beat in butter mixture. Blend in the eggs, flour, cinnamon, nutmeg, and salt, mixing until well combined. Quickly and gently stir in apple pieces.

For the Crumb Topping: In a small bowl, combine the pecans, granulated sugar, brown sugar, and cinnamon, stirring to blend well. Sprinkle evenly over cake batter. Bake for 28 to 36 minutes or until a toothpick inserted in the center comes out clean.

Cool pan on a wire rack. Serve cake warm. Serves 15-18.

Graham Crumbs Apple Snack Cake

Graham cracker crumbs sub for flour in this surprising treat of a snack cake.

3 large eggs
1 cup granulated sugar
½ cup unsalted butter, melted
2 cups graham cracker crumbs
2 medium-size, tart apples, peeled, cored, and chopped
1½ tsp. ground cinnamon
4 tbsp. confectioners' sugar, sifted

Heat oven to 350 degrees. Lightly grease an 8" square cake pan.

In a medium bowl, whisk the eggs until blended. Add the granulated sugar and butter, mixing well.

Stir in the graham cracker crumbs, apple pieces, and cinnamon until well blended.

Spread batter into prepared pan. Bake for 38 to 45 minutes or until firm to the touch. Cool on a wire rack. When ready to serve, sprinkle with confectioners' sugar. Serves 9.

Fresh Stalks of Rhubarb Cake

I love those tart stalks of fresh rhubarb . . . those harbingers of spring . . . especially when they're baked into a delectable cake.

2 cups unbleached, all-purpose flour
1 tsp. baking soda
¼ tsp. salt
1 cup firmly packed light brown sugar
½ cup firmly packed dark brown sugar
½ cup unsalted butter, room temperature, cut into pieces
1 large egg
1 tsp. vanilla extract
1 cup milk, whole
1 tbsp. fresh lemon juice
2 cups chopped fresh rhubarb stalks

TOPPING

½ cup chopped pecans, toasted
¼ cup granulated sugar
1 tsp. ground cinnamon

A SLICE OF ADVICE FROM BEV

This cake is best served warm, but room temperature will do!

Rhubarb is botanically a vegetable, not a fruit. Remember when cleaning fresh rhubarb that only the stalks are edible (the leaves can be poisonous). Choose fresh-looking stalks that are firm and crisp; depending on the type, the color should be either light pink or streaked green and cherry red.

Heat oven to 350 degrees. Grease and flour a 13" by 9" cake pan, tapping out excess flour.

In a medium bowl, whisk together the flour, baking soda, and salt.

In a large bowl of an electric mixer, beat brown sugars and butter until light and fluffy. Beat in egg and vanilla until well mixed. Scrape bowl.

In a glass measuring cup, combine milk and lemon juice. With mixer on low, alternately add milk mixture and flour mixture to butter mixture. Scrape bowl.

Quickly and gently fold in rhubarb pieces. Spread batter into prepared pan.

For the Topping: In a small bowl, combine the nuts, sugar, and cinnamon. Sprinkle evenly over batter. Bake for 38 to 45 minutes or until a toothpick inserted in the center comes out clean.

Cool on a wire rack until warm. Serves 12.

Italian Cassata

Italian bakeries and Italian weddings in New York and New Jersey were part of my formative years ... and so was this classic cassata!

2 cups cake flour, sifted
1 cup granulated sugar
1 tsp. baking powder
⅛ tsp. salt
¾ cup unsalted butter, room temperature, cut into pieces
3 large eggs
¼ cup milk, whole

RICOTTA FILLING

2 cups whole-milk ricotta cheese
½ cup granulated sugar
1 tbsp. freshly grated orange zest

GLAZE

1½ cups semisweet chocolate, coarsely chopped
½ cup unsalted butter, room temperature, cut into pieces

Heat oven to 350 degrees. Grease and flour an 8" by 4" loaf pan, tapping out excess flour.

In a large bowl of an electric mixer, combine the flour, sugar, baking powder, and salt. With mixer on low, add the butter and beat until well blended. Scrape bowl.

Add eggs, one at a time, beating well after each addition. With mixer on medium, stir in the milk and beat mixture until smooth.

Spread batter into prepared pan. Bake for 50 to 55 minutes or until a toothpick inserted in the center comes out with a few moist crumbs attached.

Cool in pan on a wire rack for 15 minutes. Then run a knife around the inside edge of pan and carefully remove the cake. Cool completely on a wire rack.

For the Ricotta Filling: In a small bowl, whisk together the ricotta, sugar, and zest. Refrigerate until ready to use.

To Assemble Cassata: Carefully slice cake horizontally into 3 even layers. Place top layer, cut side up, on a serving platter. Spread *half* of the Ricotta Filling over layer, spreading to the edges.

Place second layer of cake on top. Spread remaining Ricotta Filling over layer, spreading to the edges. Top with the third layer of cake.

Cover with plastic wrap and refrigerate overnight to allow cake to set.

For the Glaze: In a small saucepan, melt the chocolate and butter, stirring constantly, until melted and smooth. Refrigerate to allow glaze to thicken *just* to a spreading consistency.

When the cassata is set and ready to serve, spread the glaze with a thin, flexible metal spatula on the sides and top of the cake. Refrigerate for 30 minutes. Serves 8-10.

Simple Weeknight Cake

This is a simple yet delicious cake, perfect for a weeknight treat.

⅔ cup unbleached, all-purpose flour
½ tsp. baking powder
⅔ cup unsalted butter, room temperature, cut into pieces
⅔ cup granulated sugar
2 large eggs
¼ tsp. vanilla extract

WEEKNIGHT GLAZE

2 tbsp. fresh lemon juice
2 tbsp. confectioners' sugar, sifted

A SLICE OF ADVICE FROM BEV

Glazing the cake while it's in the pan helps infuse additional flavors and moisture.

Heat oven to 350 degrees. Grease an 8½" by 4½" loaf pan.

In a small bowl, stir together the flour and baking powder.

In a large bowl of an electric mixer, beat the butter until creamy. Mix in the sugar, beating until fluffy. Scrape bowl.

Add the eggs, one at a time, just until combined. With mixer on low, beat in the vanilla.

Stir in the flour mixture until combined. Spread batter into prepared pan. Bake for 25 to 38 minutes or until a toothpick inserted in the center comes out clean.

Cool in pan for 10 minutes.

For the Weeknight Glaze: In a small bowl, whisk together the lemon juice and confectioners' sugar until smooth. Spread atop cake while still warm.

Cool pan completely on a wire rack. Run a knife around the inside edge of pan and remove cake. Serves 6-8.

The Tartness of Cranberry Cake with Silky Butter Sauce

I adore the tartness that cranberries bring to a sweet cake base. This is one of my favorite quick and easy dessert cakes.

1½ cups unbleached, all-purpose flour
¾ cup granulated sugar
1½ tsp. baking powder
¼ tsp. salt
1½ cups cranberries, fresh or frozen,
    coarsely chopped
¾ cup milk, whole
2 tbsp. unsalted butter, melted

SILKY BUTTER SAUCE

½ cup firmly packed light brown sugar
1½ tsp. unbleached, all-purpose flour
¼ cup half-and-half
¼ cup unsalted butter, cut into pieces
1 tsp. vanilla extract

Heat oven to 350 degrees. Grease and flour an 8" square cake pan, tapping out excess flour.

In a large bowl, combine the flour, sugar, baking powder, and salt, stirring to blend. Quickly and gently stir in cranberry pieces.

Add milk and butter, stirring just until batter is mixed. Spread into prepared pan.

Bake for 25 to 35 minutes or until a toothpick inserted in the center comes out clean. Cool on a wire rack.

For the Silky Butter Sauce: In a small saucepan, whisk together the sugar and the flour. Stir in the half-and-half and butter and cook over medium heat, stirring constantly, until mixture is thickened and bubbly.

Remove from heat and stir in vanilla. Serve cake with warm Silky Butter Sauce. Serves 9-12.

A Hint of Whole Wheat Date Snack Cake

A hint of whole wheat and the sweetness of dates and coconut make this a perfect pick-me-up snack cake.

¾ cup unbleached, all-purpose flour
¾ cup whole-wheat pastry flour or
   whole-wheat flour
2 tsp. baking powder
½ tsp. baking soda
¼ tsp. salt
1 cup pitted, chopped dates
1 cup unsweetened applesauce
¼ cup water
2 tbsp. light olive oil
1½ tsp. ground cinnamon
2 large eggs

COCONUT TOPPING

1 cup unsweetened coconut flakes
1 tbsp. milk

Heat oven to 350 degrees. Grease and flour a 9" round cake pan, tapping out excess flour.

In a medium bowl, whisk together the flours, baking powder, baking soda, and salt.

In a food processor, combine the dates, applesauce, water, oil, cinnamon, and eggs. Pulse to combine, stopping to scrape down sides of the work bowl.

Add flour mixture to food processor, pulsing just until mixture is combined. Spread batter into prepared pan.

For the Coconut Topping: In a small bowl, quickly stir together the coconut flakes and milk. Sprinkle evenly over cake batter.

Bake for 32 to 45 minutes or until a toothpick inserted in the center comes out clean. Cool in pan on a wire rack. Serves 9-12.

A SLICE OF ADVICE FROM BEV

The best dates are Medjool dates, prized for their large size and extraordinary sweetness.

Banana Snack Cake with Cream Cheese Frosting

When you have overripe bananas on hand, this is the perfect cake to bake!

1¼ cups unbleached, all-purpose flour
1 tsp. baking powder
½ tsp. baking soda
½ tsp. salt
½ tsp. ground cinnamon
⅛ tsp. freshly grated nutmeg
⅓ cup unsalted butter, room temperature, cut into pieces
¾ cup granulated sugar
¾ cup mashed ripe bananas
¼ cup buttermilk
1 tsp. vanilla extract
1 large egg
¼ cup coarsely chopped walnuts, toasted

CREAM CHEESE FROSTING

3 oz. cream cheese, room temperature, cut into pieces
2 tbsp. unsalted butter, room temperature, cut into pieces
2 cups confectioners' sugar, sifted
1 tbsp. milk, plus more if needed
½ tsp. vanilla extract

Heat oven to 350 degrees. Grease and flour a 9" square cake pan, tapping out excess flour.

In a medium bowl, whisk together the flour, baking powder, baking soda, salt, cinnamon, and nutmeg.

In a large bowl of an electric mixer, beat butter until creamy. Add sugar and beat until light and fluffy. With mixer on low, stir in bananas, buttermilk, vanilla and egg until blended. Stir in the flour mixture until well combined. Scrape bowl, then stir in walnuts.

Spread batter into prepared pan. Bake for 22 to 32 minutes or until a toothpick inserted in the center comes out clean. Cool completely on a wire rack.

For the Cream Cheese Frosting: In a large bowl of an electric mixer, beat the cream cheese and butter until creamy. With mixer on medium, add the confectioners' sugar, milk and vanilla until mixture is smooth. Add additional milk if needed to reach desired spreading consistency. Spread over cake. Serves 9-12.

A SLICE OF ADVICE FROM BEV

Usually, 2 to 3 ripe, medium-size bananas are all it takes to make ¾ cup, mashed.

Fudgy Snack Cake

My not-too-sweet version of a chocolaty, fudgy snack cake would be perfect with fresh summer berries or a tart, fall cranberry sauce.

1 cup unbleached, all-purpose flour
½ cup unsweetened cocoa powder, sifted
½ tsp. baking soda
¼ tsp. salt
5 tbsp. unsalted butter, room
    temperature, cut into pieces
1¼ cups granulated sugar
1 tsp. vanilla extract
2 large eggs
⅔ cup buttermilk

Heat oven to 350 degrees. Lightly grease an 8″ square cake pan.

In a medium bowl, whisk together the flour, cocoa, baking soda, and salt.

In a large bowl of an electric mixer, beat the butter until creamy. With mixer on medium, beat in the sugar and vanilla until fluffy.

Add eggs, one at a time, beating just until combined. With mixer on low, alternately add the flour mixture and the buttermilk to the sugar mixture, mixing just until smooth.

Spread batter into prepared pan. Bake for 30 to 35 minutes or until a toothpick inserted in the center comes out clean.

Run a knife around the inside edge of pan and carefully remove the cake. Cool completely on a wire rack. Serves 9-12.

Lemon Rosemary Cake with Fresh Lemon Glaze

This cake has such bright flavors, and rosemary helps it cross over from a simply sweet cake to a treat that would go perfectly as a ladies' luncheon "bread."

2 cups unbleached, all-purpose flour
1½ tsp. baking powder
¼ tsp. salt
2 tsp. freshly grated lemon zest
2 tsp. finely chopped fresh rosemary
⅓ cup light olive oil
1 cup granulated sugar
2 large eggs
¾ cup buttermilk

GLAZE

¾ cup confectioners' sugar, sifted
3 tbsp. fresh lemon juice

A SLICE OF ADVICE FROM BEV

One of my testers also made this with lemon-infused olive oil for an even lighter, more flavorful cake.

Heat oven to 325 degrees. Grease a 9" by 5" loaf pan.

In a medium bowl, whisk together the flour, baking powder, salt, zest, and rosemary. Set aside.

In a large bowl with an electric mixer, beat the oil and sugar until well blended. With mixer on medium, add the eggs, one at a time, until mixture is a pale yellow. Scrape down sides and bottom of bowl.

Alternately add the flour mixture and the buttermilk to the sugar mixture, stirring just to blend.

Spread batter into prepared pan. Bake for 52 to 58 minutes or until golden and a toothpick inserted in the center comes out with a few moist crumbs attached. Cool in pan on a wire rack for 15 minutes.

For the Glaze: In a medium bowl, whisk together the confectioners' sugar and lemon juice until mixture is smooth. Spread glaze atop *warm* cake.

Cool completely on wire rack. When ready to serve, run a knife around the inside edge of pan and carefully remove the Lemon Rosemary Cake. Serves 8-10.

CAKES TO DIE FOR!

This Lemon Rosemary Cake with Fresh Lemon Glaze is perfect for a ladies' luncheon, garden party with grilled fish, or midday snack.

BUNDT CAKES AND TUBE CAKES

This Toasted Almond Cake with White Chocolate Glaze is a showpiece. Your eyes and mouth will thank you with every bite.

Cakes made in Bundt pans or tube pans, once unmolded, are perfect "centerpiece" desserts for a brunch or holiday buffet. Place on an antique cake stand, perhaps one with a family history just waiting to be revealed, and listen for the "oohs" and "aahs"—even before they taste!

There are enough flavor profiles and texture variations, with glazes and sauces and infused whipped cream, to keep you busy for some time trying to determine which might be *your* favorite.

Toasted Almond Cake with White Chocolate Glaze

This cake is a showpiece—with subtle flavors and beautiful "eye appeal." It's worthy of your finest cake stand, china, and silver (but it'll do just fine on paper plates, too).

1½ cups granulated sugar
¾ cup unsalted butter, room
   temperature, cut into pieces
2½ cups unbleached, all-purpose flour
1⅓ cups milk, whole
1 tbsp. baking powder
2 tsp. vanilla extract
½ tsp. salt
2 large eggs, lightly beaten
⅔ cup almonds, toasted and cooled, then
   very finely chopped

WHITE CHOCOLATE GLAZE

3½ oz. coarsely chopped white chocolate
2 tbsp. unsalted butter, room
   temperature, cut into pieces
2 tbsp. corn syrup
1 to 2 tsp. hot water

Heat oven to 350 degrees. Grease and flour a 12-cup Bundt cake pan, tapping out excess flour.

In a large bowl of an electric mixer, beat the sugar and butter until light and fluffy. Scrape bowl.

With mixer on low, add the flour, milk, baking powder, vanilla, salt, and eggs, blending until well combined. Scrape bowl.

Quickly and gently stir in almonds. Spread batter into prepared pan.

Bake for 42 to 49 minutes or until a toothpick inserted in the center comes out clean.

Cool in pan on a wire rack for 15 minutes. Then run a knife around the inside edge of pan and carefully remove the cake. Cool completely on wire rack.

Place cake on rack atop a large piece of waxed paper.

For the White Chocolate Glaze: In a small saucepan, heat the chocolate, butter, and corn syrup over low heat, stirring constantly, until chocolate is melted. Cool slightly.

Whisk in the hot water, 1 tsp. at a time, until glaze is the consistency of thick syrup. Drizzle atop cooled cake. Allow to set for at least 30 minutes. Place on a cake stand to serve. Serves 12-16.

Blueberry Crunch Tube Cake

All the elements of a perfect cake confection—a surprise crunch on top, a moist cake, and a burst of fresh fruit.

½ cup toasted, finely chopped walnuts
½ cup firmly packed light brown sugar
2 tbsp. unbleached, all-purpose flour
2 tsp. ground cinnamon
2 tbsp. unsalted butter, melted

TUBE CAKE

1½ cups unbleached, all-purpose flour
¾ cup granulated sugar
1 tbsp. baking powder
½ tsp. salt
¼ tsp. ground cinnamon
⅓ cup unsalted butter, cut into pieces
1 cup fresh blueberries, gently washed
  and dried
1 large egg
½ cup milk, whole
1 tsp. vanilla extract

Confectioners' sugar, sifted

A SLICE OF ADVICE FROM BEV

Don't be discouraged by this rather thick batter. Patience makes for a perfect (and very tasty) tube cake.

Heat oven to 350 degrees. Grease and flour a 9" tube pan, tapping out excess flour.

In a medium bowl, mix together the walnuts, brown sugar, flour, and cinnamon until combined. Stir in melted butter just until coarse crumbs form. Pat about half of this streusel mixture into the pan.

For the Tube Cake: In a large bowl of an electric mixer, mix together the flour, sugar, baking powder, salt, and cinnamon. Cut in butter until mixture resembles coarse crumbs. With a spatula, gently stir in blueberries.

Beat egg lightly with the milk and vanilla. Quickly and gently stir into berry mixture just until combined. Spread *half* the batter into streusel-lined pan. Sprinkle with remaining streusel, then spread with remaining batter.

Bake for 40 to 48 minutes or until a toothpick inserted in the center comes out clean.

Cool in pan on a wire rack for 25 minutes. Then run a knife around the inside edge of pan and carefully remove the cake. Cool completely on wire rack.

When ready to serve, dust cake with confectioners' sugar. Serves 12-16.

A crunch of this and a streusel of that . . . this Blueberry Crunch Tube Cake is a mouthful.

Blueberry Bundt Cake with Blueberry Syrup

Fresh blueberries swirled inside a moist cake . . . and to top it all off, the rich colors and bright flavors of a blueberry syrup.

3 cups plus 1 tbsp. unbleached, all-purpose flour, divided
1½ cups fresh blueberries
1 tbsp. baking powder
½ tsp. salt
¾ cup unsalted butter, room temperature, cut into pieces
2 cups granulated sugar
3 large eggs
¾ cup milk, whole

BLUEBERRY SYRUP

1½ lb. fresh blueberries
2 cups granulated sugar
1 vanilla bean, split lengthwise
¾ cup water
1 tbsp. fresh lemon juice

TOPPING

Confectioners' sugar, sifted
Fresh blueberries

Heat oven to 350 degrees. Grease and flour a 12-cup Bundt pan, tapping out excess flour.

In a medium bowl, gently toss together 1 tbsp. flour with the fresh blueberries. In another medium bowl, whisk together the remaining 3 cups flour, baking powder, and salt.

In a large bowl of an electric mixer, cream the butter and sugar until light and fluffy. Beat in the eggs, one at a time, until blended. Scrape bowl.

With mixer on low, alternately add the flour mixture and the milk to the butter mixture until well blended. Scrape bowl.

Quickly and gently fold in the blueberry mixture. Spread batter into prepared pan. Bake for 65 to 85 minutes or until a toothpick inserted near the center comes out clean.

Cool in pan on a wire rack for 15 minutes. Then run a knife around the inside edge of pan and carefully remove the cake. Cool completely on wire rack.

For the Blueberry Syrup: In a large saucepan, combine the blueberries and sugar. Quickly and gently toss mixture until combined. Place split vanilla bean in the center of it all. Let mixture macerate for 40 minutes.

Bring the mixture to a boil, gently stirring in the water and lemon juice. Reduce heat to a simmer and cook, stirring occasionally, until mixture begins to thicken, about 20 minutes.

Remove from heat and strain through a fine-mesh sieve. Discard solids and cool syrup to room temperature.

When ready to serve, place the Blueberry Bundt Cake on a cake stand and dust top of cake with confectioners' sugar. Place fresh blueberries in the center space of the cake.

Serve each slice with a generous drizzle of Blueberry Syrup. Serves 12-16.

CAKES TO DIE FOR!

A Plethora of Citrus Pound Cake with Lime Glaze

Should only those who can spell "plethora" be allowed to enjoy a slice of this refreshingly moist cake? Maybe we won't be so harsh, this time!

2 tsp. freshly grated grapefruit zest
2 tsp. freshly grated lime zest
2 tsp. freshly grated lemon zest
2 tsp. freshly grated orange zest
½ cup milk, whole
1 tbsp. fresh lime juice
2¼ cups unbleached, all-purpose flour
¾ tsp. baking powder
½ tsp. baking soda
¼ tsp. salt
1¼ cups unsalted butter, room temperature, cut into pieces
1½ cups granulated sugar
3 large eggs

LIME GLAZE

2 tbsp. unsalted butter, melted
¾ cup confectioners' sugar, sifted
1 tsp. freshly grated lime zest
1 to 2 tbsp. fresh lime juice

A SLICE OF ADVICE FROM BEV

Remember, no pith . . . grating just the outside colored flesh of the citrus will help ensure a refreshing (and not bitter) taste.

Heat oven to 350 degrees. Grease and flour a 12-cup tube pan, tapping out excess flour.

In a medium glass bowl, stir together the grapefruit zest, lime zest, lemon zest, orange zest, milk, and lime juice.

In a medium bowl, whisk together the flour, baking powder, baking soda, and salt.

In a large bowl of an electric mixer, beat the butter and sugar until light and fluffy. Scrape bowl.

Beat in the eggs, one at a time, until blended. With mixer on low, alternately add the zest mixture and the flour mixture to the butter mixture *just* until combined. Scrape bowl.

Spread batter into prepared pan. Bake for 42 to 55 minutes or until a toothpick inserted near the center comes out clean.

Cool in pan on a wire rack for 15 minutes. Then run a knife around the inside edge of pan and carefully remove the cake. Cool completely on wire rack.

When ready to serve, place cake on rack atop a large piece of waxed paper.

For the Lime Glaze: In a small bowl, whisk together the butter, confectioners' sugar, lime zest, and enough lime juice to reach a glaze consistency. Drizzle over cooled cake. Serves 12-16.

The delicately flavored Tea-Infused Whipped Cream is the perfect accompaniment to this "Three Lemons" Cake.

"Three Lemons" Cake with Tea-Infused Whipped Cream

Zest, juice, and extract make three . . . with a tea-infused whipped cream that will be the talk of your next "tea party."

2 cups granulated sugar
1 cup unsalted butter, room
    temperature, cut into pieces
4 large eggs, separated
3 cups unbleached, all-purpose flour
2 tsp. baking powder
1 cup milk, whole
2 tsp. freshly grated lemon zest
1 tbsp. lemon juice
1 tsp. lemon extract

CREAM

2 cups heavy cream
2 tbsp. confectioners' sugar, sifted
1 tsp. unsweetened (dry) instant tea

Heat oven to 350 degrees. Grease and flour a 10" tube pan, tapping out excess flour.

In a large bowl of an electric mixer, beat the sugar and butter until light and fluffy. Scrape bowl.

Add egg yolks, beating until creamy. Scrape bowl.

In a small bowl, whisk together the flour and baking powder. With mixer on low, alternately add the flour mixture and the milk to the butter mixture. Stir in the zest, lemon juice, and lemon extract. Scrape bowl.

In a small bowl of an electric mixer, beat the egg whites at high speed, scraping bowl often, just until stiff peaks form.

Gently fold the egg whites into the batter. Pour batter into prepared pan and bake for 54 to 66 minutes or until a toothpick inserted in the center comes out clean.

Cool in pan on a wire rack for 15 minutes. Then run a knife around the inside edge of pan and carefully remove the cake. Cool completely on wire rack.

For the Cream: In a large bowl of an electric mixer, beat the heavy cream, confectioners' sugar, and tea until stiff peaks form.

Serve cake slices with a large dollop of cream. Serves 12-16.

Whole-Wheat Lemon Poppy-Seed Cake

You'll love this loaded-with-poppy-seeds, flavorful, lemony cake, which I enjoy with a luncheon salad and a cup of tea!

1½ cups whole-wheat pastry flour
1 cup unbleached, all-purpose flour
¼ cup poppy seeds, toasted
1½ tsp. baking powder
½ tsp. baking soda
¼ tsp. salt
1 cup buttermilk
¼ cup light olive oil
1 tsp. vanilla extract
2 tbsp. freshly grated lemon zest
2 tbsp. fresh lemon juice
2 large eggs, room temperature
2 large egg whites, room temperature
1¼ cups granulated sugar

GLAZE

¾ cup confectioners' sugar, sifted
3 tbsp. fresh lemon juice
1 tbsp. lemon extract

Lemon sorbet or sherbet, optional

A SLICE OF ADVICE FROM BEV

Here's a little trick when baking with whole-wheat flour. Allow the cooled cake to sit, completely covered, for 1 day so that the bran has a chance to absorb. This way the flavors will mellow.

Toast poppy seeds in a small dry skillet over medium heat, stirring constantly, just until fragrant, 3 to 4 minutes. Transfer to a plate to cool.

Heat oven to 350 degrees. Grease and flour a 12-cup Bundt pan, tapping out excess flour.

In a medium bowl, whisk together the flours, poppy seeds, baking powder, baking soda, and salt.

In another medium bowl, whisk together the buttermilk, oil, vanilla, lemon zest, and lemon juice.

In a large bowl of an electric mixer, beat the eggs, egg whites, and sugar on medium speed until thick and pale yellow.

Using a spatula, alternately add the flour mixture and the buttermilk mixture to the egg mixture, a third at a time, until combined. Scrape bowl.

Spread the batter into prepared pan. Bake for 32 to 36 minutes or until a toothpick inserted in the center comes out clean and the top springs back when lightly touched.

Cool in pan on a wire rack for 15 minutes. Then run a knife around the inside edge of pan and carefully remove the cake.

Place cake on rack atop a large piece of waxed paper.

For the Glaze: In a small bowl, whisk together the confectioners' sugar, lemon juice, and lemon extract until smooth. With a thin wooden skewer, poke 12 to 14 deep holes over the entire cake. Using a pastry brush, coat the warm cake with the glaze.

Cool completely. Serve slices with a scoop of lemon sorbet or sherbet, if desired. Serves 12-16.

Minimal guilt, maximum pleasure . . . that's what this Whole-Wheat Lemon Poppy-Seed Cake is all about. (You'll love the flavors!)

Don't just obsess about it. Heat the oven, get out the mixing bowls and ingredients, and start baking!

Obsessed with Orange Almond Cake

A dense yet moist Bundt cake with a very intense almond flavor.

3 cups unbleached, all-purpose flour
1 tsp. baking powder
½ tsp. salt
1½ cups granulated sugar
½ cup unsalted butter, room
    temperature, cut into pieces
½ cup sour cream
2 tsp. freshly grated orange zest
3 large eggs
½ cup fresh orange juice

FILLING

½ cup orange marmalade
¼ cup almond paste, crumbled

GLAZE

¾ cup confectioners' sugar, sifted
1 to 2 tbsp. fresh orange juice

Heat oven to 350 degrees. Grease and flour a 12-cup Bundt pan, tapping out excess flour.

In a medium bowl, whisk together the flour, baking powder, and salt.

In a large bowl of an electric mixer, combine the sugar and butter, beating until creamy. Scrape down bowl.

With mixer on low, add sour cream and orange zest. Add eggs, one at a time, continuing to beat until smooth. Scrape bowl.

Alternately add the flour mixture and the orange juice until well combined.

For the Filling: In a food processor, combine the marmalade and almond paste. Pulse mixture until smooth.

Spread *half* of the cake batter into prepared pan. Spoon filling over batter in pan, then spread remaining batter on top of filling. Using a thin metal spatula, quickly and gently swirl filling into batter.

Bake for 50 to 55 minutes or until a toothpick inserted in the center comes out clean.

Cool in pan for 15 minutes. Then remove from pan and cool completely on wire rack set atop waxed paper.

For the Glaze: In a small bowl, whisk together the confectioners' sugar and orange juice until smooth and desired glazing consistency. Drizzle over cooled cake and allow glaze to set before serving. Serves 16.

Buttery Cream Cake with Citrus Slices and Orange Glaze

What better way to celebrate and congratulate an adult friend or family member than with this buttery cake with a Grand Marnier glaze?

1 cup unsalted butter, room
   temperature, cut into pieces
3 cups granulated sugar
6 large eggs
3 cups cake flour, sifted
½ tsp. baking powder
2 cups heavy cream
1 tbsp. vanilla extract
2 tbsp. freshly grated orange zest
2 tsp. orange extract

ORANGE GLAZE

2 cups confectioners' sugar, sifted
1 to 2 tbsp. Grand Marnier
1 to 2 tbsp. fresh orange juice

3 cups segments of fresh citrus fruit
   such as navel oranges, blood oranges,
   pink grapefruit

Heat oven to 325 degrees. Grease and flour a 10" Bundt or tube pan, tapping out excess flour.

In a large bowl of an electric mixer, beat butter until creamy. Add sugar and beat until mixture is light and fluffy.

Beat in the eggs, one at a time, until blended.

Stir together the cake flour and the baking powder. Alternately add the flour mixture and the heavy cream to the butter mixture, beating to combine. With mixer on low, blend in the vanilla extract, orange zest, and orange extract. Scrape bowl.

Spread batter into prepared pan. Bake for 64 to 82 minutes or until a toothpick inserted near the center comes out clean and the top springs back when lightly touched.

Cool in pan on a wire rack for 15 minutes. Then run a knife around the inside edge of pan and carefully remove the cake. Cool completely on wire rack.

When ready to serve, place cake on rack atop a large piece of waxed paper.

For the Orange Glaze: In a medium bowl, whisk together the confectioners' sugar, Grand Marnier, and orange juice, 1 tbsp. at a time, until a glaze consistency is reached. Spoon atop cake and allow to sit for 15 minutes before slicing.

Serve slices of Buttery Cream Cake with a mixture of segments of fresh citrus fruit. Serves 12-16.

CAKES TO DIE FOR!

Golden Orange Buttermilk Cake

Buttermilk always adds a moist texture to cakes, and this cake is loaded with orange flavor as well.

3 cups unbleached, all-purpose flour
½ tsp. baking powder
½ tsp. baking soda
½ tsp. salt
2 cups granulated sugar
1 cup unsalted butter, room temperature, cut into pieces
4 large eggs
¾ cup buttermilk
1 tbsp. freshly grated orange zest
1 tbsp. fresh orange juice

GLAZE

1¼ cups confectioners' sugar, sifted
2 tsp. fresh orange juice, pulp free
1 to 2 tbsp. water or additional fresh orange juice

Heat oven to 325 degrees. Grease and flour a 12-cup Bundt pan, tapping out excess flour.

In a medium bowl, whisk together the flour, baking powder, baking soda, and salt.

In a large bowl of an electric mixer, beat the sugar and butter until light and fluffy.

Beat in the eggs, one at a time, until blended. With mixer on low, gradually add the flour mixture alternately with the buttermilk until well mixed. Scrape bowl. Stir in the orange zest and orange juice until combined.

Spread batter into prepared pan. Bake for 50 to 66 minutes or until a toothpick inserted in the center comes out clean.

Cool in pan on a wire rack for 15 minutes. Then run a knife around the inside edge of pan and carefully remove the cake. Cool completely on wire rack.

When ready to serve, place cake on rack atop a large piece of waxed paper.

For the Glaze: In a medium bowl, whisk together the confectioners' sugar, orange juice, and just enough water or additional orange juice until the desired consistency is reached. Drizzle over cooled cake. Serves 12-14.

Pomegranate-Glazed Pomegranate Cake

Incredibly moist and loaded with healthful pomegranate.

2 cups unbleached, all-purpose flour
1¼ tsp. baking powder
½ tsp. baking soda
3 tbsp. unsalted butter, room
    temperature, cut into pieces
1 cup granulated sugar
2 large eggs
⅔ cup plain, nonfat yogurt
2 cups fresh pomegranate seeds, lightly
    chopped

POMEGRANATE GLAZE

½ cup confectioners' sugar, sifted
1 tbsp. pomegranate juice

Heat oven to 350 degrees. Grease a 10″ tube pan.

In a medium bowl, sift together the flour, baking powder, and baking soda.

In a large bowl of an electric mixer, beat the butter and sugar until light and fluffy. Scrape bowl.

Beat in the eggs, one at a time, until blended. With mixer on low, alternately beat flour mixture and yogurt into butter mixture, until well combined. Quickly and gently stir in pomegranate seeds.

Spread batter into prepared pan. Bake for 35 to 45 minutes or until a toothpick inserted in the center comes out clean.

Cool in pan on a wire rack for 15 minutes. Then run a knife around the inside edge of pan and carefully remove the cake.

Place cake on rack atop a large piece of waxed paper.

For the Pomegranate Glaze: In a small bowl, whisk the confectioners' sugar with the pomegranate juice until a glaze consistency is reached. Spoon over cake while still warm.

Cool completely on wire rack. Serves 12-16.

CAKES TO DIE FOR!

Cranberry Gingerbread Cake with Lemon Glaze

The sweet-tart flavor of cranberries is the perfect complement to the homey flavor of gingerbread.

2½ cups unbleached, all-purpose flour, divided
12 oz. dried cranberries
½ cup unsweetened cocoa powder
1 tsp. baking soda
½ tsp. salt
1¼ tsp. ground ginger
1 tsp. ground cinnamon
½ tsp. ground allspice
⅛ tsp. ground cloves
¼ tsp. freshly grated nutmeg
⅛ tsp. freshly ground black pepper
¾ cup unsalted butter, room temperature, cut into pieces
1¼ cups granulated sugar
1 tsp. vanilla extract
2 large eggs
1 cup molasses, preferably Barbados
1 cup hot water

LEMON GLAZE

1 cup confectioners' sugar, sifted
¼ tsp. lemon extract
1 to 2 tbsp. fresh lemon juice

Heat oven to 350 degrees. Grease and flour a 10-cup Bundt pan, tapping out excess flour.

In a small bowl, toss together 2 tbsp. flour and the dried cranberries.

In a medium bowl, whisk together the remaining flour, cocoa powder, baking soda, salt, ginger, cinnamon, allspice, cloves, nutmeg, and black pepper.

In a large bowl of an electric mixer, beat the butter and sugar until light and fluffy. With mixer on low, blend in vanilla. Scrape bowl.

Beat in the eggs, one at a time, until blended.

In a medium bowl, whisk together the molasses and hot water.

With mixer on low, alternately add the flour mixture and the molasses mixture to the sugar mixture, beating to combine. Quickly and gently fold in the dried cranberries.

Spread batter into prepared pan. Bake for 54 to 66 minutes or until a toothpick inserted near the center comes out clean.

Cool in pan on a wire rack for 15 minutes. Then run a knife around the inside edge of pan and carefully remove the cake.

Place cake on rack atop a large piece of waxed paper.

For the Lemon Glaze: In a medium bowl, whisk together the confectioners' sugar, lemon extract, and fresh lemon juice, 1 tbsp. at a time, until a drizzle consistency is reached. Drizzle over cake, and then allow cake to cool completely on wire rack. Serves 12-16.

Pieces of Pear Cake with Pear Sauce

When it comes to fall flavors, we often think apples . . . but this delicious pear-infused cake with pear sauce will change your thinking!

3½ cups unbleached, all-purpose flour
1½ tsp. baking powder
½ tsp. salt
1½ cups unsalted butter, room
    temperature, cut into pieces
2 cups firmly packed light brown sugar
1 cup firmly packed dark brown sugar
1 tbsp. vanilla extract
5 large eggs
¾ cup milk, whole
¼ cup pear nectar
2⅓ cups firm, ripe pears, peeled, cored,
    and cut into ¼" dice
1 tbsp. freshly grated orange zest

PEAR SAUCE

4 firm, ripe pears (such as Bartlett or
    D'Anjou), peeled, cored, and cut into
    1" dice
2 tsp. fresh lemon juice
¾ cup pear nectar
2 tbsp. granulated sugar

Heat oven to 350 degrees. Grease and flour a 10" tube pan, tapping out excess flour.

In a medium bowl, whisk together the flour, baking powder, and salt.

In a large bowl of an electric mixer, beat butter until creamy. Beat in the brown sugars and vanilla until light and fluffy. Scrape bowl.

Beat in the eggs, one at a time, until blended. With mixer on low, alternately add the milk, the pear nectar, and the flour mixture to the butter mixture, beating just until combined. Scrape bowl.

Quickly and gently fold pears and zest into batter until blended. Spread batter in prepared pan.

Bake for 52 to 71 minutes or until golden brown and a toothpick inserted near the center comes out clean.

Cool in pan on a wire rack for 15 minutes. Then run a knife around the inside edge of pan and carefully remove the cake. Cool completely on wire rack.

For the Pear Sauce: In a medium saucepan, combine the pears, lemon juice, pear nectar, and sugar, stirring gently to blend.

Bring to a boil. Reduce heat to a bare simmer. Cover saucepan and cook, stirring occasionally, for about 10 minutes or just until pears are soft.

Remove from heat and cool for 20 minutes. Puree mixture with an immersion blender or in a food processor. Serve cake slices drizzled with Pear Sauce. Serves 12-14.

Breakfast Polenta Cake

Yes—there are several steps to this polenta cake, but your time will be rewarded. Don't even think about saving this just for breakfast . . . you'll be missing so many tasty parts of the day.

½ cup unsalted butter, room temperature, cut into pieces
½ cup plus ¼ tsp. granulated sugar, divided
2 large egg yolks
2 tsp. freshly grated orange zest
1 tsp. freshly grated lemon zest
1 tsp. vanilla extract
⅔ cup almonds
¼ cup cornstarch or arrowroot
½ cup stone-ground cornmeal
½ tsp. baking powder
4 large egg whites, room temperature
Confectioners' sugar, sifted

Heat oven to 325 degrees. Grease a 9" Bundt pan.

In a large bowl of an electric mixer, combine the butter, ½ cup sugar, egg yolks, orange zest, lemon zest, and vanilla. Beat until mixture is light and creamy. Scrape bowl.

In a food processor, combine the almonds, cornstarch, cornmeal, and baking powder. Pulse until mixture is powdery and combined. Sift this mixture into a mixing bowl. If bits of the almond remain in the sifter, return them to the mixture.

In a clean large bowl of an electric mixer, beat the egg whites with the remaining ¼ tsp. sugar until soft peaks form.

Quickly and gently fold the dry ingredients and *half* of the beaten egg whites into the butter mixture.

Fold in the remaining whites just until incorporated. Gently spread batter into prepared pan.

Bake for 25 to 32 minutes or until a toothpick inserted in the center comes out clean.

Cool in pan on a wire rack for 15 minutes. Then run a knife around the inside edge of pan and carefully remove the cake. Cool completely on wire rack.

When ready to serve, dust cake with confectioners' sugar. Serves 8-10.

Sweet Heat Fruit and Nut Cake with Spicy Caramel Glaze

Flavorful and spicy, this cake would be the perfect ending to a Mexican meal . . . or a sweet treat with heat for an appetizer-and-margarita party!

½ cup firmly packed light brown sugar
¼ cup unsalted butter, room temperature, cut into pieces
¼ cup heavy cream
½ tsp. ground chipotle pepper
1 tsp. vanilla extract

SWEET HEAT CAKE

3 cups unbleached, all-purpose flour
2 tsp. ground cinnamon
1½ tsp. freshly grated nutmeg
1 tsp. baking soda
1 tsp. ground chipotle pepper
¾ tsp. ground ginger
½ tsp. freshly ground white pepper
¼ tsp. salt
⅛ tsp. ground cloves
1½ cups light olive oil or canola oil
1¾ cups granulated sugar
3 large eggs
1 tbsp. vanilla extract
3 cups peeled, cored, and diced sweet-tart apples
1 cup toasted, coarsely chopped pecans

A SLICE OF ADVICE FROM BEV

A chipotle is a smoked jalapeno pepper.

In a small saucepan, stir together the brown sugar, butter, heavy cream, and chipotle pepper. Bring to a boil, stirring occasionally.

Simmer and cook for 4 minutes, stirring occasionally. Remove from heat and whisk in the vanilla. Cool for 1 hour (mixture will thicken slightly).

Heat oven to 325 degrees. Grease and flour a 10" Bundt or tube pan, tapping out excess flour.

For the Sweet Heat Cake: In a medium bowl, whisk together the flour, cinnamon, nutmeg, baking soda, chipotle pepper, ginger, white pepper, salt, and cloves.

In a large bowl of an electric mixer, beat oil and sugar on medium speed until combined. Beat in the eggs, one at a time, until blended. With mixer on low, blend in the vanilla. Scrape bowl.

With mixer on low, beat in the flour mixture just until combined. Scrape bowl.

Quickly and gently stir in the apple pieces and the pecans. Spread batter into prepared pan.

Bake for 62 to 66 minutes or until a toothpick inserted near the center comes out clean.

Cool in pan on a wire rack for 15 minutes. Then run a knife around the inside edge of pan and carefully remove the cake.

Place cake on rack atop a large piece of waxed paper. Drizzle warm cake with Spicy Caramel Glaze. Cool completely on wire rack. Serves 12-16.

CAKES TO DIE FOR!

What's a little heat among cakes?

These cakes are a perfect way to celebrate "Sneak Some Zucchini onto Your Neighbor's Porch" Day.

Gad Zukes! Zucchini Cakes with Lemon Glaze

These will soon become your favorite use for all that zucchini from your garden (or your neighbor's).

2 cups unbleached, all-purpose flour
1 tsp. baking powder
½ tsp. baking soda
1 tsp. salt
2 tsp. ground cinnamon
1 tsp. ground ginger
½ tsp. freshly grated nutmeg
3 large eggs
1½ cups granulated sugar
¼ cup firmly packed light brown sugar
1 cup light olive oil
2 tsp. vanilla extract
2½ cups grated zucchini
1 cup toasted, finely chopped almonds

LEMON GLAZE

¼ cup fresh lemon juice
⅓ cup granulated sugar
1 cup confectioners' sugar, sifted

A SLICE OF ADVICE FROM BEV

My mini Bundt pan makes cakes that are 3½" wide and 2" tall.

Freeze a few of these moist and flavorful beauties to thaw and enjoy on a cold winter's night.

This recipe also fills a 10-cup Bundt pan. Bake for 44 to 66 minutes. Serves 8.

Heat oven to 350 degrees. Grease and flour a 6-cake mini Bundt pan, tapping out excess flour.

In a medium bowl, sift together the flour, baking powder, baking soda, salt, cinnamon, ginger, and nutmeg.

In a large bowl of an electric mixer, beat the eggs, sugars, oil, and vanilla until light and fluffy. Scrape bowl.

With mixer on low, beat the flour mixture into the egg mixture until thoroughly combined. With mixer on medium, blend in the zucchini and almonds. Scrape bowl.

Spread batter into prepared pan. Bake for 22 to 36 minutes or until a toothpick inserted in the centers comes out clean.

Cool in pan on a wire rack for 15 minutes.

For the Lemon Glaze: In a medium bowl, whisk together the lemon juice and granulated sugar. Whisk in the confectioners' sugar until smooth.

Run a knife around the inside edge of pan and carefully remove the cakes.

Place cakes on rack atop a large piece of waxed paper. Using a pastry brush, immediately brush the glaze over the entire surface of the warm cakes, using all of the glaze. Cool the cakes completely. Serves 12.

John's Best Angel-Food Cake with Variations on an Angel-Food Cake Theme

I don't even try to compete with John's angel-food cakes. They're simply divine, especially when served with fresh local organic strawberries and freshly whipped organic heavy cream.

1¼ cups confectioners' sugar, sifted
1 cup cake flour, sifted
1½ cups egg whites, room temperature
   (usually 12 large eggs)
1½ tsp. cream of tartar
2 tsp. vanilla extract
¼ tsp. salt
1 cup granulated sugar

A SLICE OF ADVICE FROM JOHN

Be *very* careful to have no moisture or grease get into the bowls, utensils, or cake pan, which will prevent the egg whites from whipping properly. Also, egg whites at room temperature whip to maximum peaks . . . so separate when cold and allow to warm before using.

Heat oven to 375 degrees. Set aside an ungreased 10" tube pan.

In a medium bowl, whisk together the confectioners' sugar and cake flour.

In a large bowl of an electric mixer with whisk attachment, add egg whites, cream of tartar, vanilla, and salt. With mixer at high speed, beat until well mixed.

With mixer at high speed, sprinkle in the sugar, 1 or 2 tbsp. at a time, just until sugar dissolves and whites form stiff peaks. *Don't* scrape bowl during beating.

With a rubber spatula, quickly and gently fold in the flour mixture, a fourth at a time, just until flour disappears. Spread mixture into pan, and with a thin metal spatula, quickly and gently cut through batter to break up any large air bubbles.

Bake for 30 to 35 minutes or until the top springs back when lightly touched. Any cracks on surface should look dry.

Immediately remove pan from oven and invert onto a sturdy funnel or bottle.

When the cake is cool, run a knife around the inside edge of pan and carefully remove the cake. Serves 8-10.

To keep John's Best Angel-Food Cake from deflating, you need to invert it. A bottle works well for this task—and a very cool bottle keeps your mind (temporarily!) off the cake.

VARIATION ONE: TOASTED ANGEL-FOOD CAKE

Slices of John's Best Angel-Food Cake
Fresh assorted berries
Freshly whipped cream

A SLICE OF ADVICE FROM BEV

This is my favorite way to serve angel-food cake. Toasting brings a nice crunch to the top of the cake slice, while it remains soft and moist on the inside.

Heat oven to 350 degrees. Place angel-food cake slices on a parchment-paper-lined baking sheet. Toast for 15 minutes or longer, just until tops are lightly golden in color and feel lightly crisped to the touch.

Cool on a wire rack for 10 minutes. Then serve with berries and whipped cream. Serves 8-10.

Not only is this John's Best Angel-Food Cake, it's his birthday (and unbirthday) celebration favorite—toasted and served with whipped cream and strawberries.

VARIATION TWO: SORBET 'N ANGEL

1 John's Best Angel-Food Cake
4 cups sorbet, preferably raspberry, mango, or lemon, lightly softened, divided

A SLICE OF ADVICE FROM BEV

This is perfect for a ladies' lunch or bridal shower, and sorbet lends bright colors to the plate.

Slice cake in half horizontally to form 2 layers. Return bottom layer, cut side up, to the cooled tube pan. Spread evenly with half of the sorbet. Top with remaining cake layer, cut side down, then quickly spoon remaining sorbet over top of cake.

Cover with plastic wrap and freeze for at least 4 hours or overnight.

When ready to serve, let pan stand at room temperature for about 10 minutes. Remove the cake from pan. Cut cake into slices and serve on cold dessert plates. Serves 8.

Layer John's Best Angel-Food Cake with your favorite sorbet flavor . . . and keep some in the freezer for emergencies!

Brown Sugar Toffee Cake with Maple Glaze

*Perfect for anyone who loves the flavors of butterscotch and toffee . . .
and oh! that Maple Glaze is divine.*

12 oz. toffee pieces
3 cups unbleached, all-purpose flour,
    divided
2 tsp. baking soda
1 tsp. baking powder
¾ tsp. salt
1 cup unsalted butter, room
    temperature, cut into pieces
1½ cups firmly packed light brown sugar
4 large eggs
2½ tsp. vanilla extract
1 tsp. maple extract
1 cup buttermilk

MAPLE GLAZE

1 cup confectioners' sugar, sifted
2 tbsp. pure maple syrup
¼ tsp. maple extract
2 tbsp. milk, plus more as needed

Heat oven to 325 degrees. Grease and flour a 12-cup Bundt pan, tapping out excess flour.

In a medium bowl, toss together the toffee pieces and 2 tbsp. flour.

In another medium bowl, whisk together the remaining flour, baking soda, baking powder, and salt.

In a large bowl of an electric mixer, beat the butter and brown sugar until light and fluffy. Beat in the eggs, one at a time, until blended.

In a small bowl, whisk together the vanilla extract, maple extract, and buttermilk. With mixer on low, alternately add the flour mixture and the buttermilk mixture to the butter mixture.

Quickly and gently fold in the toffee pieces. Spread batter into prepared pan.

Bake for 48 to 65 minutes or until a toothpick inserted near the center comes out clean.

Cool in pan on a wire rack for 15 minutes. Then run a knife around the inside edge of pan and carefully remove the cake. Cool completely on wire rack.

Place cake on rack atop a large piece of waxed paper.

For the Maple Glaze: In a medium bowl, whisk together the confectioners' sugar, maple syrup, maple extract, and as much milk as needed to reach desired consistency. Spoon Maple Glaze over top of cake, then let stand at room temperature until glaze firms, about 30 minutes. Serves 12-14.

CAKES TO DIE FOR!

Fudge Sauce Infused Chocolate Coconut Cake

Chocolate and coconut marry well together, and this moist coconut-infused chocolate cake is a marriage made in—well—your kitchen!

SMOOTH AND SILKY FUDGE SAUCE

4 oz. bittersweet chocolate, coarsely chopped
⅓ cup unsalted butter, room temperature, cut into pieces
1⅓ cups confectioners' sugar, sifted
¾ cup half-and-half
1 tsp. vanilla extract

CAKE

1 cup unsalted butter, cut into pieces
⅔ cup Smooth and Silky Fudge Sauce
7 oz. semisweet chocolate, coarsely chopped
2¼ cups unbleached, all-purpose flour
1 cup granulated sugar
1 cup sweetened flaked coconut
1 cup milk, whole
4 large eggs, lightly beaten
½ tsp. baking soda
1 tbsp. fresh lemon juice
1 tbsp. vanilla extract

Confectioners' sugar, sifted

A SLICE OF ADVICE FROM BEV

This perfect Smooth and Silky Fudge Sauce is from my cookbook *Brownies to Die For!* and is a taste treat with so many wonderful things (e.g., ice cream, fresh berries, or spooned directly from the container!). Leftovers are never a problem.

In a medium saucepan, combine the chocolate and butter. Let soften over low heat, stirring until mixture is almost blended.

Whisk in confectioners' sugar and half-and-half. Cook, whisking, over medium heat until mixture comes to a full boil. Reduce heat to low and cook, whisking often, for 5 minutes.

Remove saucepan from heat. Whisk in vanilla. Cool to room temperature and use immediately. Leftovers may be stored, cooled and covered, in the refrigerator.

Heat oven to 325 degrees. Grease a 10" tube pan.

For the Cake: Place butter, ⅔ cup Fudge Sauce, and chocolate in a medium saucepan. Cook over low heat, stirring, until mixture is melted and combined.

In a large bowl of an electric mixer, beat together the melted chocolate mixture, flour, sugar, coconut, milk, eggs, baking soda, lemon juice, and vanilla at medium speed until well mixed. Scrape bowl.

Spread batter into prepared pan. Bake for 58 to 74 minutes or until a toothpick inserted in the center comes out clean.

Cool in pan on a wire rack for 15 minutes. Then run a knife around the inside edge of pan and carefully remove the cake. Cool completely on wire rack.

When ready to serve, dust with sifted confectioners' sugar. Serves 12-16.

White Chocolate Chip Pecan Pound Cake

Be sure your white chocolate chips contain cocoa butter for a truly fragrant, not-too-sweet white chocolate flavor.

3 cups unbleached, all-purpose flour
½ tsp. salt
¼ tsp. baking soda
1 cup unsalted butter, room
    temperature, cut into pieces
3 cups granulated sugar
6 large eggs
1 cup sour cream
1 tbsp. vanilla extract
12 oz. white chocolate chips
2 cups toasted, coarsely chopped pecans

Heat oven to 350 degrees. Grease and flour a 3-qt. Bundt pan, tapping out excess flour.

In a medium bowl, whisk together the flour, salt, and baking soda.

In a large bowl of an electric mixer, beat the butter and sugar until light and fluffy. Scrape bowl.

Beat in the eggs, one at a time, until blended. With mixer on low, blend in the sour cream and vanilla. Beat in the flour mixture just until combined.

In a medium bowl, stir together the white chocolate chips and pecans.

Spread *half* of the batter into prepared pan. Sprinkle *half* of the chip/pecan mixture over batter.

Spread remaining batter over chip/pecan mixture, spreading evenly. Sprinkle with remaining chip/pecan mixture.

Bake for 68 to 90 minutes or until a toothpick inserted in the center comes out clean.

Cool in pan on a wire rack for 15 minutes. Then run a knife around the inside edge of pan and carefully remove the cake. Cool completely on wire rack. Serves 8-10.

CAKES TO DIE FOR!

Buttermilk Cake Poked with Butter Sauce

A silky butter sauce is poured atop this cake while it's still warm, for an easy, flavorful cake that's always a hit.

3 cups unbleached, all-purpose flour
1 tsp. salt
1 tsp. baking powder
½ tsp. baking soda
2 cups granulated sugar
1 cup unsalted butter, room
   temperature, cut into pieces
1 cup buttermilk
2 tsp. vanilla extract
4 large eggs

BUTTER SAUCE

¾ cup granulated sugar
⅓ cup unsalted butter, cut into pieces
3 tbsp. water
1 tsp. vanilla extract

Heat oven to 325 degrees. Grease and flour a 10" tube pan or 12-cup Bundt pan, tapping out excess flour.

In a medium bowl, whisk together the flour, salt, baking powder, and baking soda.

In a large bowl of an electric mixer, beat the sugar and butter until light and fluffy. With mixer on low, blend in the buttermilk and vanilla. Scrape bowl.

Alternately beat in the eggs, one at a time, with the flour mixture until well blended.

Spread batter into prepared pan. Bake for 52 to 74 minutes or until a toothpick inserted in the center comes out clean.

For the Butter Sauce: In a small saucepan, combine the sugar, butter, and water. Whisk over medium heat until butter melts, being careful not to boil mixture. Remove from heat and stir in vanilla.

Prick warm cake (in pan) 12 times with a long-tined fork. Slowly pour Butter Sauce over cake. Cool pan completely on a wire rack.

When ready to serve, run a knife around the inside edge of pan and carefully remove the cake. Serves 10-12.

MY MIXES CAKES PLUS FROSTINGS

Frosted and swirled and colorful, baby!

This chapter offers up some basic cakes or what I like to call "my mixes." Why? It's no secret that I'd like you to rise above the mix . . . to break out of the box. You get the idea. Cakes are simple and satisfying, and you often already have all the ingredients you need at home. And frostings? If you want flavor, *real* flavor, don't skip taking time to gather together your sifter (or sieve), mixing bowl, and whisk. Frosting should be lick-your-fingers sweet, with buttery overtones.

The following four recipes—Chocolate Cake, Yellow Cake, White Cake, and Lemon Cake—all offer you the opportunity to make a plain cake and frost it to your liking. They're perfect for spur-of-the-moment celebrations or when you're just craving something sweet.

Following those is a varied assortment of some of my favorite frosting recipes, for you to mix and match and slather and enjoy.

All of my cake recipes in this book contain their own versions of what I consider to be the best frosting choice for the cake. However, feel free to mix and match and experiment.

It takes 2½ to 3 cups frosting to ice a two-layer cake. Vary the flavors by adding 4 oz. bittersweet chocolate or 2 oz. white chocolate, melted and completely cooled, to a prepared buttercream. You can add 1 tsp. freshly grated orange zest and Grand Marnier to taste for a bright orange, adult buttercream.

Just how much can you enjoy the frostings? Well, consider this. Some bakeries across the U.S. have been known to sell "frosting shots": creamy dollops of buttercream in small paper or plastic sampler cups. These are especially appealing to children (of all ages—who are we kidding?!) and those who have purchased a cupcake but need that instant, sweet splurge. Frosting Anonymous, anyone?

My Mixes Chocolate Cake

This recipe is the perfect basic cake when only chocolate will do.

2 cups unbleached, all-purpose flour
1¼ tsp. baking soda
½ tsp. salt
1½ cups granulated sugar
½ cup unsalted butter, room
   temperature, cut into pieces
1 tsp. vanilla extract
2 large eggs
4 oz. unsweetened chocolate, coarsely
   chopped, melted
1 cup milk, whole

Heat oven to 350 degrees. Grease and flour 2 9" square or round cake pans or a 13" by 9" baking pan, tapping out excess flour.

In a medium bowl, whisk together the flour, baking soda, and salt.

In a large bowl of an electric mixer, beat the sugar and butter until light and fluffy. Scrape bowl. Add vanilla and eggs, beating until well combined. With mixer on low, blend in cooled, melted chocolate.

Alternately add flour mixture and milk, beating well after each addition.

Spread batter evenly into prepared pan(s). Bake for 28 to 32 minutes or until a toothpick inserted in the center(s) comes out clean.

Cool in pan(s) for 10 minutes. Then run a knife around edge of pan(s) to loosen cake(s). Cover a pan with a large, lint-free towel-covered plate (or place a large tray atop baking pan) and invert pan. Remove pan from cake. Re-invert cake onto cooling rack. Repeat with remaining cake, if applicable. Allow to cool completely on wire rack(s).

My Mixes Yellow Cake

With its golden color and moist texture, this buttermilk-based yellow cake is perfect for a multitude of uses!

2½ cups cake flour, sifted
1¼ tsp. baking powder
¼ tsp. baking soda
¾ tsp. salt
1¾ cups granulated sugar, divided
10 tbsp. unsalted butter, melted
1 cup buttermilk
3 tbsp. light olive oil or canola oil
2 tsp. vanilla extract
6 large egg yolks, room temperature
3 large egg whites, room temperature

Heat oven to 350 degrees. Grease 2 9" round cake pans and line bottoms with parchment paper rounds. Grease parchment paper and dust pans lightly with flour, tapping out excess flour.

In a large bowl of an electric mixer, whisk together the flour, baking powder, baking soda, salt, and 1½ cups sugar.

In a large bowl, whisk together the melted butter, buttermilk, oil, vanilla, and egg yolks.

In a large bowl with a handheld mixer, beat egg whites until foamy. With mixer on high, gradually add remaining ¼ cup sugar, 1 tbsp. at a time, until stiff peaks form.

With mixer on low, slowly pour the butter mixture into the flour mixture and mix until almost incorporated. Scrape bowl.

Using a rubber spatula, fold one-third of the egg whites into the batter to lighten. Quickly and gently add remaining whites, folding into batter until no white streaks remain. Divide batter evenly between prepared pans. Lightly tap pans against counter 2 or 3 times to dislodge any large air bubbles.

Bake for 20 to 22 minutes or until toothpick inserted in the centers comes out clean.

Cool in pans for 10 minutes. Then run a knife around edge of pans to loosen cakes. Cover a pan with a large, lint-free towel-covered plate and invert pan. Remove pan from cake. Peel off parchment and re-invert cake from plate onto cooling rack. Repeat with remaining cake. Allow to cool completely on wire racks.

My Mixes White Cake

A white "canvas" of a cake, just waiting for the creative baker in you to emerge with some filling and frosting.

3 cups unbleached, all-purpose flour
1 tbsp. baking powder
¼ tsp. salt
1 cup unsalted butter, room
   temperature, cut into pieces
2 cups granulated sugar
6 large eggs
1 tsp. vanilla extract
1 cup milk, whole

Heat oven to 350 degrees. Grease 2 9" round cake pans and line bottoms with parchment paper rounds. Grease parchment paper.

In a medium bowl, whisk together the flour, baking powder, and salt.

In a large bowl of an electric mixer, beat the butter and sugar until light and fluffy. Scrape bowl.

Add the eggs, one at a time, mixing well after each addition. Beat in the vanilla to combine.

With mixer on low, add the milk alternately with the flour mixture. Beat only until smooth. Scrape batter into prepared pans.

Bake for 28 to 34 minutes or just until a toothpick inserted in the centers comes out clean and tops spring back when lightly touched.

Cool in pans for 10 minutes. Then run a knife around inside edge of pans to loosen cakes. Cover a pan with a large, lint-free towel-covered plate and invert pan. Remove pan from cake. Peel off parchment and re-invert cake from plate onto cooling rack. Repeat with remaining cake. Allow to cool completely on wire racks.

My Mixes Lemon Cake

Tart, sweet, and moist—yum!

2 cups cake flour, sifted
1½ cups plus 1½ tsp. unbleached, all-purpose flour
2¼ tsp. baking powder
1 cup unsalted butter, room temperature
3 cups granulated sugar
1 tbsp. vanilla extract
1 tbsp. fresh lemon juice
¾ tsp. salt
1 cup egg whites (about 6 large eggs), room temperature
1½ cups milk, whole
1½ tsp. finely grated lemon zest

Heat oven to 350 degrees. Grease 3 9" round cake pans and line the bottoms with parchment paper rounds. Grease parchment paper.

In a large bowl, whisk together the flours and baking powder.

In a large bowl of an electric mixer, beat the butter and sugar until light and fluffy. Add the vanilla, lemon juice, and salt.

With the mixer on low, gradually add the egg whites, stopping to scrape the bowl often.

Alternately add the flour mixture and the milk to the butter mixture. Scrape bowl. Add the lemon zest. Beat until thoroughly combined.

With the mixer on medium high, beat the mixture for 30 seconds. Scrape bowl.

Divide the batter evenly among the cake pans. Bake for 30 to 35 minutes or until a toothpick inserted in the centers comes out clean.

Cool in pans for 10 minutes. Then run a knife around edge of pans to loosen cakes. Cover a pan with a large, lint-free towel-covered plate and invert pan. Remove pan from cake. Peel off parchment and re-invert cake from plate onto cooling rack. Repeat with remaining cakes. Allow to cool completely on wire racks.

Luscious Buttercream Frosting

A cake baker's secret weapon—fluffy and moist and ready to slather!

4 cups confectioners' sugar, sifted
¼ cup milk, whole
½ cup unsalted butter, room
   temperature, cut into pieces
2 tsp. vanilla extract

In a large bowl of an electric mixer, beat together the confectioners' sugar, milk, butter, and vanilla until blended. Scrape bowl.

With mixer on medium, beat mixture until light and fluffy.

A SLICE OF ADVICE FROM BEV

For a chocolate version, add 3 oz. unsweetened chocolate, melted and cooled. Beat in an additional 1 to 2 tbsp. milk to reach desired spreading consistency.

For a lemon version, decrease milk to 1 tbsp. and omit the vanilla. Add 1 tbsp. freshly grated lemon zest and 3 tbsp. fresh lemon juice.

Does anyone have dibs on the frosting bowl?

"Burst of Lemon" Buttercream

The intense lemon flavor in this buttercream comes from the addition of lemon curd. It's a perfect layer-cake frosting!

BEV'S LEMON CURD

Zest of 6 lemons
1 cup plus 2 tbsp. fresh lemon juice
2½ cups granulated sugar
6 large eggs
2 cups unsalted butter, cut into pieces

"BURST OF LEMON" BUTTERCREAM

2 cups granulated sugar
¾ cup plus 2 tbsp. egg whites (about 4 to 5 large eggs), room temperature
1¾ cups unsalted butter, room temperature, cut into pieces
¼ tsp. vanilla extract
2 cups Bev's Lemon Curd, *completely cooled*

A SLICE OF ADVICE FROM BEV

You can use pasteurized egg whites in liquid form for the egg whites in this recipe.

When making the meringue, don't rush the process. It will take about 10 minutes.

Sometimes this frosting is too liquidy to spread. In that case, refrigerate until completely cool and stiff, then beat until the desired spreading consistency is reached.

In a large heat-resistant bowl, combine the lemon zest, lemon juice, and sugar.

In a bowl large enough to hold a second large heat-resistant bowl, combine ice cubes and cold water, leaving enough room to add the second bowl later. Set both the ice bath and the second bowl aside.

Whisk the eggs into the lemon mixture and set this bowl over a pot of boiling water. Stir constantly until the curd begins to thicken.

Strain the curd through a fine sieve into the second large heat-resistant bowl. Add the butter pieces, a few at a time, whisking until smooth.

Place the bowl in the ice bath and chill, stirring frequently to speed up the cooling process.

If the curd is made ahead, keep it covered and refrigerated until ready to use.

For the "Burst of Lemon" Buttercream: In a large bowl of an electric mixer, beat the sugar and egg whites until combined.

Set the bowl over a pot of boiling water. Whisking constantly, heat the mixture until all the sugar crystals have dissolved and the mixture is hot, getting mixture as hot as you're able without "cooking" the eggs.

Return the bowl to the electric mixer. With mixer on high, beat the mixture until it forms a stiff meringue and the bottom comes to room temperature.

With mixer on low, add the butter, a little at a time, until combined. With mixer on medium, beat mixture until fluffy.

With mixer on low, add the vanilla and Bev's Lemon Curd. Scraping bowl, mix until blended to a smooth, creamy texture.

CAKES TO DIE FOR!

Fluffy Boiled Icing

Perfect not only for icing cakes but for border decorations and cake writing as well.

3 tbsp. meringue powder
1 cup cold water, divided
2 cups granulated sugar
¼ cup light corn syrup

In a large bowl of an electric mixer, beat the meringue powder and ½ cup cold water until stiff.

In a small saucepan, bring the sugar, corn syrup, and remaining ½ cup water to a boil. With mixer on low, slowly add this syrup to meringue mixture. With mixer on high, beat until stiff and glossy.

A SLICE OF ADVICE FROM BEV

Meringue powder consists of dried egg whites, sugar, and a gum for stabilizing.

Be patient! It will take about 4 minutes of beating to get a stiff icing.

Rich Chocolate Frosting

A deep chocolate flavor and a light, satiny consistency that spreads like a dream.

1¼ cups unsalted butter, room
   temperature, cut into pieces
1 cup confectioners' sugar, sifted
¾ cup unsweetened cocoa powder, sifted
⅛ tsp. salt
¾ cup light corn syrup
1 tsp. vanilla extract
4 oz. bittersweet chocolate, melted
4 oz. milk chocolate, melted

In a large bowl of an electric mixer, beat the butter and confectioners' sugar until light and fluffy. Scrape bowl.

With mixer on low, beat in the cocoa powder, salt, corn syrup, and vanilla until blended. Scrape bowl.

Stir in the chocolates (being sure they are completely cool before adding!) just until combined. Scrape bowl.

A SLICE OF ADVICE FROM BEV

You can use 8 oz. of just 1 type of chocolate—anything from unsweetened to semisweet to white chocolate.

White Chocolate Buttercream

When John and I had our own catering business, we would make this for our from-scratch wedding cakes. It was well worth every minute, and everyone raved about the cake and frosting! I've halved the recipe for this book, so you can use it to frost a cake for an anniversary, small wedding, or everyday celebration. Make it a day or two before you want to use it. Don't rush the process; it takes time. Cover and refrigerate until ready to use.

4⅛ cups granulated sugar, divided

1⅛ cups water, divided

⅜ cup light corn syrup, divided

9 egg whites, room temperature, divided

3 cups plus 3 tbsp. unsalted butter, room temperature, divided

1 lb. white chocolate, coarsely chopped, divided

2¼ tsp. vanilla extract, divided

A SLICE OF ADVICE FROM BEV

It goes without saying that you should use the very best white chocolate for this recipe!

Patience is a must when beating the egg whites with the hot syrup. The mixture can take as long as 20 minutes to cool down.

Combine 1 cup sugar, ⅜ cup water, and ⅛ cup corn syrup in a small saucepan. Stir over low heat until the sugar dissolves. Increase heat and boil without stirring until mixture reaches soft-ball stage (234 to 240 degrees on a candy thermometer).

In a large bowl of an electric mixer, beat 3 egg whites with ⅜ cup sugar until soft peaks form. Beat in the hot syrup in a slow steady stream. With mixer on medium, beat until egg white mixture cools to room temperature.

In another large bowl of an electric mixer, beat 1 cup plus 1 tbsp. butter until light and fluffy. Gradually beat into the egg white mixture and continue to beat until smooth, light, and fluffy.

In the top of a double boiler, melt ⅓ lb. white chocolate. Remove from heat and allow to cool slightly.

With mixer on low, beat melted chocolate into buttercream. Mix in ¾ tsp. vanilla. Transfer to a large bowl.

Repeat the entire process 2 more times with remaining ingredients. Once you've completed this process 3 times, mix all of the batches together for 1 large final batch of White Chocolate Buttercream.

White Chocolate Cream-Cheese Frosting

This provides a perfect jolt of sweetness when slathered atop a gingerbread cake or carrot cake.

16 oz. cream cheese, room temperature, cut into pieces
½ cup unsalted butter, room temperature, cut into pieces
4 cups confectioners' sugar, sifted
4 oz. white chocolate, melted

In a large bowl of an electric mixer, beat the cream cheese and butter until light and fluffy. Scrape bowl.

With mixer on low, add confectioners' sugar, a little at a time, until well blended. Scrape bowl. With mixer on medium, beat mixture until well blended.

Beat in the cooled, melted white chocolate until well blended. Refrigerate the frosting for 30 minutes or until desired spreading consistency.

Cinnamon Cream-Cheese Frosting

A rich frosting with bursts of cinnamon flavor.

8 oz. Neufchatel cheese, room temperature, cut into pieces
4 tbsp. unsalted butter, room temperature, cut into pieces
3 cups confectioners' sugar, sifted
2 tsp. ground cinnamon

In a large bowl of an electric mixer, beat the Neufchatel and butter until creamy. Scrape bowl.

With mixer on low, beat in the confectioners' sugar and cinnamon, a little at a time, until well combined. Scrape bowl.

With mixer on medium, beat the mixture until desired spreading consistency.

A SLICE OF ADVICE FROM BEV

Regular cream cheese (not whipped) can be used in place of the Neufchatel.

Store any leftovers, covered, in the refrigerator. Bring to room temperature and gently rebeat before using.

Milk Chocolate Whipped Cream Frosting

This frosting is rich, rich, rich, so a little goes a long way.

3 oz. cream cheese, room temperature, cut into pieces
1 tbsp. milk
2 cups heavy cream
⅔ cup confectioners' sugar, sifted
4 oz. milk chocolate, melted

In a large bowl of an electric mixer, beat cream cheese and milk until smooth. Scrape bowl.

With mixer on low, add the heavy cream and confectioners' sugar. Scrape bowl. With mixer on high, beat mixture until stiff peaks form.

Quickly and gently fold in cooled, melted milk chocolate. Use immediately.

A SLICE OF ADVICE FROM BEV

The beaten cream cheese and milk mixture may look curdled, but all is well. Continue with the recipe.

Milk Chocolate Ganache

Not a fan of bittersweet or semisweet chocolate? Then the rich sweetness of this Milk Chocolate Ganache is for you.

½ cup plus 3 tbsp. heavy cream
16 oz. milk chocolate, coarsely chopped

In a small saucepan, bring the heavy cream to a simmer.

Place the chocolate pieces in a large bowl and immediately pour the simmering cream over them. Allow mixture to steep for 5 minutes.

Whisk until mixture is melted and smooth. Allow to thicken slightly at room temperature before using.

A SLICE OF ADVICE FROM BEV

It goes without saying, but . . . there are only 2 ingredients in this recipe, so use organic heavy cream and top-quality milk chocolate for the best results!

White Chocolate Whipped Cream

When you have an extraordinary cake that doesn't require frosting, but you want to take it over the top, a dollop of this cream will do the trick!

4 oz. white chocolate, coarsely chopped
1 cup plus 4 tbsp. heavy cream, divided

In a small saucepan, combine the white chocolate and 4 tbsp. heavy cream. Stir constantly over low heat until chocolate is melted and mixture is smooth. Remove from heat and cool for 15 minutes.

In a large bowl of an electric mixer, beat the remaining 1 cup heavy cream until soft peaks form. Quickly and gently whisk in the cooled white chocolate mixture. Use immediately.

Bev's Butterscotch Filling

You could (but I wouldn't recommend it!) slather this incredible filling between two pieces of cardboard and people would rave about it. When I make this, I use the very best organic brown sugar and organic dairy . . . and the results simply shine.

½ cup firmly packed dark brown sugar
2 tbsp. plus 2 tsp. cornstarch or arrowroot
¼ tsp. salt
1½ cups milk, whole
½ cup heavy cream
2 tbsp. unsalted butter, cut into pieces
1 tsp. vanilla extract

In a medium saucepan, whisk together the brown sugar, cornstarch/arrowroot, and salt. Whisk in the milk and cream and bring mixture to a boil, stirring constantly, over medium heat.

Whisk for 1 additional minute.

Remove saucepan from heat and whisk in the butter pieces and vanilla. Pour into a medium bowl, covering surface with buttered waxed paper. Chill until cold.

A SLICE OF ADVICE FROM BEV

Don't use anything but whole milk for this filling.

Set a little aside to enjoy right out of a custard cup once the butterscotch has chilled!

BIBLIOGRAPHY

Corriher, Shirley O. *BakeWise*. New York: Scribner, 2008.

Editors of Sunset Books. *Good Cook's Handbook*. Menlo Park, Calif.: Lane, 1986.

Herbst, Sharon T. *Food Lover's Companion*. 2nd ed. Hauppauge, N.Y.: Barron's Educational Series, 1995.

McCarty, Meredith. *Sweet and Natural*. New York: St. Martin's Griffin, 1999.

Riley, Elizabeth. *The Chef's Companion*. 2nd ed. New York: John Wiley & Sons, 1999.

Shaffer, Bev. *Brownies to Die For!* Gretna, La.: Pelican, 2006.

Shaffer, Bev and John. *No Reservations Required*. Wooster, Ohio: Wooster Book Company, 2003.

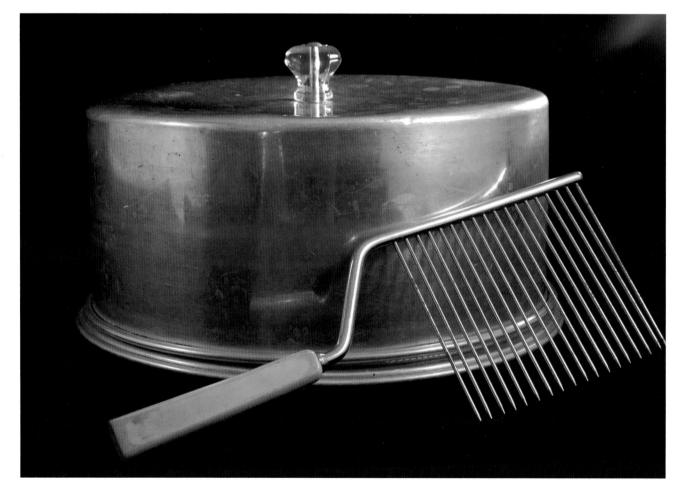

Thanks, Mom (John's mom, Jane's, cake keeper and angel-food cake slicer—the perfect way to slice an angel-food cake without crushing the slices).

286

INDEX